Politics of Migration

This book studies the politics surrounding Indian emigration from the nineteenth century to the present day. Bringing together data and case studies from across five continents, it moves beyond economic and social movers of migration, and explores the role of politics – both local and global – in shaping diaspora at a deeper level.

This work will be invaluable to scholars and students of migration and diaspora studies, development studies, international politics and sociology, as well as policymakers and non-governmental organisations in the field.

A. Didar Singh is Secretary General, Federation of Indian Chambers of Commerce and Industry (FICCI), New Delhi, India, and former Secretary to the Government of India.

S. Irudaya Rajan is Chair Professor, Ministry of Overseas Indian Affairs Research Unit on International Migration, Centre for Development Studies (CDS), Thiruvananthapuram, Kerala, India.

'*Politics of Migration* is an in-depth analysis of the growing influence of the Indian Diaspora abroad, explaining the reasons for emigration and dispelling a number of myths and misconceptions. There is no better work on the politics of migration from an Indian perspective. Singh and Rajan see the Indian Diaspora as a growing global powerhouse and compellingly advocate the adoption of a national diaspora policy. Thought-provoking, insightful, thoroughly researched and impressively argued, this volume is indispensable to all academics and policymakers concerned with migration.'
– **Shashi Tharoor**, Member of Parliament for Thiruvananthapuram, Lok Sabha, and Chairman, Parliamentary Standing Committee on External Affairs, India

'This is a remarkably well-written and informative book on Indian migration, a phenomenon that everyone is interested in, but one which is often plagued by absence of data, information and facts. But the book goes beyond data and probes the political economy, a facet missing in some existing books on cross-border migration.'
– **Bibek Debroy**, Professor, Centre for Policy Research, New Delhi

'Migration is an integral element of economic development. And yet, because it evokes strong feelings in the destination communities, whether in the richer countries or in the richer states within India, migration is often neglected by the policymakers. *Politics of Migration* presents pioneering analysis of the complexity of the Indian migration phenomenon and related policymaking. In doing so, it highlights the great developmental benefits that India can reap by elevating the importance of managing labor mobility to the same level as policies related to trade, investments and other forces of globalization.'
– **Dilip Ratha**, Migration and Remittances Unit and Head, KNOMAD, Development Prospects Group, World Bank

'Human migration has been a natural process from time immemorial. In the 20th Century, however, even as trade and capital flows have been liberalised, people flows have been constrained by political and geo-political factors. Didar Singh and Irudaya Rajan have written an important book on the politics of migration that deserves to be read widely because governments will not be able to control for too long what has always been a natural human phenomenon.'
— **Sanjaya Baru**, International Institute of Strategic Studies

'*Politics of Migration* provides valuable insights on contemporary migration in general and the Indian diaspora. In particular, the excellent analysis by Didar Singh and Irudaya Rajan offers very interesting and thought-provoking perspectives on migration and Indian diaspora nexus in a globalizing world. It also sheds light on the importance of diaspora engagement as it relates to and impacts diplomatic relations between countries.'
— **Ovais Sarmad**, Chief of Staff, International Organisation for Migration, Geneva, Switzerland

'*Politics of Migration* is a timely and much needed analytic publication in view of the history and continuing trend of Indian first migration, second migration and re-migration which are unprecedented, with more people of Indian origin in increasing numbers in more countries than ever before. Simultaneously, the issues, concerns and interests of the Indian Diaspora increase accordingly, including assimilation and adaptation, co-existence in multi-ethnic societies, new social and cultural experiences, as well as academic, economic, inter-generational and political issues. [This book] provides in-depth analyses of the underlying and visible political aspects of Indian migration. A highly recommended textbook for Indian Diaspora studies.'
— **Ashook Ramsaran**, President, Global Organisation of People of Indian Origin International, United States of America

'The *Politics of Migration* is a refreshingly original contribution to research on Indian international migration. It is engaging, rigorously analysed and compellingly argued.'
— **Dharmalingam Arunachalam**, Monash University, Australia

Politics of Migration

Indian emigration in a globalised world

A. Didar Singh and
S. Irudaya Rajan

NEW DELHI LONDON NEW YORK

First published 2016
by Routledge
2 Park Square, Milton Park, Abingdon, Oxon OX14 4RN

and by Routledge
711 Third Avenue, New York, NY 10017

Routledge is an imprint of the Taylor & Francis Group, an informa business

© 2016 A. Didar Singh and S. Irudaya Rajan

The right of A. Didar Singh and S. Irudaya Rajan to be identified as authors of this work has been asserted in accordance with sections 77 and 78 of the Copyright, Designs and Patents Act 1988.

All rights reserved. No part of this book may be reprinted or reproduced or utilised in any form or by any electronic, mechanical, or other means, now known or hereafter invented, including photocopying and recording, or in any information storage or retrieval system, without permission in writing from the publishers.

Trademark notice: Product or corporate names may be trademarks or registered trademarks, and are used only for identification and explanation without intent to infringe.

British Library Cataloguing in Publication Data
A catalogue record for this book is available from the British Library.

Library of Congress Cataloging-in-Publication Data
A catalog record has been requested for this book.

ISBN: 978-1-138-92288-4 (hbk)
ISBN: 978-1-315-68546-5 (ebk)

Typeset in Galliard
by Apex CoVantage, LLC

Dedicated to our wives

Poonam Khetrapal Singh
Hema Rajan

whose support and encouragement symbolises that of our larger Indian family – the Great Indian Diaspora.

Contents

List of figures		x
List of tables		xi
List of appendices		xii
Foreword by Karan F. Bilimoria		xiii
Preface		xv
Acknowledgements		xix
1	Introduction: myths of movement	1
2	Politics in migration	16
3	Migration and politics in countries of destination	41
4	Political mainstreaming of the Indian Diaspora	88
5	The political economy of migration in Indian states	112
6	Conclusion: migration in a globalised world	145
	Appendices	155
	Bibliography	179
	About the authors	191
	Index	193

Figures

1.1	Number of migrants in the North and South	7
3.1	Bar graph representing estimated population of Indian Diaspora (PIOs and NRIs) in five European countries in the year 2011	60
3.2	Bar graph representing increase in the number of Indian Diaspora in five European countries from 2001 to 2011	61
3.3	Immigrants in the United States, 1995–2007	69
3.4	Immigrants in the United States, numbers and per cent, 1900–2007	69
4.1	Region of birth of immigrants by period of immigration, Canada, 2011	90
4.2	Number of Canadians whose mother tongue is one of the twenty-two immigrant languages reported by more than 100,000 persons in Canada, 2011	94

Tables

3.1	Top 25 countries of birth in 2007	70
3.2	Total and Indian foreign-born populations, 1960–2008	71
3.3	Percentage per religion by country of birth, Western Australia, 2001	77
4.1	Inflow of the immigrants in Canada, 2011	91
4.2	Total number of immigrants, 1946–80	92
4.3	Immigrant population by languages family speak	93

Appendices

I	Year of beginning of migration of Indians	155
II	Population of Indian Diaspora: countrywise	156
III	History of migration and immigration laws in the United States	157
IV	List of Indian associations in the United States	168

Foreword

The recent years have been conflicting time for matters of international migration. While recognising the important economic contributions that migrants make to their countries of origin and their destination countries, the politics associated with migration policy has created new barriers for people wishing to move around the globe.

Notwithstanding this fact, migrants and Diasporas have assumed vital importance in the general conversation on globalisation and development owing to their potential as powerful development actors. Despite this, political participation and democratisation are concepts that have only recently began to emerge from these movements. Following the 2001 report of the High Level Committee (HLC) on the Indian Diaspora, the Government of India has recognised the significance of Diaspora remittances, investment and philanthropy, as well as their potential for facilitating international economic collaborations and realising the country's political objectives. Given the diverse characteristics and professional dynamism of India's overseas communities, the country has made multi-level efforts to harness the social, human and financial capitals of overseas Indians through the creation of conducive legal frameworks, partnerships and institutions. This work by Dr Didar Singh (administrator) and Dr S. Irudaya Rajan (researcher) profiles and evaluates different dimensions of the emigration from India and the nature of migrants' political linkages with their homeland. It outlines, for the reader, the institutional architecture through which India interacts and networks with its Diaspora with a view to assessing present practices and suggesting future points of intervention. The book maps different avenues through which overseas Indians benefit from opportunities and engagements in India and the role of trans-border networks and Diaspora organisations in mediating the immigrant experience evaluating how the Diaspora acts on matters of foreign policy interests and homeland politics.

Even though international migration is a complex phenomenon, more often than not, international migration policy is left at the mercy of political rhetoric and the whim of public opinion. In this book, the authors debunk the myths of migratory flows and deconstruct the political economy of migration, advancing a nuanced analysis both from the emigration origin states and its Diaspora's destinations. Their approach challenges previous theories of migration as primarily economically motivated and accounts for the diversity and multidirectionality of complex human movements. This book educates and illustrates how engagement with the Diaspora has undergone transformation in the years since independence. It provides the reader a thorough and interesting historical context to some of the most prominent Diaspora communities in the world – especially that of the United Kingdom. The authors question the assumed linearity between migration and development and dispel common misconceptions regarding migratory flows. Combining decades of research and policy experience, the authors deftly traverse the perceptions, policies and politics on emigration management, Diaspora engagement and the legal and political structures of the home and host countries. Recognising the need to bring a strategic dimension to the relationship between India and its overseas community, the book adds momentum to the political mobilisation of the Indian Diaspora as a strategic asset for India's expanding development trajectory. With the new government's renewed interest in the Diaspora, this book is both timely and appropriate.

Karan F. Bilimoria
Friday, 12 December 2014

Preface

Mobility of individuals, groups and peoples has been intertwined in the history of mankind since time immemorial. Such movement has been seen to be a natural part of the growth and evolution of societies. The question arises whether such movement is entirely 'natural' and whether it be explained in primarily economic or social provisos.

Migration is quite simply defined in the dictionary as the process or act of migrating. The definition of the word can be 'the movement of people from one place to another'. There are of course two main types of migration: first, internal migration, that is, migration within one country, and secondly international migration, which means the movement from one country to another – the second is usually referred to as 'emigration' and is the focus of this book.

The reasons for migration can be divided into two main aspects, the so-called push and pull factors. Push factors are those factors at the source that force people to move. For example, there may be civil wars or general unrest in the country, political or religious oppression, climate changes or lack of jobs or poverty, all of which are important push factors. Pull factors are factors in the target country that encourage people to move; these include peace and safety, a chance of a better job, better education, social security, a better standard of living in general as well as political and religious freedom.

It is the premise of this book that a comprehensive understanding of both the rationale and impact of migration needs to be considered in the political context of its environment. Such an analysis will be attempted in the Indian context – both from the emigration origin states as also the Diaspora destinations.

The book is divided into six chapters. In Chapter 1 we discuss the *Myths of Movement*. Migration theory itself has led to myths about movement. One such premise for movement of people has been to consider economic compulsion as *the* major cause for migration and thereby assume that migration usually occurs from poorer or less-developed regions to richer or more developed areas. Could it simply be that larger populations are mostly found in the developing or poorer countries and several reasons therefore could be in play in such movement? If the premise was true, it should also hold that as countries and regions get more developed, mobility should slow down or halt. Industrialisation in Europe tells a different story, as do growth stories in several developing countries. Most such economic changes have in fact led to increased migration besides creating greater disparities of wealth. Quite obviously, the relationship between migration and development is complex and not direct. This chapter discusses several existing myths and theories of migration and analyses the ground reality of actual movement.

Chapter 2 of the book talks about *Politics in Migration*. Migration is not without politics; sometimes obvious and apparent, at other times hidden and veiled. Migration also produces its own politics as do Diaspora and return migrants. This chapter seeks to examine some of these concealed trends in the context of Indian migration. Human mobility is not all about numbers; it is also about social conditions, cultural contexts and economic compulsions. In order to obtain a comprehensive understanding of mobility, it is necessary to deliberate on the political milieu of such movements – movements that have over the course of recent history evolved from slavery to indenture to workers to student mobility. This chapter seeks to understand the politics behind such movements, particularly from the perspective of Indian emigration.

Besides dealing with above questions, it also discusses India's emigration policy. The first question we need to address is – Does India have a migration or emigration policy? Is it clearly stated or written somewhere? Is it clear, transparent and apparent in India's dealing with its own emigrants? There is of course the Emigration Act 1983, but that piece of legislation is dated and outmoded. It is a policy that originally applied to all emigration from India but today, by executive order, stands restricted to just 17 countries and to emigrants that have less than Class 10 educational qualification. Formally, there exists no 'white-paper' on 'Indian Migration Policy' or 'Indian Diaspora Policy'.[1] That however does not mean that India does not have a specific policy on emigration management and Diaspora engagement. It is the view of this book that India does in fact have a robust emigration policy as also a Diaspora engagement policy, one that is evolving with active involvement of the emigrants themselves.

Chapter 3 of the book explores the connection between *Migration and Politics in Countries of Destination*. Migration is all about two ends of the 'rainbow' – the pulls and pressures from destination to origin countries. This chapter takes into account regional and country-wise case studies of major destination countries of Indian migrants to understand the legal and political frameworks such migrants have to contend with. It will discuss immigration policies of the destination countries that have impacted such movement. The legal and political structures at the host country have considerable implications on the nature, duration of stay and migratory status of migrant communities. The chapter covers questions of inclusion, integration and incorporation of migrants into civic life along with barriers to entry and stay. It brings to light the socio-legal underpinnings of migrant environments and the methods through which migrants negotiate their living. The focus of this chapter is on countries or regions that include Gulf Cooperation Council (GCC) countries, Europe, the United States and Australia.

Chapter 4 of the book analyses *Political Mainstreaming of the Indian Diaspora*. The chapter looks at the size, spread, nature and composition of the Indian Diaspora in some key destination countries and seeks to analyse the changing role the Indian Diaspora communities have been through in these countries. It covers the ways in which migrants gain access to political systems in host countries, their representation/marginalisation in civic life and the changing context of barriers to political activity. Also to be considered is migrant contribution to the economic, cultural and political fabric of host countries. The chapter comments not only on the political role that the Indian Diaspora has had in the destination nations, but also its potential implications for India and, more specifically, the ways in which these communities can help India realise its interests in these regions. The chapter highlights the need to bring a strategic dimension into the relationship between India and its overseas community. It opens up space to consider the Indian Diaspora as a strategic political asset for the nation.

This chapter carries out an in-depth study of Diaspora civic participation and political involvement in the following countries: Canada, the United States, Trinidad and Tobago and Mauritius.

Chapter 5 looks at the *Political Economy of Migration in Indian States*. While migrants continue to contribute to India's development through cross-border flows of trade, investment and other channels, this chapter analyses the role of the Indian Diaspora in home politics. It seeks to understand the legal and political framework at the state level in India that creates the possibility of the Diaspora influencing local politics. The research has focused on three key states – Punjab, Kerala and

Gujarat. Some questions which have been looked at include the following: Is there any evidence of Diaspora engagement with local politics? Has it seen any marked success? What are the implications of increasing domestic political leverage among migrants? How can India effectively harness the political potential of its return migrants and Diasporas? The chapter seeks to contextualise such Diaspora engagement in the *Political economy* of the state seeing it as an interdisciplinary study encompassing the socio-economic environment in the context of domestic politics and set to understand what role the Diaspora could play in the local environment.

Chapter 6 is titled *Conclusion: Migration in a Globalised World*. Where does migration fit into the rapidly globalising world? Is it a significant representation and product of globalisation? The Indian Diaspora is certainly one of the most globalised communities around the globe considering Indian migrants are found across some 160 countries. Is this fact of Indian migration itself creating hitherto unrecognised (or addressed) political and diplomatic conditions?

This concluding chapter draws on the chapter-wise conclusions and findings and seeks to place them in a global context. It also comments on the changing global environment where means and tools of engagement itself are changing. In the old days, the principal means for migrant communities to retain contact with their country of origin and their culture were through language, religious practices, cooking recipes and occasional letters or visits (Naim, 2002). Globalisation and its concomitant communication systems have greatly expanded the means through which people in one country can remain actively involved in another country's cultural, economic and political life. People were suddenly able to maintain strong ties with their country of origin and assert their ethnic identities in their country of settlement. Today media, telecommunications and other technologies have become so extensive that a different level of human interaction has been achieved (Gupta and Fugerson, 1992), characterised by Internet, films, telecommunications and television. This chapter seeks to analyse these instruments of Diaspora–homeland linkages and situate it within the broader picture of global Diaspora engagement.

Note

1 Aspects of the Indian diaspora policy can be seen as publically first spelt out at the inaugural Pravasi Bhartiya Divas, 2003, in the speech of the then prime minister Vajpayee. Available at http://indiandiaspora.nic.in/ch2.pdf, accessed 15 May 12. The emerging diaspora policy and various initiatives are found outlined in the Annual Reports of MOIA at http://moia.gov.in/.

Acknowledgements

While working on the book, several young researchers have helped us in the endeavour. We would like to acknowledge Smita Tiwari (Indian Council of World Affairs, Delhi), Jolin Joseph (York University, Canada), Soumi Roy Chowdhury (The University of New Mexico, United States of America), Vishnu Narendran (Centre for Development Studies, Kerala) for research assistance, Ambassador Paramjit S Sahai of Centre for Research in Rural and Industrial Development (CRRID) for the Punjab section and Natasha Chhabra (Federation of Indian Chambers of Commerce and Industry) for editorial assistance.

Chapter 1
Introduction
Myths of movement

Migration is a natural, continuous and spatial phenomenon. People move from one place to another, alone or with others, for a short visit or for a long period of time. Migrants reshape their societies and influence the economic and political systems of two countries: the country of origin and the country of settlement. Along with the large amount of movement now being seen, the very notion of migration has itself been changing in this century. In ancient times, most of the migration is seen as the lifestyle of certain communities, determined by their geographical environment. In the modern era, when people are migrating willingly for betterment of life, the concept of migration has come to be seen as more positive and dynamic. This phenomenon of migration is now regarded as normal and as a structural element of human societies that evolved throughout history. Migration is no longer viewed as a 'sign of crisis' (Potts, 1990),[1] as a phenomenon exclusive to the industrial period. It is considered as part and parcel of a general human pattern, essential for the functioning of families and crucial to the operation of labour markets. It is a complex social, political and economic issue which Rodriguez has referred to as, 'a dramatic socio-geographical picture' (Rodriguez, 1996). It is not only a physical transition of a group or individual that involves leaving one's social setting and entering into another one, but also creating a transnational network.

Rapid population growth, uneven economic development and improved transportation have accelerated migratory movements. But through a combination of preferences, these migrants maintain their distinct identity. Along with internal cohesion, they mostly remain connected with their country of origin. Communication with kinfolks and financial remittances to relatives are the most common forms of contact. They may also take vital interest in the political development of the country of origin and even try to influence it. Thus, a migrant community not only tries to retain its group identity but also maintains its links, both material and sentimental, with its country of origin. These links become a dimension of politics.

International migration implies movement of people from one place to another for the purpose of taking permanent or semi-permanent residence, usually across a political boundary. Eisenstadt defines migration 'as physical transition of an individual or group from one society or another'. This transition usually involves abandoning one social setting and entering another and different one (Eisenstadt cited in Dutta, 2003). The UN Convention on the Rights of Migrants defines a migrant worker as a 'person who is engaged or to be engaged in remunerated activity in a state of which he or she is not a national'. This definition indicates that 'migrant' does not refer to refugees, displaced or others forced or compelled to leave their homes. Migrants are people who make choices about when to leave and where to go, even though these choices are sometimes extremely constrained.

According to the International Organisation for Migration's World Migration Report 2010, the number of international migrants was estimated at 214 million in 2010. While the number of migrants is expected to rise in future, the question that arises is, why do so many people migrate? Migration occurs for many reasons. Many people leave their home countries in order to look for economic opportunities in another country. Others migrate to be with family members who have migrated or because of political conditions in their countries. Education is another reason for international migration, as students pursue their studies abroad. The reasons for migration may be various, ranging from population pressures, poverty, structurally caused unemployment and underemployment, political conflicts to ecological factors. However, there is no causal links between such variables and international migration (Tamas, 1996).

Though the causes and consequences of migration are not the same throughout history, the new wave of emigration flows from countries in Asia, Africa and Latin America has emerged in a process closely linked to economic development. The population increase in these countries has not been matched with a growth in employment opportunities. The present level of unemployment and underemployment will continue and probably grow, and thereby give new incentives to a future increase in migration from South to North (Hammar et al., 1997). Migration is an important factor in the erosion of traditional boundaries between languages, cultures, ethnic group and nation states. Even those who do not migrate are affected by movements of people in or out of their communities, and by the resulting changes (Rajan, 2013). Migration is not a single act of crossing a border, but rather a lifelong process that affects all aspects of the lives of those involved.

Migration and development

Migration and development are highly interdependent processes. Today, both are increasingly viewed through the prism of the many links that exist between these two spheres. While development-oriented actions can sometimes help tackle the root causes of migratory flows, migration can, in turn, contribute positively to development, including economic growth, social empowerment and technological progress. On the other hand, if not well managed, migration can also pose challenges to countries' development efforts. Such phenomenon popularly referred to as 'brain drain', experienced by a number of developing countries in key development sectors, calls for more cohesive and sustainable policies. Greater partnership between countries of origin, transit and destination as well as the full integration of the migratory dimension in development policies and dialogue on all levels are crucial steps in enhancing the development potential of migration. Here, it is pertinent to understand what we mean by 'development'.

According to the World Bank, 'development' is a dynamic process implying growth, advancement, empowerment and progress, with the goal of increasing human capabilities, enlarging the scope of human choices and creating a safe and secure environment where citizens can live with dignity and equality. In the development process, it is important that people's productivity, creativity and choices are broadened, and that opportunities are created. Economic development is essentially improving the economic well-being of a community, through efforts focused on investment attraction and job creation leading to improvement in the quality of life of the community. Skeldon, in his seminal work *Migration and Development* (1997), has correctly pointed out that while we intuitively know what 'development' and 'migration' mean, defining these two terms can raise several issues. Both of course are dynamic terms and imply change, with development suggesting an advancement of human condition and migration a shift in human residence. Migration or human mobility encompasses a whole spectrum of movements, which is why Diasporas are not homogenous and represent different waves and types of migration from the homeland. Similarly, development comprises many dimensions ranging from technological change to institutional, social and political. In fact, it can be argued that migration and therefore Diasporas are an integral part of the development process – both caused and causing change themselves.

For the purpose of this book, the meaning of development is used in a broader sense to include overall development of the life of human beings instead of the traditional meaning, which include statistics like gross domestic product (GDP) and national income (NI) for individuals and society. Evidence suggests that migration can be a powerful driver of development both for migrants and their households. The development impacts of migration at a more aggregate, community or national level tend to be more tangible, both at origin and destination.

Myths of movement or migration

Migration has also been used to describe the experience of movement and to analyse socio-cultural and political formations that result from this movement. Movement of people across national borders has emerged as a subject of considerable policy debate amongst nation states in the twenty-first century (Kumar and Rajan, 2014). It has been argued that if global development was dominated by the movement of goods in the nineteenth century and by the movement of capital in the twentieth century, the development imperatives of the twenty-first century will be dominated by the movement of people across national borders (Bhagwati, 1999). Though migration or movement of people has been seen to be a natural part of the growth and evolution of societies, migration theory has led to several 'myths' about the movement or migration of people.

These beliefs or in some cases even misconceptions influence both the social relationships and the political responses for emigrants and Diasporas. Indian emigrants also encountered them – and in fact continue to. We will discuss these here and see if they hold good with the experience of migration. In the concluding chapter, we will refer back to this listing and examine if they are in fact valid for Indian emigration.

Myth # 1: People migrate mostly because of economic compulsion

This is a popular myth about the movement of people implying that they essentially migrate because of the economic compulsions of the country of origin. According to this, the traditional 'push–pull model' on the assumption of neo-classical economics (Lee, 1966) has remained an influential perspective on migration. The premise behind this is that migrants respond to primarily economic conditions in the places of origin and destination and the decision to migrate is based on a rational economic calculation. Thus, people migrate from insecure to comparatively securer regions and from areas lacking employment and good living opportunities to areas which offer better economic, political and social prospects. This would imply that migrants would move essentially from poor nations to the rich and developed nations.

Fact

Data shows that international migrants do not originate in the world's poorest nations, but in those that are developing and growing dynamically. Very few transcontinental migrants originate in Sub-Saharan Africa, for example, even though it is generally the poorest region of the world. Given their poverty, most Africans lack the means to finance international migration. Rather, today's global migrants are much more likely to come from the rapidly developing and relatively wealthy economies of Asia and Latin America than from the marginalised regions of Africa. Because it is the structural transformation accompanying development and the creation of markets that influences international migration and not poverty per se, there is no empirical relationship between per capita income and rate of emigration. It is the initiation of economic development under market mechanisms that causes mass migration to occur, not its absence.

People generally do not leave their countries of origin because of a lack of economic development. Rather, they often emigrate owing to the onset of development itself. The shift from a peasant or command economy to a market system entails a radical transformation of social structures at all levels: a revolutionary shift that displaces people from traditional ways of life and creates a mobile population on the lookout for alternative ways of making a living. Historically, some of those displaced by industrialisation and development migrated internally, going to burgeoning cities and thereby bringing about the urbanisation of society. But in most countries a large share of the economically displaced emigrated internationally, thus yielding large-scale migration. As a result, there is a close empirical correspondence between the onset of industrialisation and the beginnings of international migration.

The largest single source of US immigrants, Mexico, is not a poor nation by global standards. Mexico has a $1 trillion economy, a per capita income of almost $9,000, a fully industrialised economy, a high level of urbanisation and an advanced life expectancy (Meissner, 2010). Within Mexico, moreover, it is not the poorest and least-developed communities that send the most migrants. On the contrary, other factors being equal, the communities with the highest rates of out-migration are those that are most developed. In contrast, the Congo is truly impoverished and underdeveloped, with an economy that is still predominantly agrarian, a low rate of urbanisation, a per capita income of just $600, a low life expectancy and a high rate of fertility (Meissner, 2010). The Congo hardly records any significant migration to the West.

Myth # 2: Migration mostly takes place in South–North direction

Another prevalent myth about migration is that following post–World War II de-colonisation and rapid economic growth in Western societies, there has been a trend of global migration movements, in which South–North migration has strongly increased. This confronted many Western societies with the unprecedented settlement of non-Western, culturally and physically distinct immigrants. This increasing visibility of global migration for the resident populations of Western societies might partly explain the popular perception that current migration is at unprecedented levels and the concomitant 'flooding' images associated with migration.

Fact

That migration takes place mostly in South–North direction is a myth. Data in recent World Migration Reports indicate that around 60 per cent of all global migration takes place within the developed world. Migration is frequent in these countries because of several factors which include: highly developed transportation system; migration on account of profession, education, tourism etc. The data also show that more than 40 per cent of international migration takes place between developing countries, that is, South to South. This misperception about migration in an era of growing human mobility results in increased public concern over inflows of migrants and over irregular migration, and smuggling and trafficking, in particular, and as a consequence affects the image of migrants in general.

Income, proximity and networks are the major drivers of migration from developing to industrial countries. As South–South income differentials are relatively modest, proximity and networks likely have a proportionally greater impact, while the role of income is more complex. The costs (financial, social and cultural) of migrating to nearby countries are likely to be lower than those of moving farther away. Also because many South–South migrants lack adequate travel documents, they are restricted to overland migration (Ratha and Shaw, 2007). Further, ethnic, community and family ties reduce the uncertainties involved in migration. This type of South–South migration might include a

Introduction: myths of movement 7

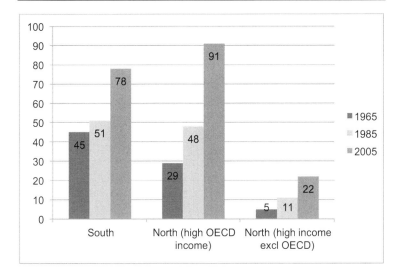

Figure 1.1 Number of migrants in the North and South
Source: Ratha and Shaw (2007).

Bangladeshi labourer moving to India. Migrants escaping from war usually go to other neighbouring developing countries, often as a first step in seeking asylum. In fact, most refugees and asylum seekers are located in developing countries (Figure 1.1) (Ratha and Shaw, 2007).

Myth # 3: Migration is a simple move from an origin to a destination

Another myth is that migration is a simple move from an origin to a destination country. It is considered to be a simple process of leaving one social setting and entering into another one, with little or no complexity. The reasons or motivation of migration may differ but the process is a fixed pattern, that is, moving, physically, from one place to another.

Fact

Migration is a complex process and has been a feature of human societies for many centuries. There are many reasons why people choose to migrate including poverty, armed conflict, social strife, political turmoil, economic hardships etc. These incidents are not a simple phenomenon; in many instances they involve human emotion and human hardships. The travails of such movement are not conducive to organised and planned mobility. In many instances, the movement is dependent on external factors that may change suddenly, resulting in change of plans and change of destination. Many of today's migrants are mere components of transnational networks that influence both domestic politics and foreign relations of a state. Such networks not only charge huge sums of money but also treat the migrants as human cattle being herded from one location to another until they are surreptitiously pushed across borders.

Professionals also move along with economic opportunity. As global trends make for better economic growth in different regions and countries, pull factor for students and professionals attracts them to different destinations. Where such migrants finally settle is therefore a factor of several variables – complex and unpredictable. Movement and mobility therefore take place in diverse and varied forms and cannot be considered as a simple shift from origin to destination country. Movements are more complex and they may involve several destinations including regular contact with the homeland. Sometimes, they may lead to eventual return migration.

Myth # 4: Migration hurts the economy of the country of origin

The primary cost associated with migration for the country of origin is the 'brain drain', or the loss of some of its brightest citizens. When migrants are skilled and/or highly educated, the sending country experiences the loss not only of that worker and his contribution to society, but also the investment made in his education or training, and the potential for him to mentor and teach others. Considering that making an international move requires some financial solvency and entrepreneurship from anyone, even unskilled workers who migrate are considered a loss to their country of origin.

Brain drain has for long been considered solely as a vicious event depriving sender countries, often less- and least-developed countries, of professionals needed for national development. The effect of 'brain drain' is acute in many developing nations where doctors and nurses are in short supply locally because they have been so heavily recruited to make up for shortfalls in developed countries.

Fact

Most views on international migration tend to be one-sided, because of their one-sided focus on the interest of, and consequences of, migration for 'receiving societies'. This is striking since migrants contribute significantly to the social and economies development of their country of origin. It is also unfortunate as the neglect of the 'other side' of migration hampers a proper understanding of the development causes and consequences of migration.

Migration can also benefit the country of origin. Relieving a country of some of its inhabitants can reduce the pressure on resources – from land to water to food – particularly in densely populated and impoverished regions. Migration of certain demographic groups in society can relieve pressure on labour markets and ease intergenerational tensions. Countries with large youth/working age populations experience downward pressure on wages, especially among unskilled labourers, if labour supply significantly exceeds demand. Unemployed youth populations are politically destabilising as well, and their migration is often welcomed by their home countries (World Savvy Monitor, 2009).

Migrants perhaps benefit their home countries most when they send home a portion of their wages to family and friends, or make investments in their countries of origin. These remittances sent to developing countries are estimated at $251 billion year in 2007,[2] $328 billion in 2008[3] and $307 billion in 2009.[4] In 2010, after the global financial crisis showed signs of recovery, the recorded remittances flow to developing countries reached to $325 billion.[5] In 2014, it was predicted that these would rise to $436 billion.[6] The total value of remittances – including unofficial remittance flows – money and goods sent through family, friends, informal or semi-formal channels – is thought to be much higher. Diasporas also invest in their countries of origin and are an important source of ideas and technologies.

Myth # 5: Migrants take away jobs of locals in the country of destination

Another popular myth surrounding migration is that of migrants moving, en masse, into so-called richer countries for taking up jobs in their country of destination. The argument follows that with more immigrants, there is bound to be rising unemployment in their country of settlement.

Fact

To date there is no strong evidence to support such claims. Migrants generally travel to where there are jobs available, often filling vacancies where there are skill shortages. Migrants in developed countries are permitted to take jobs only where there are recognised skill shortages and if they can prove before entering that they have the relevant qualifications. Low-skilled workers fulfil a need by taking jobs that others do not want, letting natives move up the scale. Without them employers would need to pay higher salaries, making those products and services more expensive. Numerous statistical studies have shown that there is no link between immigration and unemployment. Also due to demographic change, developed countries need increased immigration in the medium and long term. Predictions indicate that there will be shortages of labour in the European Union (EU), in several sectors including healthcare. In the EU, between 2008 and 2060, the population aged over 65 will increase by 79 per cent, while the population aged over 80 is expected to increase by 181 per cent.[7]

Although immigrants account for 12.5 per cent of the US population, they make up about 15 per cent of the workforce. They are overrepresented among workers largely because the rest of our population is ageing. Immigrants and their children have accounted for 58 per cent of US population growth since 1980 (Meissner, 2010). This probably would not change anytime soon. Low US fertility rates mean that immigration is likely to be the only source of growth in what we call the 'prime age' workforce – workers between the ages of 25 and 55 – in the decades ahead. As record numbers of retirees begin drawing Social Security checks, younger immigrant workers will be paying taxes, somewhat easing the financial pressures on the system (Meissner, 2010).

Moreover, immigrants tend to be concentrated in high- and low-skilled occupations that complement – rather than compete with – jobs held by native workers. And the foreign-born workers who fill low-paying jobs are typically first-hired/first-fired employees, allowing employers to expand and contract their workforces rapidly. As a result, immigrants experience higher employment than natives during booms – but they suffer higher job losses during downturns. It is true that an influx of new workers pushes wages down, but immigration also stimulates growth by creating new consumers, entrepreneurs and investors. As a result of this growth, economists estimate that wages for the vast majority of American workers are slightly higher than they would be without immigration (Meissner, 2010).

Myth # 6: Migrants are a drain on public services

Besides high wages, potentially attractive to immigrants are public-benefit programmes in their country of settlement such as Aid to Families with Dependent Children (AFDC), food stamps, Social Security, Medicare etc. Prominent in the popular imagination is the notion that immigrants in general and undocumented immigrants in particular consume more in public services than they contribute in taxes, thus burdening native citizen taxpayers. Indeed, Proposition 187 in California was organised precisely around this belief, as its preamble states, in that it seeks '. . . to prevent illegal aliens in the United States from receiving benefits or public services in the State of California' (Massey et al., 2002).

Although Proposition 187 was approved by voters in 1994, its provisions were voided by the federal courts. Nonetheless, it served as a model for federal legislation enacted by Congress. Taking a cue from Proposition 187, the Illegal Immigration Reform and Immigrant Responsibility Act of 1996 declared undocumented immigrants ineligible for Social Security while limiting their eligibility for educational benefits even if they had paid the requisite taxes. The legislation also granted states the authority to limit public assistance to US citizens alone. At the same time, the Personal Responsibility and Work Opportunity Reconciliation Act of 1996 (better known as the Welfare Reform Act) barred *legal* immigrants from receiving food stamps or Supplemental Security Income and prohibited them from receiving AFDC for at least five years after admission to the United States (Massey et al., 2002).

Fact

However, research on the foreign-born finds that immigrants are less likely than natives to use public services and most of those who do use them are refugee groups, such as Russians, Cubans and Indochinese. Studies that focus specifically on undocumented immigrants suggest they use public services at rates far below those of legal immigrants. A 1987 study, for example, found that just 2 per cent of illegal Mexican immigrants had ever received welfare or Social Security payments and just 3 per cent had ever accepted food stamps and, in contrast, 84 per cent paid taxes (Massey et al., 2002).

Data from the Mexican Migration Project (MMP) of Princeton University and the University of Guadalajara indicate rates of tax withholding and public-service use by undocumented Mexican migrants. Nearly 6,000 migrants provided this information on their last trip to the United States. Some 66 per cent of migrants reported the withholding of Social Security taxes and 62 per cent said that employers withheld income taxes from their pay cheques. While the vast majority paid taxes into the federal treasury, however, far fewer withdrew funds: only 10 per cent even reported filing a tax return. Whereas nearly three-quarters paid taxes, very few made use of any public service in the United States. Around 10 per cent said they had ever sent a child to US public schools and

7 per cent indicated they had received Supplemental Security Income. Just 5 per cent or less of all migrants reported ever using food stamps, AFDC or unemployment compensation.

It is also possible to measure the influence of expected welfare benefits on the likelihood of undocumented migration. This is accomplished by estimating each migrant's probability of using welfare and food stamps given his or her socio-economic and demographic characteristics, and then multiplying this probability by the average value of monthly AFDC and food stamp payments in the leading migrant-receiving states. Instead of finding a positive correlation between the expected value of welfare benefits and undocumented migration, a 1997 study found a rather strong *negative* association. That is, the greater the potential benefit, the less likely the migration. Summarising the results of this and other studies, the Carnegie Endowment for International Peace concluded that 'there is no reputable evidence that prospective immigrants are drawn to the United States because of its public assistance program'. By and large this will hold true across the Western world.

Myth # 7: Migrants cause unnecessary population growth in country of destination

Another prediction of the new economics of labour migration is that most international migration is permanent. Because neoclassical economics presumes that people come to the developed countries to maximise income over their working lives, it necessarily assumes migration to be permanent. After all, if people seek to maximise income, and wages are higher in the United States, then return migration is illogical. Under neoclassical assumptions, return migration is only predicted if there is a decline in US wages or an increase in Mexican or other sending country wages. However, because return migration is often observed in the absence of such conditions, those who return are often categorised as 'failed' migrants. Unable to find suitable employment, they are assumed to have been 'forced' to return.

Fact

In contrast, because the new economics of labour migration presumes that people migrate in order to solve economic problems at *home*, they are predicted to return a significant share of their earnings to their families in the form of remittances or savings and then to return home themselves. Those who return are thus the 'successes'. If they migrate to overcome missing mortgage markets in Mexico, for example, they remit or save the money they need to finance the acquisition of a home and, having done so, they return to inhabit it.

Patterns of migration are more consistent with the new economics of labour migration than neoclassical economics to the extent that we observe a widespread repatriation of earnings and high rates of return migration among Mexicans. One study found that 85 per cent of undocumented migrants from Mexico during the period 1965–85 were offset by departures, yielding a relatively modest net inflow of just 5.1 million persons over 20 years (around 255,000 persons per year). According to estimates by a variety of researchers, the annual probability of return migration fluctuated around 33 per cent through the early 1990s. If, within any given year, the likelihood of returning to Mexico is one in three, then 70 per cent of immigrants will have returned home within five years. Of all Mexicans who have ever migrated to the United States, therefore, the vast majority currently live in Mexico. In other words, Mexico–US migration has historically been circular. Moreover, the fertility rate in Mexico is about 2.3 children per woman, which is only slightly above 'replacement' level. The highest fertility levels are generally observed in the Arab world and Sub-Saharan Africa, but these regions contribute few migrants to global streams.

Myth # 8: Undocumented migrants are criminals

The fight against irregular/undocumented migration continues to be top priority in developed countries. In the era of globalisation, free flow of capital, goods and services are expanding, on the one hand. On the other, the flow of labour has been the subject of massive enforcement efforts and legal restrictions. Migrants are vulnerable in their countries of settlement but when they are undocumented, they are treated as illegal and criminals. But again this is a myth and there are no obvious links between illegal migrants and criminalisation.

Fact

The first point to note is that many of the so-called illegal migrants are actually 'irregular migrants'. In that they have travelled on a legal visa (usually tourist visa) but stayed back or not adhered to the visa conditions. They join the work force or find some economic activity to sustain themselves until such time as there is an amnesty or they get sponsored for a work visa. They are not criminals as we understand the term. Their only crime, if any, is that they may not have a legal visa status in the country. They are irregular migrants now workers and professionals in the country of destination. In most cases, the countries concerned provide some sort of legal avenue such as amnesty schemes, which attract such strategies by migrants. Ultimately they contribute to the local economy.

Myth # 9: Migrants do not integrate with the host societies

The integration of immigrants remains a hallmark of America's vitality as a society and a source of admiration abroad. Although some people complain that today's immigrants are not integrating into US society as quickly as previous newcomers did, the same charge was levelled at virtually every past wave of immigrants, including the large numbers of Germans, Irish and Italians who arrived in the nineteenth and early twentieth centuries. The same charge is repeated in the United Kingdom, Europe and elsewhere.

Fact

Today, as before, immigrant integration takes a generation or two. Learning English (or whatever the local language is) is one key driver of this process; the education and upward mobility of immigrants' children is the other. In the United States, for example, today's immigrants consistently seek English instruction in such large numbers that adult-education programmes cannot meet the demand, especially in places such as California. On the second count, the No Child Left Behind Act has played a critical role in helping educate immigrant children because it holds schools accountable for teaching them English.

However, the unauthorised status of millions of foreign-born immigrants can slow integration in crucial ways. For example, illegal immigrants are ineligible for in-state tuition at most public colleges and universities, putting higher education effectively out of their reach. And laws prohibiting unauthorised immigrants from getting driver's licences or various professional credentials can leave them stuck in jobs with a high density of other immigrants and unable to advance.

Myth # 10: Migrants are caught in a time-warp in the context of their connect with home country

Much of the traditional writing treats Diasporas as culturally ancient, blinkered and dogmatic in their views and culture, as if they are all frozen in time and relate only to rituals and customs of days bygone. This impression gains from the misinformation that Diaspora communities have little or no contact with their home countries and also that they are not 'modern' in their outlook.

Fact

In the old days, the principal connect of migrated communities with their country of origin and their culture was through language, rituals, cooking recipes and occasional letters or visits (Naim, 2002: 95–6). Globalisation has greatly expanded the means through which people in one country can remain actively involved in another country's cultural, economic and political life. This has had far-reaching effects on migrant communities and has changed their relationship with their country of origin. It also led to reconstitute their identities. People were suddenly able to maintain strong ties to their country of origin and assert their new ethnic identities in their country of settlements.

Modern Diasporas are 'ethnic minority groups of migrant origins residing and acting in host countries but maintaining strong sentimental and material links with their countries of origin – their homelands' (Sheffer, 1986). In an era of accelerated globalisation, the relationship between Diaspora and the economic and social development of many countries is increasingly relevant.

Notes

1 Potts Lydia (1990), in her *World Labour Market: A History of Migration*, depicted migration (be it slave, indentured labourers or guest workers) as a sign of crisis within the capitalist world.
2 The World Bank (2008), *Migration and Development Brief 5* (The World Bank: 2008), The World Bank, http://siteresources.worldbank.org/INTPROSPECTS/Resources/334934-1110315015165/MD_Brief5.pdf, accessed on March 2011.
3 The World Bank (2009), *Migration and Development Brief 10*, The World Bank, http://siteresources.worldbank.org/INTPROSPECTS/Resources/334934-1110315015165/Migration&DevelopmentBrief10.pdf, accessed on March 2011.
4 The World Bank (2010), *Migration and Development Brief 13*, The World Bank, http://siteresources.worldbank.org/INTPROSPECTS/Resources/334934-1110315015165/MigrationAndDevelopmentBrief13.pdf, accessed on May 2012.
5 The World Bank (2011), *Migration and Development Brief 16*, The World Bank, http://siteresources.worldbank.org/EXTDECPROSPECTS/Resources/476882-1157133580628/MigrationandDevelopmentBrief16, accessed on July 2012.
6 http://www.worldbank.org/en/news/press-release/2014/04/11/remittances-developing-countries-deportations-migrant-workers-wb, accessed on 23 August 2014.
7 Busting Migration Myth, http://www.solidar.org/IMG/pdf/54_booklet_migration_myths.pdf.

Chapter 2

Politics in migration

Introduction

The reality of migration is found best portrayed in the reality of politics. Politics is the counterpoise that both defines and portrays it for the force it is in society. There is little doubt that there is politics in migration. Sometimes it is obvious and apparent, sometimes hidden and veiled. Migration also creates its own politics as do Diasporas and return migrants. Human mobility is all about the numbers that move. It is also about social conditions, cultural contexts and economic compulsions. In order to obtain a comprehensive understanding of mobility it is necessary to deliberate on the political milieu of such movements. Emigration has moved, in recent history, from slavery to indenture to workers to student mobility. This chapter will seek to understand the politics behind such movements from the perspective of Indian migration.

Indians have been a major source of human resource for many countries of the world for long. Migration of people from the Indian subcontinent has been occurring for several centuries. Emerging in the ancient period and expanding in the medieval period – it exhibited a fascinating evolution in colonial and post-colonial times. Large-scale *economic* migration dates from the 1830s in the colonial period which led thousands of Indians to colonial destinations, and in fact still continues. However, the later migrants differ markedly, particularly from the earlier migrants of the nineteenth century, in terms of various socio-economic attributes, their compulsions and intentions to migrate, and the diversity in destinations as well.

Presently, the Indian Diaspora may well be regarded as an international phenomenon – with a strong presence of some 27 million persons of Indian origin in over 150 countries globally (Ministry of Overseas Indian Affairs, 2013). Today, it constitutes a significant and successful economic, social and cultural force in the world. Its vastness and diversities, at an international level, grew out of a variety of causes – mercantilism, colonialism and globalisation – and over several hundreds of years of migration in different waves. The origins and roots of the migration have been different and the routes and patterns of the migration and settlement have been divergent. The level of their interaction with the new country of settlement and the emergence of new identities make the Indian Diaspora unique (see also Appendix II). They reflect a growing self-consciousness that has been further strengthened by the development of new communication technologies. With increasing globalisation, the Indian Diaspora is growing and becoming more visible and influential worldwide.

Migration of the Indian Diaspora

Phases and patterns

The movements of Indian migration can be broadly classified into three phases: ancient, colonial and modern. During the ancient period, migration was mainly intended to promote trade, conquer and spread the teachings of Buddha. In that period, traders from India crossed the seas to the Persian Gulf region and the east coast of Africa and over land to Central and West Asia and South East Asia in search of fame and fortune (Jayaram, 2004). R. K. Jain has distinguished between two main phases of Indian migration (Jain, 1993):

- Overseas emigration in the late nineteenth and early twentieth centuries (colonial period).
- Late twentieth-century migration to industrially developed countries (post-colonial period).

During the colonial period, much of the migration to other colonies was as 'indentured labour' for plantations and mines in the Atlantic, Pacific and the Indian Ocean regions. The other form, *Kangani* (meaning foremen or overseer) system, prevailed in the recruitment of labour for emigration to Ceylon and Malaya and a variant of this called *Maistry* (meaning supervisor) system was practiced in Burma (Jayaraman, 1975; Zachariah et al., 2003). The modern phase begins after the Second World War when India gained independence and its people began to move, to participate in the modern mercantile and industrial world. The present chapter focuses on the last two phases of migration and strives to recognise their distinctive nature, causes and the politics of this migration.

Colonial emigration

The establishment of de facto political control by the English East India Company in Bengal after the Battle of Plassey in 1757 inaugurated a period of gradual conquest of the subcontinent leading ultimately to the establishment of direct imperial control. The 'Plassey plunder' set in motion a process which witnessed a 'drain' of resources or wealth from India. Experimentation with the revenue policy resulted in higher demand and ruthless collection of land-revenue without always due regard to the capacity of the land to pay. The revenue settlements subjugated the peasantry to local despotism of moneylenders and riches landowners. The land revenue experimentations, the basic aim of which was the maximisation of revenues, resulted in severe burden on the peasants in general. The new structures of tenures forced the small peasants/ agricultural labourers to migrate. To this may be added the process of de-industrialisation, commercialisation of agriculture and the introduction of the plantation economy – all of which resulted in enhancing the misery of the smallest peasants in particular. Gail Omvedt (1980) has suggested that an examination of colonial migration reveals both the specific characteristics of the colonial working class it produced and the continuing existence of feudal ties of dependence in agriculture. The situation is best conceptualised in terms of the existence within the Indian social formation of feudal (agrarian) and proto-capitalist (mines, plantations, factories) modes of production, articulated in such a way that the main costs of reproduction of labour power that was sold in the capitalist sector were borne in the non-capitalist agrarian sector.

In terms of the magnitude of emigration and its spread, the European colonisation was the most crucial phase in Indian migration. Large-scale emigration of Indians into far-off lands was facilitated by the integration of peripheral economies into the emerging world capitalist system (Jayaram, 2004). Tinker provides one of the most comprehensive surveys of the emigration of Indian labour overseas during the colonial era (Tinker, 1993). Broadly three distinct patterns of Indian emigration are identifiable in this period:

a. 'Indentured'[1] labour emigration,
b. 'Kangani'[2] and 'maistry'[3] labour emigration and
c. 'Passage' or 'free' emigration.

In the late nineteenth and the early twentieth centuries, there was large-scale emigration of Indians to East Africa and other parts of the world, mainly as indentured labourers (see more details, Appendix I). The indentured system was introduced by British, under which the worker went on contract of five to ten years on a very meagre salary (Agrawal, 2001). The British colonial authorities arranged a system of indentured Indian emigration established in Calcutta and Madras (Lall, 2001). It was a form of social contract in which the labourer remained under the personal jurisdiction of the master. Labour was recruited and asked to sign contracts of at least five years, which guaranteed them basic pay, accommodation, food, medical facilities and free or partly paid return passage to India. At the end of the five years, he or she was free to re-indenture or to work elsewhere in the colony and at the end of ten years, depending on the contract, he or she was entitled to a free or partly paid return passage to India or a piece of crown land in lieu of the fare (Clark et al., 1990). In the event of the original contract of indenture expiring, the labourer was usually re-indentured (Kondapai, 1951).

The phenomenal trade surpluses earned by the European mercantile class were invested in mines and plantations in Asia, Africa and elsewhere. This created a huge demand for a cheap and regulated labour force. In the starting of the nineteenth century, the demand for labour was increased by the ever-expanding colonial economy, the growing opposition to slavery and its eventual abolition and the inability of the European countries to meet the shortfall in labour by deploying their own labour force (Jayaram, 2004). A combination of factors made India an excellent reservoir of cheap, docile and dependable labour, especially to work on the plantations. During this period, cheap Indian indentured labour was sent to countries like Guyana, Trinidad and Tobago, Fiji and Mauritius (Yadav, 2005). In the 1840s and 1850s, labour was supplied under the indentured system to Mauritius and British Guyana from Chhota Nagpur (Sahadevan, 1995). In the following decades, a large proportion were exported from the rural district of Bihar and Eastern Uttar Pradesh to various colonies including several Caribbean countries, and the South Indian labourers continued to respond to the demands from South Africa (Polak, 1909) and Fiji (Gillion, 1971). These labour emigrants were also taken to the French colonies of Guadalupe and Martinique, and the Dutch colony of Suriname (Jayaram, 2004). The indentured system was finally abolished in 1920 when the British Indian government implemented the Abolition of Indentured Act, 1916 (Sahadevan, 1995).

The second type of recruitment of 'cheap labour' was for South East Asia and Sri Lanka under the *Kangani* and *Maistry* systems. The

Kangani system prevailed in the recruitment of labour emigration to Ceylon and Malaya. Under this system, the British Indian government controlled the labour migration through *Kanganis* (labour headman) who were not only the leaders of the labour corps but also the principal agents for the recruitment and placing of Indian labours abroad for the colonial government (Kapur, 2010). *Kanganis* were authorised to get hold of recruits only from their own district of origin (Kondapai, 1951). As the system operated mostly in South India, a great majority of emigrants were drawn from impoverished and depressed section of people in Tamil Nadu. As far as labour recruitment to Burma was concerned, the *Maistry* system was followed (Chakravarti, 1946). The labourers so recruited were legally free, as they were not bound by any contract or fixed period of service. During the period between 1852 and 1937, 1.5 million Indians went to Ceylon, 2 million to Malaysia and 2.5 million to Burma (Davis, 1951). Since these colonies were situated not far from India, majority of the migrants returned home after serving as plantation labourers. These systems, which began in the first and third quarter of the nineteenth century, were abolished in 1938 (Jayaram, 2004).

Emigration from India did not stop with the abolition of indenture and other systems of organised export of labour, nor was it limited to that system alone. There emerged 'free' and 'passage' migration of Indians in response to enormous job and commercial opportunities in several parts of the British Empire. The emigrants under this pattern 'paid their own passage and were free in all respect' (Jain, 1990). The members of trading communities were 'from Gujarat and Punjab to South Africa and East Africa (Kenya, Tanzania and Uganda), and those from South India to Southeast Asia' (Jayaram, 2004). Most labourers immigrated to East Africa to work on the construction of railroads (Jain, 1989). These emigrations were not officially sponsored, they themselves paid their passage and they were free in the sense that they were not bound by any contract.

Indian emigration also took place to Europe and North America under the voluntary system of migration. Most of these emigrants were labourers, professionals and students. Sikhs who made up the majority of Indian emigrants to America in the early twentieth century were workers and farmers (Leonard, 1989). As regards Britain, the Bengali Muslims and Gujaratis were the prominent groups of Indian emigrants during the nineteenth century (Sahadevan, 1995). Some of the members of the Indian community went abroad along with their British officials who served in India as civil servants (Helweg, 1993). To a small number of emigrants in a few colonies, the pattern of migration had been involuntary – kidnapping, forceful deportation and forced banishment of convicts. It was carried out mostly to the West Indies through Pondicherry and Calcutta in the later part of the nineteenth century (Tinker, 1993). The British government also considered convicts as cheap labour when the demand for labour in the colonies had a steep rise (Sahadevan, 1995).

Post-colonial emigration

A new and significant phase of migration began after India became independent in 1947. Broadly, two patterns of emigration can be identified in the post-independence emigration:

a. The emigration of professionals to the industrially advanced countries like the United States, England and Canada, and
b. The emigration of skilled and unskilled labourers to West Asia.

The large-scale and steady emigration of doctors, engineers, scientist, teachers and the other semi-professionals to the industrially advanced countries of the West is a post-independence phenomenon, particularly in the late 1960s and 1970s. This pattern of emigration is often described as 'brain drain', and is essentially voluntary and mostly individual in nature (Jayaram, 2004). This 'second' and subsequent generation of emigrant population enjoyed economic prosperity and socio-cultural rights. This stream of emigration resulted in vibrant Indian communities abroad. The knowledge of English and contact with other Indians, who had already settled in the countries of Europe and North America, have increased the interest in migration to these countries. Initially, the receiving countries in Europe and North America easily accepted these immigrants because they found them useful for the development of their industrial economies, particularly their contribution to science and technology. Later, when this professional migration gathered momentum, the receiving countries started restricting the flow of immigrants (Wood, 1983).

The emigration of skilled and unskilled labourers to West Asia is entirely different in its economic and social implication from the nineteenth- and early twentieth-century emigration. The process of migration to West Asia has been voluntary and temporary in its nature (Pant, 1998). In the wake of the oil price boom in the 1970s in the Gulf region, the demand for labourers grew stupendously. The fixed temporary contacts attracted labourers from the South Asian countries to work in the oil-producing countries of the Middle Eastern region. By the year

1975, the labour supplies from Arab countries seemed to have been depleted (Knerr, 1990). This created an increasing demand for expatriate labour in these oil-exporting countries of the Gulf region such as Saudi Arabia, United Arab Emirates (UAE), Oman, Bahrain, Qatar and Kuwait. This demand could not be satisfied locally because of small domestic populations (Weiner, 1982). Most of the emigrants here were semi-skilled and skilled workers (as construction workers, housemaids, cooks and drivers) recruited by agents operating in major cities of India.

In different periods, the magnitude of people emigrating and their destination has varied. In other words, time, magnitude and destination are the important variables in the analysis of the Indian Diaspora. The reason to leave their homeland and to settle down in an alien land is influenced by various factors. This includes 'the motivating factors of – push and pull' (Sahadevan, 1995). Unemployment, under-employment, poor working conditions, low wages, competition for higher posts, natural calamities etc. have been the 'push' factors. European influence and their domination had created severe economic upheavals, disturbances and deprivations among peasants. The prospect of a paid job was the only way to get rid of their depressed conditions. This was one of the 'push' factors. The British colonial administration needed cheap labour, which was readily available in India (Knerr, 1990). The 'pull' factors include attraction of people to the new location, better living and working conditions, handsome salaries, employment opportunities as well as educational and cultural facilities for personal enrichment. The persons having good professional and commercial positions also migrated largely for better social and economic gains. Behind all these factors always remains the political scenario, both internal and external. It was this scenario that determined both the choice and the opportunity in the emigration.

On the whole, the Indian emigration pattern had been both assisted and unassisted in almost all the countries. Despite various patterns and modes of migration, a considerable number of Indians migrated only under the indentured system. A majority of present-day overseas Indians are the descendants of the indentured labourers. Further, the colonial and post-colonial migrations were a two-way process. After the completion of their contract period, many Indians returned to their motherland and re-emigrated to either old destinations or new places. Out of some 30 million Indians who had migrated to different parts of the world during 1834–1937, around 24 million returned home, resulting in the net migration of only 6 million (Davis, 1951). Yet it was a migration that was spread far and wide across continents. Thus, this whole process of emigration created a heterogeneous Diaspora in terms of their origin, period of migration and destination.

India's Diaspora policy

Historical background

India's imperial legacy had led to the creation of the Indian Diaspora. India's nationalist leadership first turned its attention to the issue of Indian overseas as far back as 1890s (Lal et al., 2006). Racial discrimination and restrictive immigration policies in the colonies were forging an emotional bond between Indians overseas and emerging nationalist leadership. Both groups considered themselves engaged in opposing colonial regimes. Before independence, the Indian National Congress (INC) demanded equal rights and status to the overseas Indian nationals with other local people of the land (Sahadevan, 1995). It included those Indians who had migrated to other countries under the British, 'indentured labour system'. British Imperial policy had no such compulsion. Its only interest had been in replacing 'slavery' by recruiting 'indentured' labour from India (Dubey, 2003). The indentured labour was based on a supposed 'voluntary' contractual system and after finishing their term, labourers were free to return to their homeland. In many cases, however, the colonial rulers actively discouraged the returning of the labour by charging heavy amounts of money for their return passage (Dubey, 2003). They were further discouraged from returning by offers of a plot of land. Behind the economic compulsions, the political strategies were always played out.

Until 1908, the Congress ardently asked the Imperial government to adopt a tough attitude towards those self-governing colonies which were ruthlessly dealing with Indian emigrants by denying them their just rights as the citizens of the Empire (Zaidi, 1985). In its annual sessions in 1911 and 1912, the INC asserted its solidarity with Indian settlers in Africa and in 1916 in Lucknow, it expressed its 'ever growing sense of dissatisfaction at continued ill treatment of Indian settlers' (Lal et al., 2006). Many Indian leaders cited the deceitful ways of labour recruitment – by fraud and by force – and the treatment they were meted with, both during the long journeys and in plantations, and called it as 'a system of slavery in disguise' (Ghai and Ghai, 1970). The Congress also raised the issue of their conditions of work. At the Imperial Conference of 1921, the Indian delegation lobbied for equal rights with the British population to be granted to the overseas Indian population living in the Dominions (Lall in Østergaard-Nielsen, 2003). But when the Imperial administration did not pay heed to the INC's demands, it pressurised the British Indian government to fight for the rights of the Indian settlers.

For the INC leadership, the cause of Indians overseas was an extension of the anti-imperialist struggle in other parts of the empire and presented an opportunity to highlight colonialism's underlying racist dimension. The 38th Indian National Congress Annual Session in December 1923 declared that unless India became independent, the grievances of Indian Diaspora could not be properly remedied (Tinker, 1993). Nation-wide *hartal* was organised by the INC followed by public meetings and boycott of British goods to mobilise support for the cause of Indians overseas (Sahadevan, 1995). In 1929, the INC institutionalised this aspect by setting up an Overseas Department under Jawaharlal Nehru, who showed special interest in international affairs (Lal et al., 2006). The department would stay 'vigilantly aware of all legislations and enactments that adversely or otherwise affect Indian settlers abroad' (Lal et al., 2006). Further, Indian settlers were encouraged to develop a harmonious relationship with the natives in the colonies so as to ensure success in their struggle against the colonial government (Zaidi, 1985). In the 1940s, the Second World War and its adverse effects on Indian communities in South East Asia gained widespread sympathy for them. Subhash Chandra Bose's formation of the Indian National Army (INA) and his call to Indians overseas to take up arms to liberate the motherland gave a further boost to the patriotic sentiments.

Simultaneously, expatriate Indians also made a contribution to the movement for independence. The Overseas Indian community published papers and generated political and public opinion in America to favour the Indian freedom struggle (Sheffer, 1986). Funds from the Diaspora supported the movement, demonstrating that the solidarity was mutual (Lall, 2001). At the same time, the Congress exhorted the overseas Indians to treat the interests of original population, superior to all other interest and continue to cooperate with them for mutual advancement and removal of disabilities (Sahadevan, 1995). Several efforts were made to improve the condition of Indian nationals abroad but nothing substantial was achieved. Hence, the attainment of India's independence was considered as pre-condition for the effective protection and improvement in the status of Indians abroad. Even Gandhi, who initially made India's Diaspora a major issue, shifted his energy towards gaining freedom from British rule (Sheffer, 1986). The settlement of the problems of Indian community abroad was set aside to be decided on the basis of 'mutual agreement with independent countries' (Zaidi, 1985). Thus we see in the first half of twentieth century a marked beginning and strengthening of a vital ideological link between Indian political leadership and overseas Indians only to be somewhat reduced in the focus of the national freedom struggle. Domestic politics had prevailed.

The Nehruvian era

India's independence in August 1947 was a result of the long-term struggle of Indians against British colonialism. All Indians contributed in this struggle whether they resided in India or elsewhere. India's independence was a matter of delight among Indian emigrants, because in many of the colonies they were still ruled by the British. They hoped that India's independence would bring a relief to their plight. However, contrary to the expectations of the expatriate community, Indian independence in 1947 did not prove to be any relief to their miserable conditions. India's policy towards them changed after the withdrawal of the colonial power. India's foreign policymakers adopted a policy which was different from the policy of pre-independence. Jawaharlal Nehru, after taking over the leadership of India in post-independence as prime minister, advised the expatriate community of India to be loyal to their country of residence in order to maintain national sovereignty, amicable international relations, non-interference to the affairs of other nations and for the pursuit of non-alignment. Support to Afro-Asian countries came to be considered more important than support to Indian communities overseas. He not only excluded the issue of expatriate Indians from Indian foreign and domestic policy formulation, but also actively encouraged the Diaspora to integrate into their host societies (Lall in Qstergaard-Nielsen, 2003). Domestic politics mixed with national foreign policy again prevailed!

These overseas communities were advised to join the mainstream of the country of their adoption and completely identify themselves with the local aspirations. This happened even in the face of persecution and expulsions (Singh, 1979). After India gained independence, the definition of India shifted from an identity based on nationalism to an identity based on territory. In the name of its fight against imperialism and with the aim of creating a third path in international relations through non-alignment, India avoided any indulgence, particularly to defend the interest of its expatriate community. Nehru maintained that overseas Indians should decide whether they would continue as Indian nationals or adopt the nationality of the country of their domicile (Sahadevan, 1995). He further stated, 'if they opted for the former, all they could claim abroad was most favoured alien treatment' (Gopal, 2014). He added, 'if they opted for the latter (i.e. foreign nationality), they should be given all rights of citizenship and India's connection with them will be cultural and not political' (Gopal, 2014). This way Nehru had made 'the expatriate Asians aliens in a legal sense' (Lall, 2001) and their status did not allow for any special relationship between them and the Indian state. The Indian economic setup also contributed to such a policy towards overseas Indians. The government only bothered about political and economic issues, and did very little to nourish the overseas community with cultural food. Thus India could not develop any concrete policy towards expatriate Indians and mostly behaved according to the demand of international circumstances.

One of the important elements that guided India's approach towards overseas Indians has been the emphasis on the development of harmonious relationship with the natives. Jawaharlal Nehru with his broad historical perspective was deeply aware of the problems of overseas Indians. His thoughts on this matter fall into two clearly defined phases (Singh, 1979). There was the pre-independence phase when he was championing the rights of the colonial people for freedom not only in India but throughout the world. He looked upon overseas Indians as a part of that great struggle. And then, as a prime minister and foreign minister, he advised Indian settlers abroad, who had adopted foreign nationality, to identify themselves with the urges and aspirations of their countries of adoption. Nehru announced clearly that the Indians who had left India to seek fortune abroad had to integrate with the local population, support the struggle of that nation and even put the indigenous needs first. He felt the necessity of such relationship because he was of the view that the promotion of the overseas Indian's interests actually rested with the political machinery dominated by the natives of the countries they were in. He hoped that Indian community would not be treated as 'unwanted import' (Lall, 2001) because India was fighting for the cause of anti-racialism. According to Nehru, this policy 'was right and practical, not only in the point of view of opportunism, but also in the long and short term' (Gopal, 2014). To a certain extent this policy was related to the fact that the problems concerning the overseas Indians were no longer anti-imperial matters to be solved under one regulatory power. In the post-independence period most of the states were sovereign states with independent interests, which had to reconcile with

India. India could not afford to be vociferous about the fate of Indians abroad, putting good diplomatic relations at risk.

It is noteworthy that during the colonial period, there was no serious problem encountered by Indians in the country of their domicile or adoption (Yadav, 2005). It was because of the protection and the privileges provided to overseas Indians by the colonial empire. Nevertheless, in the wake of de-colonisation in the countries of Asia, Africa and Latin America, the overseas Indians faced a number of problems on the political, economic and socio-cultural front (Yadav, 2005). The plight of Indians as a Diaspora community abroad is to a considerable extent determined by ethnic, religious and socio-economic composition of the 'host' country (Jayaram, 2004). The birth of Indophobia (fear of Indians) in Kenya, Ghana and Uganda resulted in the mass expulsion of Indians which created problems of ethnic and economic nature. While the ethnic relations between overseas Indians and the country of settlement deteriorated considerably, the economic system of these countries also collapsed (Yadav, 2005).

Africa

Africa had become one of India's foreign policy priorities. One of India's first foreign policy strategies was to develop a policy towards Africa. Many thousands of Asians from the East African countries of Kenya, Uganda and Tanzania had become a 'floating' population in search of a home. India's post-independence relationship with Indians in Kenya stood in marked contrast to that in the twenties and the thirties. While in the pre-independence era, it was thought that if Kenya was lost everything was; in the sixties, at the time of the Asian exodus, the attitude of the Indian government was not influenced by any such feelings (Singh, 1979). India took the legalistic stand that as British passport holders, the Kenyan Indians were British responsibility. The Indian government did not compromise even on the ground of inconvenience to the people of Indian origin due to the trade embargo and absence of diplomatic representation (Lall, 2001).

Wherever in Africa Indians had established themselves, they became indispensable as the main arteries of trade and shopkeepers to the nation. Their success was however envied and they were blamed with the charge that they had done well through illicit activities, by marginalising the local population, and with no other thought than of enhancing their own interests and prosperity.[4] These charges were outrageous but were used to justify the cruel and brutal treatment meted out to Indians in such places as Uganda and Kenya. In Uganda, Indians were charged of taking away livelihood from the black man and Idi Amin asked for their immediate removal. In Kenya too the eviction was only slightly less callous. Even in such critical conditions, India's overall policy stand continued to be supportive of the decolonisation in Asia and Africa and left the Diaspora mostly to fight for itself.

Indians in South Africa too faced severe racial discrimination. They were not only seen on the black side of the colour divide, but least able to influence political change and the most vulnerable minority in South Africa. Their position started deteriorating steadily after losing parliamentary and municipal franchises in various elections in early twentieth century (Lall, 2001). Later, when the racial discrimination increased greatly the Government of India imposed economic and cultural sanctions on South Africa just after the Second World War. The Indians living in South Africa had always maintained cultural and commercial ties with their country of origin. This was a severe blow to the local Indian population as it affected their commerce, religious and cultural activities. The actions of Government of India were, at first, to protest against the treatment of people of Indian origin, and later lobbying against the apartheid system as a whole. The political message was clear; local Indians were expected not to rely on India for any kind of support or special treatment.

India did not view the racial discrimination against overseas Indians as an 'internal problem' of their adopted country, but a matter of international concern because what involved in it was the violation of human rights (Sahadevan, 1995). In the pre-independence era, Nehru pushed Congress, several times, to pass resolutions against racial inequalities prevailing in South Africa and Kenya. Even after independence, the 1952 Foreign Policy Resolution called for the removal of all forms of colonialism from Asia and Africa. And the Indian residents in those countries were encouraged to emphasise African interests. Motivated by this spirit, Indian government sought the United Nations intervention in settling the South African Indian problem after moving a resolution in the UN General Assembly in 1946 (Sahadevan, 1995). Many tend to believe that the reason behind India's fight against apartheid was based on the fact that the large number of people of Indian origin were victims of the racial segregation. India though was very clear that even if the Indian minority were given racial equality and privileges, it would not end the fight until racial segregation was totally abolished (Grover, 1992). This was quite clearly an international foreign policy position.

Fiji

In case of Fiji, India adopted a similar stand. The crisis had started after the victory of the labour coalition in the general elections on April 1987. The election campaign was the most bitter in Fijian history and fought on racial, social and economic issues (Lall, 2001). After the formation of the government, which included both Indians and Fijians, demonstrations were started, backed by the Alliance Party (Lall, 2001). The inclusion of Indians in the government was seen as threat to the powers and privileges of the Fijian chiefs. In the aftermath of the May Coup, Fiji Indians lost all control and influence over the political process in the country. Like Africa, India did not consider the Fijian crisis as an internal matter of the country. The policy of racial discrimination adopted by the military-controlled Fijian government jeopardised the interests of Fiji Indians. The Indian government criticised the 1990 Constitution of Fiji, which sought to reduce Fiji Indians' parliamentary representation (Sahadevan, 1995), but that was mostly all.

Government of India demanded restoration of democracy, racial harmony and civilian rule on the basis of the racially structured constitution of 1970 and the insurance of equality of right to the Indians in Fiji (Sahadevan, 1995). Besides pressuring the Fijian government, India also urged countries like Australia, Britain and New Zealand to take a joint international action against Fiji. Despite Indian effort, nothing substantial came out of this and the racist government in Fiji continued to remain in power. India's hope that Britain, Australia and New Zealand would put a unified economic and political pressure on the regime in Suva proved false as none of them paid any heed to its request (Gupta, 1987).

Ceylon (Sri Lanka)

The case of Ceylon might seem to be an exception in as much as it did involve a diplomatic clash for the rights of Indians, where Nehru unsuccessfully tried to negotiate rights for Indian residents in the neighbouring country. India strongly protested against the Ceylonese Citizenship Act, which decreed that nationality could only be claimed by descent, or registration (registration requiring continuous residency since at least 1946 or earlier), which excluded most of the Ceylonese Indians (Lall, 2001). The reasons behind the resistance put up by the Indian government were as follows: first, unlike Burma, the Indian community in Ceylon suffered no disruption and could maintain a certain degree of continuity; and second and most important, the Tamil community in

India was directly interested in upholding the cause of the predominantly Tamil Indian population in Ceylon (Singh, 1979).

After independence, India continued to uphold the cause of the Indians in Ceylon. Nehru took a tough stand when he met Ceylonese prime minister Senanayake in 1947. He was not agreeable to Senanayake's proposal that only all Indian married men with 'seven years' stay and single men with 'ten years' stay be given the vote (Singh 1979). Nehru did not approve of this distinction and suggested that anybody with 'eight years' stay should be given the vote. In 1949, the Ceylon government came up with a proposal that it would take up to 40,000 Indians as its citizens and 250,000 as its permanent residents and the permanent resident could work in the country until retirement but had to leave after that with all their savings and belongings (Singh, 1979). Ceylon wanted India to take back a sizeable portion of the expatriate population. The Government of India rejected this proposal.

Burma

The fate of Burmese Indians was quite similar, yet in this case India did not put any pressure on the Burmese government and even signed a treaty of friendship in 1951 (Lall, 2001). Anti-Indianism has a long history in Burma. Riots had taken place even before independence, but after independence the situation further deteriorated. Indian shops were transferred to Burmese traders and they were excluded from the public services. General Ne Win's nationalisation drive deprived the Indians of their source of livelihood (Singh, 1979). In Burma, Indians were forced to leave because of danger or government order (Sheffer, 1986). When the Indian community appealed for assistance, Nehru took the position that this was a matter between them and Burmese state, and India was unable to intervene in the internal affairs of a foreign state.

In several other cases, the policies remained inconsistent. In 1948, a year after Indian independence, several Trinidadian Indians threatened to commit mass suicide unless their government agreed to facilitate their return to India. In spite of Nehru's appeal they came to India but most of them went back. In 1947, hundreds of Indians in Jamaica organised 'back to India' demonstrations, but nothing came out of it (Parekh, 1993).

Administrative arrangements post-independence

At the time of independence, the Government of India had no department dealing with emigration or overseas Indians. In fact even the Department of Overseas Indians that had been set up in 1941 had been transformed into that of Commonwealth Relations in 1944 (Mahajani, 1976).

A separate administrative wing dealing with overseas Indian affairs was located within the Ministry of External Affairs until the mid-1970s, and was revived later, but most of its work remained classified (Dutt in Lall, 2001). This department's role, besides looking at diplomatic issues concerning overseas Indians, was also probably linked to addressing the issue of 'brain drain'. Such 'brain drain', as it is commonly known, in the Indian context, was the phenomenon where young doctors, scientist, lawyers and computer specialists left India for the United States, Canada or Australia to have a better life (Lall in Qstergaard-Nielsen, 2003). As a policy to address this issue, we see Indira Gandhi for the first time raising the idea of promoting Indian scientists, settled abroad, to contribute to India's development. On the other hand, she made herself rather unpopular with overseas Indians during the East African crisis of 1968–72 when she endorsed the Nehruvian policy of non-interference and stressed on India's relations with the African nations first over her concern for the treatment meted out to the Indians there.

The first time any special department or agency was mentioned was in 1986 when a special approval committee was constituted within the Department of Industrial Development for the expeditious clearance of industrial proposals of non-resident Indians (NRIs) (Lall, 2001). Also in 1987, an Indo-NRI Chamber of Commerce and Culture was set up to promote overseas Indians' case (Lall, 2001). Thus, the Government of India had no central machinery to deal with overseas Indians until the mid-1980s. The expatriate Indians became aliens like any other foreigners, and the Government of India restricted their rights in buying property and investing in their country of origin.

Political policy perspectives post-independence

It is regrettable that the overseas Indians, who played such an important role in the history of India, particularly in the colonial period, no longer engaged the attention of the policymakers of independent India. As mentioned earlier, this marks a shift in Indian foreign policy towards the Diaspora in comparison to the pre-independence period. A leading Indian Journal like *Modern Review* of Calcutta, for instance, carried at least one feature on overseas Indians in every issue (Singh, 1979). Shri Banarasi Das Chaturvedi had a journal titled *Vishal Bharat*, which was entirely devoted to overseas Indians (Singh, 1979). But after independence, interest dwindled.

There were many downsides in the policies towards the Diaspora adopted by Nehru. He emphasised on the harmonious relations of Indians who had settled abroad with natives and the promotion of interests of the natives, suggesting that this may create favourable conditions for the Indians. This suggestion of Nehru was relevant to those who belonged to the mercantile class of the society but it was not suitable for those who were underprivileged in the society and subjected to exploitation. By following this policy, Nehru subordinated the expatriate Indians to the natives. Secondly, India did not get involved when part of the Indian Diaspora was going through political, economic and social discrimination or even such a severe crisis as expulsion. As in the case of Burma, Fiji and Uganda, the Indian government showed its helplessness to take care of the expatriate community (Lall, 2001). India feared spoiling its relations with the newly decolonised world and did not even take up the issue of human rights violations. Third, despite the continued informal ties, which remained between the members of the Diaspora and their families in the place of origin, they were not encouraged to take part in the economic development of India; rather the overseas community was viewed with suspicion because of the colonial past. In sum, the Nehruvian policy lacked both clarity and precision. In fact, 'Nehru believed that an Indian identity could emerge only within the territorial and institutional frame of the state' (Khilnani, 1997).

The Nehru policy was based on the unrealistic hope that within the broad pattern of African-Asian nationalism, the separate identity of Indian emigrants would be forgotten. This did not happen. Instead of pan Afro-Asianism, several individual nationalisms emerged. Thus the cry 'Burma for Burmese', 'Ceylon for Ceylonese' reverberated in the 1960s. He treated the question of African freedom in the abstract. He himself was not clear about the magnitude of the specific nature of the problem of Indian settlement in Africa (Gupta cited in Bhatia, 1971). This was the position of successive Indian governments for almost four decades. Though India acquired more muscle power or image as a major player in the world, it still did not attempt to use its influence to protect the interests of overseas Indians. In reality, post-independence, India was caught in a dilemma in how to engage with overseas Indians. The Government of India prompted its expatriates to integrate with the host societies. The reason was the concern of independent India's new diplomatic relations towards the newly decolonising world.

Though the policy adopted under Nehru continued, there has been considerable change in government's approach *vis-à-vis* overseas Indians in the post-Nehruvian period. The later governments of Lal Bahadur

Shastri and Indira Gandhi maintained continuity with regard to the problems of Burmese Indians and the Asians in the Kenya and Uganda. They more or less took the same stand adopted by Nehru. Change, however, occurred in the case of the problems of Tamils of Sri Lanka and somewhat at the time of the Fiji Indians crisis. The conclusion of the Sirimavo–Shastri (Lal Bahadur Shastri and Sirimavo Bandarnaike) Pact in 1964 to repatriate a large number of stateless Indians from Sri Lanka was a remarkable shift on the part of the Indian government from the Nehruvian stand on the question of statelessness.

Indira Gandhi's era

Indira Gandhi's government largely followed the policies initiated by Prime Minister Nehru with minor deviations. Her government notably deviated from Nehruvian principles while dealing with the Fiji Indian questions. The Minister of State for External Affairs Natwar Singh stated, 'India believed that the loyalty of overseas Indians should be to the country whose citizens they are. But we are responsive to their problems and cannot remain unconcerned where their safety and welfare are at stake'.[5] This shows India's concern to the Fiji Indian's problems that it was not merely cultural, emotional and sentimental but to a certain extent political too (Sahadevan, 1995). Moreover, Nehru never raised the problems of overseas Indians in Commonwealth conferences, as he did not consider it a place to discuss the mutual problems of the state. Besides, it would also violate the unwritten principles of foreign policy (Sahadevan, 1995). But subsequent governments raised the problems of overseas Indians prominently in the Vancouver Summit and made a brief mention in Kuala Lumpur (Sahadevan, 1995).

India followed an open-door policy on the matter of international migration of higher skilled workers to the industrialised countries that gained momentum in 1970s and 1980s. Besides deploring the effect of this brain drain, the Indian government never attempted to forbid such movement. Immigration to the United States came in two waves: the first from 1907 to 1924 and the second, much larger wave started in 1965 and continues until the present day. In the first wave, there was significant presence of Indians in the United States, 'when peasants from the province of Punjab began appearing on the west coast, seeking work in Washington's lumber mills and California's vast agricultural fields' (Mishra and Mohapatra, 2002). It was the Immigration and Nationality Reform Act, 1965, that marked the beginning of the second wave of immigration. Under this wave, nearly 1 million South Asians had migrated to the United States, by 1990.[6] In 1970, Asian Indians were the victim of a racial riot in Bellingham, Washington, and therefore concerted attempts were made by the Asiatic Exclusion League and other associations to prevent further immigrations from India in the United States and to restrict the capacity of those already in the country to own property (Tinker, 1977). In this second wave, the migrants from South Asia were largely professional and skilled.

In the middle of the 1970s, the oil-rich Middle East had become a focus for South Asians especially artisans. In the Middle East, Indians have gone mostly as labourers on short-term work permits, and the Indian government has been duty bound to protest about their ill-treatment and to protect their lives and property. Throughout the period of the 1970s to 1990s, the Indian members of parliament raised questions about the welfare of these Indians living in the Gulf. Their situation in the Gulf countries, with poor educational or medical facilities, and without proper accommodation provided, was a reason of concern for the Indian government. At the end of 1970s, these poor working conditions and the unequal wage structure initiated riots in Bahrain (1974), Saudi Arabia (1977) and Dubai (1977) (Knerr, 1990). The situation for women workers was the worst as they were rarely allowed to go out of their working place. This led the Indian government to sign a number of treaties/agreements, impacting deportations, labour conditions etc., with various Gulf governments as well as change its own Emigration Act in 1983 (Gangopadhyay, 2005). When Kuwait was invaded by Iraq in 1990 and again before the beginning of war between Iraq and the United States in 1991, the Indian government took upon itself the mammoth task of evacuating the greater part of the Middle East's Indian population, and it did so on the request of the people who could claim their Indian citizenship as a passport to safety.[7] This was the first time that India fully recognised in responsibility to take care of Indian citizens overseas and actually arranged such mass return of its peoples to safety.

Slowly a discernible change in policy was occurring. On occasion the Indian government did exhibit a concern and positive approach towards its Diaspora; however, the fact remains that India could do little more than indicating its displeasure with the allegedly offending party. It is alleged that this Indian lack of interest in overseas Indians had its roots in its patronising attitude to them. For the politically minded Indians, overseas Indians were either poor or illiterate and this was a liability, or they were rich men who exploited the local population and thereby an embarrassment (Parekh, 1993). There was also a belief that overseas Indian migrants had developed a habit of clinging on to their Indian-ness and as a result they neither integrated with the local population nor evolved an autonomous life of their own.

The Janata government brought some changes in the policy towards the Diaspora. The government for the first time expressed the view that Indian foreign policy would try and attain the right balance between pursuing its diplomatic goals and the issues concerning overseas Indians. This change in policy is symbolised in the changed rules especially in the areas of buying properties between foreigners/aliens and NRIs. For the first time we see a specific enunciation that NRIs with Indian passports did not need the approval of the Reserve Bank of India to buy property, which was still a requirement for other foreigners or NRIs or persons of Indian origin with foreign passport (Lall, 2001). Legally this was rather obvious and nothing new but the RBI's policy clarification was important. It was hoped that allowing NRIs to own property would increase investments flowing into the country. Other financial facilities, which were developed in the same period, were the holding of stocks and shares, and the holding of bank accounts in India. These measures were the result of an early phase of liberalisation in the 1980s. When Rajiv Gandhi came into power, 'NRI' became the buzz word and the consciousness of 'another India' abroad started to grip the Indian mind. His approach towards the Fijian crisis exemplified that the Indian government was becoming attentive of its responsibilities and a debate about the overseas Indian community started in the country.

This change in the attitude of the Indian government towards overseas Indians can mainly be attributed to two reasons. First, stereotypes were broken as more Indians came in contact with overseas expatriates. This also led to a sense of 'pride in their struggles and achievements, a desire to reciprocate their affection, and a sense of guilt for having neglected them for so long' (Parekh, 1993). Second, India's self-interest also played a vital role. India's foreign exchange situation was worsening from the 1970s and the Indians who had moved out after independence into the developed countries were successful and prosperous. India looked to benefit not only by their 'remittances but also by their technological, scientific and managerial and other skills' (Parekh, 1993). With the changing attitude of government, overseas Indians became extremely important and were given the status of NRIs.

Narasimha Rao's government

The Diaspora communities in late twentieth century were in a position to extend their connections to their country of origin with ever-greater intensity and to establish networks globally. Further the Internet, reasonably priced economy airfare and low-cost telecommunications have extended these networks among the Diaspora communities. All these have compelled the government to think and formulate a more constructive policy regarding the Diaspora. In the post–Cold War period, India's foreign policy has undergone a drastic change. This has made an impact on its policy towards its Diaspora. It had developed a particular attitude towards foreign policy in general and Indian Diaspora in particular. Though the Nehruvian policy (not to include Diaspora within the purview of Indian domestic and foreign policy formulations) made sense at the time of independence, it failed to provide scope for advancement and flexibility in the changing global environment. As the world developed, changing from bi-polar to multi-polar, emphasising economic aspects rather than political, India's position proved to be obsolete and obstructed its economic development.

A shift in domestic policy, which was largely delayed, took place in the light of global changes in the early 1990s. With the fall of the Berlin Wall and the subsequent demise of the Soviet Union, the only alternative to the capitalist system was removed. Economically, it disrupted the 'barter system'[8] (Lall, 2001) that India had with the Soviet Union. It also resulted in the diversion of Western aid to the former Communist bloc, especially Eastern Europe for fear that their collapse might trigger off mass migration to the Western Europe (Khilnani, 1997). The collapse of the Soviet Empire had further political and ideological consequences. India's traditional stand of non-alignment in internal affairs became irrelevant as there were no clear-cut blocs to oppose economic and political systems of each other. In fact, different kinds of trade blocs were emerging as dominate groupings to sequence new and complex international relations. The region of South Asia got left behind with its regional problems whereas others co-operated to further regional economic development, welfare and foreign relations. India's moralistic stand which guided its foreign policy on anti-imperialism and other non-economic issues seemed outdated, having no place within the international fora of economic realpolitik. In fact, India did not have much of an international economic policy at all since economic nationalism and independence had been on the agenda since 1947 (Lall, 2001). The early 1990s economic and trade relations were taking precedence over ideological ties and India had to find a place in a trade group and consequently had to rethink its international and regional foreign policy.

The Narasimha Rao government introduced a new economic policy that called for immediate and extensive reforms. The government's first priority was to stop the economic slide and restore India's credibility both domestically and internationally (Lall in Qstergaard-Nielsen, 2003: 129). To achieve this, immediate measures had to be taken to avert default in international payments and restore the macroeconomic balance (Lall in Qstergaard-Nielsen, 2003). The economy was for the first time opened up to outside investors who could acquire a majority shareholding in the Indian companies. A plan to dismantle the public sector loss-making units was also decided upon by the government. Subsequently, tariffs were slashed and the rupee was made convertible on the trade account. Thereafter, the rupee was also devalued. On India's balance of payment position, R. Thakur, Minister of State of Finance, stated: '. . . the resulting improvement in our balance of payments will restore the confidence of NRIs in Indian economy and encourage the inflow of foreign exchange from the NRI sources' (Ministry of External Affairs, 1991)

The term 'NRI' first appeared in the parliamentary debates in 1984, but did not replace the other headings in the indexes of 'Indians Abroad' or the 'People of Indian Origin' or even the 'expatriate Indians' (Lall, 2001). Moreover, there was no clear demarcation of the term 'NRI' until 1991, when the definition was linked to citizenship. (In fact, the legal definition of the term 'NRI' or non-resident Indian is only a tax-related definition in the Income Tax Act.) From the Nehruvian period to the Narasimha Rao government's era, the policy towards Diaspora continued with both continuity and change until 1998. The two major shifts from the Nehruvian policy were: first, the foreign policy priorities changed from a global, ideological to a regional and more realistic one (from Nehru to Rajiv Gandhi) and second, a change in foreign economic policy from a closed economy to a relatively open one (Rajiv Gandhi to P. V. Narasimha Rao).

But by 1991, the end of the Cold War had brought significant transformation globally, and India had to face new political, economic and security challenges. India's economic condition until this time was very poor and its foreign exchange reserves had reached an all-time low. The implementation of the policies during the early part of 1980s gradually liberalised the imports of raw materials and capital goods. A degree of flexibility was introduced in the policy concerning foreign participation. In view of these economic developments, the government had to reformulate its economic strategy, something better known as economic reforms or liberalisation. These economic reforms resulted in decontrolling of the private sector, reform of the public sector, liberalisation of financial markets, de-licensing of industries, decontrol of foreign trade and allowing the entry of foreign capital. This shift in the policy of the Indian government implied that India was now targeting its expatriates who had left in post-independence period mostly to the developed countries of the West for individual advancement to now return or contribute to the nation's economic advancement.

A number of special concessions were given to the NRIs to invest in the Indian industry, to set up new industrial ventures or to deposit their foreign currency in Indian banks. Some important incentives were (Lall, 2001): NRI investment in real estate development; 100 per cent incentives in 34 high-priority industry; maximum limit of portfolio investment increased from 5 per cent to 24 per cent; investment in India development bonds; approval of investment and technical collaboration on automatic basis; establishment of chief commissioner for NRIs; exemption of FERA (Foreign Exchange Regulation Act) to NRIs on various issues etc. Despite these relaxations, there remained the blockades associated with repatriation of profits along with the overwhelming bureaucratic hurdles. Policy implementation was slower than political declarations of the government because the majority of the Indian population or the politician who was not ready yet to break away from the Nehruvian practice, and to jump into a new eco-system where external capital would dictate the Indian state of affairs and development. As a result of these structural changes in policy, implementation and regular administration became slow and the loss-making PSUs continued to function. The result was the prevalence of prejudice towards foreign investment (because of the colonial past), and even stagnation in the local bureaucracy and local industrial lobby.

Simultaneously, the NRIs also placed their demands for a bailout plan of the Indian economy. They wanted the reforms to include measures to protect their investments and use them efficiently. The question of dual citizenship also arose. The NRIs (in this case, 'persons of Indian origin' with foreign passports) felt that granting of Indian citizenship would make investing in India easier. Under the existing rules they could not stay in India for more than 180 days without being liable to local taxes. Confusion prevailed within the government and the media as contradictory statements were made by a large number of government officials (Gangopadhyay, 2005). This uncertainty ended when Minister of State for Parliamentary Affairs M. M. Jacob stated, 'The concept of dual citizenship is not consistent with the Constitution of India and Citizenship Act, 1955 . . . citizenship was not clearly defined before the passage of Independence of India Act' (Varadarajan 2010). The government was of the view that such a step would be hazardous to national security as Pakistani citizens could in effect claim Indian citizenship (Lall, 2001: 168). Therefore, mistrust continued between the government and NRIs. It was felt that the Government of India had shown disregard towards expatriates. The government's inability to create the right economic environment was the cause of the estrangement between India and her Diaspora. In the past, only on two occasions had the Indian government asked the expatriates to contribute towards the defence efforts during India's war with Pakistan and China, and many were not willing to take up this third request.

The policy of the Indian government seemed to be targeting its expatriates who had left in the post-independence period mostly to the developed countries for economic reasons. The term 'NRI' itself therefore became synonymous with that of an Indian who moved to the West to improve her/his economic status, and not those who left the country as indentured labour, or as petty traders especially under colonial rule. The latter group was no longer the focus of interest as far as economic priority was concerned. The attention towards the older Diaspora was largely cultural, patchy and patronising whereas the present concern was largely economic and political (Parekh, 1993). Here, the preoccupation appeared to focus on the emigration to the West with a view to attract their capital and skills and to mobilise their political influence. It is the latter, much pampered group, which enjoy disproportionate public attention in India (Parekh, 1993). Unfortunately, the overall perception continued to be that even after liberalisation and the public realisation that the Diaspora could lift India out of economic problems, there was little the government was prepared to do to establish a relationship in order to cash the asset. This applied even more to the overseas Indians that had emigrated in the nineteenth and early twentieth centuries. The discernment was that the relations of India and NRIs or overseas Indians were a case of 'mutual abandonment' (Lall, 2001).

Conclusion

The present chapter has attempted to outline the emergence and stages of Indian emigration and focus on the relationship between the Indian government and overseas Indians in the post-independence era. It has traced the historical and geographic landmarks where India's policy towards the overseas Indians shows some variations though it is more or less consistent with the political or diplomatic position that emerged. The foregoing analysis shows that India adopted no planned policy towards the Diaspora but its reaction was mostly based on reactions to the emerging overseas developments. It failed to develop a strong relationship with the Diaspora throughout the post-independence period and to use this asset to assist the Indian economy. Both pre- and post-independence analyses show a clear political stance that overrides all others.

It is only since the emergence of an Indian elite in the Western world during the 1970s, especially in the United States, Canada and the United Kingdom, that India evinced keen interest in NRIs, the New Diaspora, in so far as to attract their investment for developmental programs in India. During the 1990s, following the policy of liberalisation, half-hearted attempts were made to secure the involvement of affluent NRIs in setting up industries and to tide over the foreign exchange crises through attractive financial schemes. India's policy of foreign non-involvement slowly changed over the years to allow the overseas Indians to take part in the economic development of the country. However, the barriers remained high while the process remained slow. The shift in India's policy towards its Diaspora certainly has doses of pragmatism, as it is trying to economically and politically harness the Indian network and resources that until now only existed in the cultural domain through familiar relation and the nostalgic search for roots.

Notes

1 Indentured System: It was a system of contract by which the emigrants agreed to work for a given employer for specific period and performing the task assigned to him/her for a specific wage.
2 Kangani: The Kangani system of recruitment was used to supply South Indian labour to Malaya and Sri Lanka. Tradesman known as Kangani recruited the migrants. Each Kangani recruited people belonging mainly to his own caste and kin group.
3 Maistry: Indian labour contractors involved in construction work moved from village to village exhorting labourers to migrate to Burma.
4 http://www.sscnet.ucla.edu/southasia/Diaspora/future.html, accessed on 29 July 2009.
5 *The Hindu*, 17 November 1987.
6 www.IndianDiaspora-History.htm
7 http://www.sscnet.ucla.edu/southasia/Diaspora/future.html, accessed on 22 December 2007.
8 Barter system allowed for international trade without expanding foreign currency.

Chapter 3

Migration and politics in countries of destination

Introduction

Migration policies by definition (and certainly in practice) are rarely implemented to facilitate free movement of people. They are generally designed to control, regulate or limit mobility of persons. Most countries have policies that are designed to restrict access to citizenship and residence by foreigners (Skeldon, 1997). Often, racial or religious bias is tied to immigration policy. This chapter takes into account regional and country-wise case studies of major destination countries of Indian migrants to understand the legal and political frameworks such migrants have to contend with. It discusses immigration policies of the destination countries that have been impacted by such movement. The legal and political structures at the host country have considerable implications on the nature, duration of stay and migratory status of migrant communities. This chapter covers questions of inclusion, integration and incorporation of migrants into civic life along with barriers to entry and stay. It brings to highlight the socio-legal underpinnings of migrant environments and the methods through which migrants negotiate their lives, both at the personal and societal levels. Destinations chosen for focus of this chapter are as follows: The Gulf, Europe, the United States and Australia.

Country case studies

As the world becomes increasingly global, borders have become progressively permeable and cross-border movements are steadily on the rise. As a result, policies that govern the number, characteristics and terms under which foreigners can enter a country have become salient policy and political issues (Massey, 2009). Within this context, India has emerged as a lead country of immigration, emigration and transit. The World Bank classifies India among the top emigrating countries worldwide, where migration is a reality for a large section of population: 5.4 million Indians migrated from India in 2010 alone (World Bank, 2011). Additionally, India figures in three of the top five migration corridors in the South Asian region – India–United States, India–Saudi Arabia, India–United Arab Emirates. India also ranks first in the list of top remittance receiving countries with $69.8 billion followed by China ($66.3 billion), and the Philippines with the United States $24.3 billion in 2012 (World Bank, 2011). With a favourable demographic pattern, the International Organisation for Migration (IOM) (2010) predicts that India is likely to emerge as one of the largest migrant-sending countries by 2050, and the number of international migrants is expected to reach 405 million by this period (IOM, 2010). This rising deployment of overseas workers from India raises fundamental methodological and theoretical questions, as well as major policy issues both at the origin and the destination. Given this upward momentum, it is imperative to examine the nature of these flows and interrogate state responses and the policy climate surrounding India's emigration movements. In this section, we focus on the policies and institutions, at the destination countries, which frame the movement of India's overseas workers, and the implications of these legal and regulatory structures.

Country case study: GCC region (cooperation council for the Arab states of the Gulf)

According to the World Bank (2011), the United Arab Emirates (UAE) registers the highest migrant stock, followed by the United States and Saudi Arabia. The Centre for Development Studies (CDS) estimates place the Indian migrant stock at 12 million in 2011 based on projections from research conducted at the time of the global financial crisis (Rajan and Naryana, 2012). As of now, it is estimated that the Gulf region accounts for 6 million or 50 per cent of the Indian emigrants. Migration to the Gulf began in 1970s and gained momentum over the years. Indians in the Gulf constitute nearly 6 million with a majority of them in the UAE, Saudi Arabia and Kuwait, working in the construction, oil and natural gas, trading and financial sectors. Although a clear majority are low- and semi-skilled labourers, the presence of professional emigrants cannot be ignored. The Indian expatriate population in West Asia increased from 0.2 million in 1975 to 3.3 million in 2001 and is estimated at around 5 million in 2010 (Rajan and Narayana, 2010) and 6 million in 2013. Moreover, the opportunities for skilled workers are poised to increase further as recruitment becomes open for nearly 300,000 jobs, with new refineries and power plants being set up in Saudi Arabia and Abu Dhabi in the course of the next five years. The boom in the investment sector and the associated migration of skilled workers refute the former notion that Indian emigration to the West Asia comprises exclusively of unskilled and semi-skilled labour (Khadria, 2009). Having considered the historical and contemporary proclivity of Indian migrants towards the Gulf region, the importance of the India–GCC corridor cannot be overemphasised.

The Gulf Cooperation Council (GCC) includes the six countries of the Persian peninsula: Bahrain, Kuwait, Oman, Qatar, Saudi Arabia and the UAE. The GCC countries have some of the world's highest shares of migrant workers in their labour force, as migrants are over 75 per cent of private-sector workers in these countries (Hussain, 2011). A majority of GCC countries exhibit demographic imbalances, to different degrees, owing to this high percentage of non-nationals in the population on one hand, and their expanding youth populations on the other hand. Demographic trends have a decisive influence on a country's economic, labour and population policies, and migration is a key social policy intervention that allows governments to control and regulate the volume and nature of its demographic base. States play a central role in regulating the unfettered flow of capital, ideas and labour. Since the 1970s, the GCC has woken up to the challenges posed by its shifting demographics and implemented a series of corrective policy measures that aim to bring about governmentally administered changes in population – both quantitative and qualitative (Zachariah and Rajan, 2014).

Immigration is a sensitive policy issue for any country. It is no mean task to manage the growing expectations of citizens while balancing the social and economic developments of a country that relies primarily on foreigners to drive development. This is especially true for the UAE and Saudi Arabia. With this in view, it is important to analyse how government laws and policies influence migration patterns, concerning both unauthorised migration and legal immigration. While a majority of industrialised countries of the developed world have set up long-standing legislation surrounding issues of immigration, settlement and integration, state policies on migration are still in a nascent stage in the Gulf countries (Shah, 2012). The relatively newly industrialised countries of the GCC (e.g. Saudi Arabia and the UAE) have avoided an explicit immigration policy altogether, preferring rather to import foreigners strictly as workers, without recognising their rights as residents or citizens (Massey, 2009).

Let us first consider the dynamics of Indian migration to the UAE and then seek to understand the shifting politics of migration to Saudi Arabia, and the rest of the Gulf region.

Indian presence in the UAE

Historically, migration to the UAE has been driven by economic factors and to fulfil the growing demand for cheap, flexible labour. As among all GCC countries, rapid development financed by oil revenues resulted in robust economic growth, infrastructure development and the expansion of public goods provisions in the UAE. In order to support and sustain this growth, in the wake of a shortage of supply of native labour, foreign workers primarily from the Indian subcontinent were imported to fulfil this role. The UAE attracts both low- and high-skilled migrants, comprising over 90 per cent of the country's private workforce, due to its economic attractiveness, relative political stability, and modern infrastructure – despite a drop in oil prices and the international financial crisis in 2008 (Malit and Ali Youha, 2013; Narayana and Abraham, 2012). Of the large number of jobs that were created in the wake of the oil boom of the 1970s, those towards the relatively lower end of the skill spectrum were sought by immigrants from South Asian countries. Today, this trend has significantly increased and diversified across multiple sectors. Indian migrant workers fill UAE's critical labour gaps, primarily in manufacturing, construction, services and domestic work sectors. This relationship has evolved into a significant partnership in the economic and commercial sphere with the UAE emerging as the second-largest market globally for Indian products. At the same time, Indians have emerged as important investors within the UAE with over 500 Indian companies having registered in Abu Dhabi, 6,000 companies in Dubai, 3,800 in Sharjah and more than 300 in Jebel Ali Free Trade Zone. India is the sixth-largest export destination for the UAE-manufactured goods. Indo-UAE trade, valued at US$180 million per annum in the 1970s, is today valued over US$18 billion (Consulate General of India, Dubai, 2012). Consequently, the strategic significance of the India–UAE corridor as the site of study cannot be overemphasised. UAE's location at the epicentre of present-day geopolitics, its position as one of the biggest labour destinations in the world and the size of the migrant Indian population underscore the need to further examine the conditions within which migrants operate in the region (Rajan, 2013).

According to the United Nations (2009), the UAE has seen a sharp increase in international migration over the past two decades. In 1990, there were 1.33 million international migrants who comprised about 71 per cent of the UAE's entire population. The following decade, in 2000, this figure increased to 2.286 million. In 2010, number of international migrants in the UAE increased to 3.293 million. It is noticed that the per cent of international migrants was almost constant in the whole period (70 per cent or slightly more), which means that the growth rate of citizens was almost the same as the growth rate of immigrants. In 2013, the UN estimates that the UAE had the fifth-largest international migrant stock in the world with 7.8 million migrants (out of a total population of 9.2 million). Of this, Indians comprise the vast majority of the immigrant population in the UAE (66.4 per cent), followed by Pakistanis and Sri Lankans (13.8 per cent and 4.9 per cent, respectively), while migrants from Egypt comprise 4.3 per cent. Most of the UAE national workforce is absorbed in the public sector, while foreigners constitute the bulk of the private sector workforce (Knapman, 2012). Furthermore, during the 1970s and 1980s the composition of migrants from India was largely restricted to South Indian migrants from Kerala (Venier, 2007). Migrants from the southern states of Kerala, Andhra Pradesh, Karnataka and Tamil Nadu comprised over 50 per cent of emigration clearances from India to UAE in the 1990s and early 2000s (ICOE, 2009). In light of the un-quenching demand for expatriate workers in the region, a more varied array of Indian states have made sizeable contributions to these migratory flows – newly emerging states such as Rajasthan, Uttar Pradesh, Maharashtra and Punjab (Kumar and Rajan, 2014).

The UAE relies heavily on its transient population due to the low literacy rates and subsequent high unemployment rates of the native population (Fargues, 2011). The abundance of capital on one side and the shortage of local labour on the other hand led to a mass influx of workers from the Indian subcontinent (Hussain, 2011). For over three decades, Indian migrant inflows have helped to correct UAE's demographic imbalances and workforce requirements. At the same time this migration is characterised by its contractual nature. The temporary status of migrant workers leads to protracted implications on remittance behaviour, duration of stay and level of socio-economic integration. Despite the fact that 70 per cent of the population in the UAE is foreigners, the UAE does not regard itself as a country of immigration. Instead, it labels non-citizens as contract labourers or guest workers. This indicates that expatriate workers with the UAE do not accumulate legal or citizenship rights by virtue of their duration of stay; rather, all immigration policies and labour laws are tailored to deal with fluctuating influx of workers and regulate their 'temporary' engagement in the labour force.

The UAE government in 1971 introduced a temporary guest worker program called the 'Kafala Sponsorship System', under which nationals, expatriates and companies were allowed to hire migrant workers (Longva, 1999). In domestic legislation, the key instrument related to the immigration is this sponsorship system that requires foreigners to have local citizen sponsors known as *kafeel*. A *kafeel* grants permission for foreigners to enter the country, monitors their stay and approves their exit. Since the *kafeel* is responsible for all aspects of the foreigner's stay, if the *kafeel* withdraws sponsorship, the foreigner has no legal right to stay in the country. Disputes over wages, accommodations, working conditions or other work-related issues can prompt the sponsor to withdraw sponsorship. The Kafala system has posed a number of challenges for UAE policymakers both at home and in the eyes of international stakeholders (Longva, 1999). Primary among them are the need to ensure economic opportunities for UAE nationals, and the demand to close policy and implementation gaps in addressing concerns that migrants fall victim to labour and human rights abuses in the UAE (Malit, Jr and Ali Youha, 2013).

In 1999, the UAE government first announced policies targeting to decrease its heavy and unsustainable dependence on foreign workers, and restore demographic balance within the UAE. This first move was directed against the nationalities that constituted the largest percentage of the workforce, specifically Indian and Pakistani workers. This initial attempt was unsuccessful owing to a new trend where other nationalities immediately replaced these workers, notably Nepalese and Bangladeshis. In August 2000, the government decided to double the fees for labour permits. This was followed by the introduction of an employment visa requirement specifying that all foreign workers must hold, in the least, a secondary education diploma (Knapman, 2012; Zachariah and Rajan, 2008). When considering migration policies and institutions in the UAE, it is important to bear in mind that laws differ between the Emirates and immigration requirements frequently change.

The main state institution dealing with migration and immigrant concerns is the Ministry of Labour and Social Affairs. The ministry aims to implement and create labour policy within the UAE, including organising and supporting labour relations at international level. While there are no other formal domestic policy documents dealing with labour emigration, it has been argued that a de facto policy exists that is apparent in bureaucratic procedure and Labour Laws. The Labour Law of 1980 also provides for a special section 'at the Ministry of Labour and Social Affairs for the employment of non-nationals and the functions of said Section shall be regulated by a Ministerial Resolution' (Article 16). The Federal Law No. (8) of 1980, On Regulation of Labour Relations or the UAE Labour Law regulates all aspects of labour relations between employers and employees within the country. A summary of key considerations and implications of the Labour Law has been compiled below (Al-Tamimi and Company, 2010):

Article 3

The provisions of this Law shall not apply to the following categories:

1. Employees of the Federal government and of governmental departments of the emirates of the Federation, employees of municipalities, other employees of federal and local public authorities and corporations, as well as employees who are recruited against federal and local governmental projects.
2. Members of the armed forces, police and security.
3. Domestic servants employed in private households, and the like.
4. Farming and grazing workers, other than those working in agricultural establishments that process their own products, and those who are permanently employed to operate or repair mechanical equipment required for agricultural work.

Domestic workers are not covered by the UAE Labour Law and are therefore not entitled to labour protection; 'domestic servants' are not considered employees, households where they work are not considered workplaces, private persons who hire them are not considered employers and consequently, labour inspectors are forbidden from visiting private households. Laws also render running away from a sponsor's home and hiding or protecting runaway domestic workers as illegal (Shah, 2005). These complex dynamics combine to make domestic service a precarious sector that operates within a legal and institutional vacuum, leaving domestic workers especially vulnerable to exploitation and according them little legal recourse to justice. In the same way, farm workers, cattle-herders, fisher folk and seamen are exempt from legal provisions and do not enjoy statutory coverage. These legal grey areas allow a multitude of Indian workers to fall through the cracks of labour laws and protective policy measures.

Article 10
Where national workers are unavailable, preference shall be given to the following:

1. Arab workers who are nationals of an Arab Country.
2. Workers of other nationalities.

The stated preference for national workers over non-nationals ensures that despite their sizeable numbers and significant contributions, immigrant workers are not accommodated into the labour market or society on equal terms (Fargues, 2011). The unfavourable dynamics of migrants' socio-economic position relative to nationals is further compounded by underlying discrimination and xenophobia of laws and norms that impede migrant's progress in the country (Jureidini, 2003).

Article 13
Employees who are not UAE nationals may be employed in the UAE only after approval of the Labour Department and the obtainment of a work permit in accordance with the procedures decided by Ministry of Labour and Social Affairs. Work permits may only be granted if the following conditions are fulfilled:

a. That the employee has the professional competence or educational qualifications that the country is in need of.
b. That the employee has lawfully entered the country and complies with the conditions stipulated by the residence regulations in force in the State.

The incidence of irregular, undocumented flows in this high-volume corridor have led to increased surveillance and restrictive policies by the UAE. Policies aiming to curb irregular migration, in particular unskilled workers, have further resulted in evasive strategies and illegal pathways to entry and employment. This situation further hinders the employment of nationals as well as the safe, secure migration experience for Indian workers – in many cases, the only stakeholders to benefit from such restrictive policies remain the recruitment agents who charge a premium to help migrants circumvent legislature.

Article 14
The Labour Department may not approve the employment of employees who are not UAE nationals unless its records show that there are no nationals registered as unemployed with the Labour Section who are qualified and capable of performing the job.

While such arbitrary clauses populate the Labour Law, they have not yet been fully enforced. With the introduction of the 'Emiratisation' strategy in the early 1990s, certain private sector roles were reserved for nationals and a quota system was initiated for non-nationals to enter the workforce. The aim of such measures was to promote employment of the domestic labour force and draw them in the region's development trajectory (Al Ali, 2008).

Article 15
The Ministry of Labour and Social Affairs may cancel work permits granted to non-nationals in any of the following cases:

a. If the employee remains unemployed for a period exceeding three consecutive months;
b. If the employee fails to meet one or more of the conditions on basis of which the permit is granted;
c. If the Ministry is satisfied that a certain national employee is qualified to replace the employee; in this case the employee shall continue to carry out his work until the expiry of his contract of employment or his work permit, whichever occurs earlier.

It should be noted that Labour Laws in the UAE are clearly skewed in favour of the employer – a citizen – over the foreign immigrant worker. The kafala system of migrant labour sponsorship does not operate like a free labour market in which workers can sell their work to the highest bidder (Longva, 1999). Any competition happens prior to arrival in the country. Once a work contract and permit for entry and residence is agreed upon, migrants are bound to their sponsors by contract. This system also involves that contractors hold the labourers' passport (Knapman, 2012). This is the only way that the residency is considered legal. If the migrant worker attempts to break the contract, they find themselves bearing the burden for travel home and very often are stopped at the border.

Article 128
A non-national worker, who abandons his work without a valid reason before the expiry of his definite term contract, may not, even with the employer's consent, take up other employment until the lapse of one year from the date on which he abandons his work. No other employer may knowingly recruit such worker or keep him in his service before the lapse of such period.

Article 129
A non-national, who notifies the employer of his desire to terminate his indefinite term contract but abandons his work before the expiry

of the statutory period of notice, may not, even with the employer's consent, take up other employment until the lapse of one year from the date on which he abandons his work. No other employer may knowingly recruit such worker or keep him in his service before the lapse of such period.

The UAE now has a complex system of order and resolutions regarding the issuing of work permits for foreign workers. Some of these include discrimination as to which groups of labourers may bring their families. They also have policies designed to control entry into territory by specific migrants, such as iris scan technology which is used to detect whether former deportees attempt to enter the country illegally (Shah, 2005). In recent years, the database on expatriate workers has been linked between and among GCC countries, therefore disallowing deportees and workers given bans in one country from working in another Gulf country (Knapman, 2012). As is evident from Articles 128 and 129, the UAE labour migration management system structurally safeguards the employer and mitigates nationals from risk and loss of employees. This systemic support guaranteed to sponsors consequently undermines the immigrant workforce, leaving them at the margins of the labour market. The vulnerability of immigrant labour in the Gulf region and the lack of statutory provisions and protection have been identified as an important terrain for investigation and intervention by international organisations.

In recent years, the UAE government has substantively reformed its laws and policies to address and accommodate the concerns of those who condemn the Kafala system for exposing migrant workers, especially domestic workers, from exploitative practices. Recent measures have ranged from outlawing employer confiscation of workers' passports to allowing workers to transfer employer sponsorship and introducing wage protection measures. Despite these efforts, human rights and migrant organisations maintain that abusive labour practices have persisted at alarming rates, largely due to poor enforcement and scrutiny of human rights violations. Furthermore, the Kafala system poses many domestic challenges for UAE policymakers, from effectively controlling the costs of the program. According to researcher Mouawiya Al Awad, the UAE government invests approximately $3000 per foreign-born worker to maintain its national infrastructure and services (e.g. police security and subsidised programmes) to, more generally, ensuring economic opportunities for its own nationals (Malit, Jr and Ali Youha, 2013).

Glaring policy and enforcement gaps in the UAE enable foreign and local employers and recruitment agencies to violate local and international labour standards, and also undermine the UAE's efforts to uphold international human rights obligations. The Kafala system has also presented a number of domestic challenges stemming from the country's dependence on foreign labour (Malit, Jr and Ali Youha, 2013). While the UAE has not changed the kafala system, it has implemented incremental changes in the form of a wage protection system requiring employers to pay the wages of migrant workers directly into bank accounts to make it easier to resolve claims of non-payment of wages. In the light of demographic imbalances and stark unemployment, the UAE has adopted nationalisation policies since the 1990s, to increase the proportion of nationals in the labour market. This move, however, has hitherto been unsuccessful (Al Ali, 2008). 'Emiratisation' policies to date have largely been unsuccessful, but more recently, the UAE government has been trying to revitalise the policy.

The UAE experienced major challenges during its process of nation building and economic development. One of these challenges was, and remains, the education, training and development of the national human resource to enable it to play an active role in supporting and contributing to the country's rapid development. In terms of Emirati employment, government sector jobs are considered most favourable by most Emiratis. Compared to the private sector, salaries are generally higher, non-monetary benefits are better and hours of work tend to be shorter. Many private sector establishments operate on ten-hour days, six days per week, with a split shift day. In contrast, the government sector operates on a single shift, eight-hour day and is a five-day week system. Finding experienced Emiratis is also a challenge. Organisations face difficulties in identifying well-qualified and experienced national employees to occupy positions in sectors such as technology, construction and manufacturing (Al Ali, 2008). In addition, when suitable individuals are identified for these positions, they are in a strong position to negotiate high salaries, with demands often exceeding the salary and benefits awarded to their expatriate superiors. In light of these dynamics, expatriate human resource is a factor that cannot be neglected. Cheap, flexible and skilled foreign workers from the Indian subcontinent have undeniably contributed to the UAEs nation building.

Although the UAE does not have a comprehensive migration strategy, a number of legal and policy measures are in place that includes international, regional and national provisions for the regulation of migration, including irregular migration. For example, the UAE is party to the set of conventions related to labour protections; conventions ratified by UAE include Worst Forms of Child Labour Convention, 1999; Minimum Age Convention, 1973; Abolition of Forced Labour Convention, 1957; Equal Remuneration Convention, 1951; Night Work (Women) Convention (Revised) 1948; Labour Inspection Convention, 1947; Forced Labour Convention, 1930; and Hours of Work (Industry) Convention. However, the UAE has not yet ratified the International Convention on the Protection of the Rights of All Migrant Workers and Members of Their Families or the International Labour Organisation (ILO) Convention C189 concerning decent pay and working conditions for domestic workers adopted in June 2011.

In the twenty-first century, more than ever, competition is global. Whether the UAE continues to be one of the most attractive migrant destinations will depend on whether or not the government makes concerted attempts to attract, train and retain the best future workforce from around the world. Recognising the strategic significance of contractual labour mobility between the India and the UAE, the UAE Ministry of Labour and the Ministry of Overseas Indian Affairs, Government of India, signed a historic Memorandum of Understanding on Manpower recruitment in 2006 and updated it in 2011. A history of positive bilateral linkages through the Abu Dhabi Dialogue, diplomatic visits and labour agreements has paved the way for future productive partnerships between India and the UAE.

There is little prospect of a reduced demand for migrant workers in Middle Eastern countries or a complete overhaul in migrant worker policies. Labour migration flows to GCC countries are expected to grow in the coming decades, and will therefore remain a critical public policy challenge. The UAE – although one of the most liberal GCC countries and one that is seemingly proactive in addressing migration and human rights issues – still struggles to balance labour market needs with native-born employment and a host of other pressing concerns. An important first step will be to strengthen efforts in data collection and knowledge sharing across the Emirates, for example, to probe further into career trajectories of UAE nationals versus foreign-born professionals, or to identify the victims of human trafficking. Building on existing initiatives like the Abu Dhabi Dialogue, origin and destination countries could also expand data collection efforts to collectively ensure evidence-based policymaking and improved labour migration governance across the region (Malit, Jr and Ali Youha, 2013). In light of its paramount position as a destination of choice among South Asian workers, it is important that the UAE sheds its slant towards technocratic governance and bordering of immigrant workers, in favour of a more inclusive and efficacious immigration strategy that is built on mutual cooperation and a joint emigration-expatriate effort for development.

Saudi Arabia

Saudi Arabia occupies a pre-eminent position in the history of Indian emigration. Indian workers have been economically and socially entrenched in the Kingdom since the pre-oil boom era and continue to contribute significantly to the country's development. Today, Saudi Arabia hosts approximately 2.8 million Indian workers (Saudi Gazette, 2012), which is roughly 35 per cent of the 8 million foreign workers present in the Kingdom. Indians constitute one of the highest contingents of foreign workers in the country, and the Indian community in Saudi Arabia has been identified as the largest Indian passport holding community abroad (MOIA, 2010). India and Saudi Arabia enjoy cordial relations that have been strengthened through trade, ministerial delegations and MoUs (Memorandums of Understanding) over the years. However, migration is only one component of a complex chain of processes that shape the socio-political landscape of a country. A comparative evaluation of the demographic dynamics of Saudi Arabia and India affords critical insights into labour market characteristics, current government policies and the potential outcomes of these policies for India and the wider Indian subcontinent.

Migrant associations

The Kingdom of Saudi Arabia prohibits unions and collective organisations. In the absence of workers' unions, a burgeoning number of social and cultural associations have been set up in the major cities. These associations play a vital role in community life in the Kingdom. Although migrants' participation in such organisations appears to be for predominantly social, cultural and religious reasons, some of these organisations, as part of their wider welfare agenda, raise funds towards migrant upliftment (Rajan and Joseph, 2013). A number of key Indian associations have been listed as under:

1. Indian Doctors Forum (IDF)
2. Indian Engineers Forum (IEF)
3. Tamil Cultural Society

4. Riyadh Indian Association
5. Kerala Muslim Cultural Centre (KMCC)
6. Indian Cultural Congress
7. World Malayalee Council (WMC)
8. Navodaya Fine Arts
9. Pleace India (Pravasi Legal Aid Cell)
10. Indian Youth Welfare Association (IYWA)
11. Tamil Sangam (Jeddah, Riyadh, Dammam)
12. Navayugam
13. Hyderabad Association
14. Indian Cultural Association
15. Alumni Associations of various educational institutions.

Demographic indicators

The Indian Diaspora community in Saudi Arabia is ethnically and economically diverse, originating from key states such as Tamil Nadu, Andhra Pradesh, Kerala and more recently Rajasthan, Uttar Pradesh and Maharashtra. Expatriate workers range from low- and semi-skilled workers to high-skilled migrants, professionals and entrepreneurs. The Kingdom of Saudi Arabia is the largest country in Western Asia by land area, constituting four-fifths of the Arabian Peninsula. However, it has a small population relative to total land area of 2,148,690 km. Saudi Arabia is among the fastest growing nations in the world in terms of population growth. The Kingdom's population grew three-fold from 7.3 million in 1975 to 27.1 million in 2010. Of this, foreigners account for upwards of 8.4 million.

In Saudi Arabia, much like other countries of the GCC, demographic factors such as ageing, small or shrinking populations together with burgeoning economic opportunities and vast resources have long acted as pull factors for migrant workers from the Indian subcontinent. Saudi's GDP in 2011 was US$693.73 billion, its per capita GNP was US$9163. Low per capita income and slow economic growth induced many Indians to seek their fortunes on Gulf shores. Alongside exponential population rise, the Kingdom's labour markets have witnessed specific demographic pressures that triggered the move towards immigration caps and workforce regulations. First and most noticeable is the Kingdom's youth boom. Secondly, these new entrants into the labour market lack adequate skills and training required to participate in the economy and effectively contribute to economic growth. As a result, the Kingdom continues to be directly dependent on expatriate human resource.

Lastly, the irregular entry and stay of unauthorised migrant workers have further undermined the position of citizens in the Kingdom.

These demographic realities are unavoidable. Given the growing need to employ local youth and balance new and emerging challenges, it seems instrumental to analyse the localisation policies against the backdrop of broader demographic and development processes.

One of the defining characteristics of contemporary Arab societies is the large and expanding youth population. The size and trend of population in the young working ages in Saudi Arabia are critical factors in determining the country's migration policy. Given the growing need to employ local youth and balance new and emerging challenges, it seems instrumental to analyse the localisation policies against the backdrop of broader demographic and development processes.

Status of immigrants

Although entry and stay of foreign workers is regulated under the kafala or 'sponsorship system', loopholes exist that allow workers to bypass state controls and join the labour market without being tied to a specific job or employer. In addition, annual pilgrimages to Mecca (Haj and Omra) open doors to thousands of foreigners for overstaying the visa making it impossible to accurately estimate the stock of foreign workers in Saudi at any given time. The operation of informal economies and migration intermediaries has further encouraged both irregular and regular migration flows (Shah, 2009) and the large-scale settlement of illegally resident immigrants. As a result, low-wage sectors are vastly expanding, thus perceptibly flattening the wages across such sectors and escalating the need to resolve the status of the illegally resident population.

Saudi's labour localisation policies and the Nitaqat law

While policymakers recognise the lasting contribution of expatriates to the country, a revamp of the size and quality of the foreign workforce is long overdue. The Saudi Arabian government has framed institutional arrangements and programmes through which it aspires to influence demographic change and shed its current migrant-dependant economic model by increasing the proportion of native workers in Kingdom's labour force. Two such policy measures were introduced to hedge the economy against impending demographic downfall: 'Saudisation' and 'Nitaqat'.

Saudisation

Saudisation refers to an implicit policy programme undertaken by the Saudi government since 1994, in order to amend the imbalances in the labour market and increase workforce participation of citizens. This is also an attempt to recapture and reinvest the immense capital fleeing the country through foreign labour remittances, estimated at 20 billion SAR annually.

The basic principle of the system was the requirement to appoint a certain percentage of Saudi citizens in all the establishments existing in the Kingdom. The percentage varied in accordance to the activity of the establishment. Generally the percentage was fixed at 30 per cent. The system, however, did not achieve the desired objective. These quotas were widely resented by businesses that were forced to pay above-market rates for low-skilled and unmotivated local workers. More than 6.5 million expatriates are currently working in the private sector. This compares with only 700,000 Saudi workers, constituting 10 per cent of that value. Moreover, 2 million work visas were issued during the preceding two years. The continued overwhelming dependence of the private sector on foreign workers outweighed the bureaucratic controls on both foreign and national companies in obtaining visas and ongoing government efforts to promote labour nationalisation. The government required a strategic rethink to mitigate, if not solve, the local unemployment quandary.

Nitaqat

More recently, the Saudi Arabian government has been trying to revitalise the localisation policy, considered critical to the long-term stability of the country. KSA's latest indigenisation strategy, 'Nitaqat', came into effect in September 2011. The main obstacle faced under the previous system was that it was impractical to apply one fixed percentage across all sectors and industry verticals. Nitaqat's requirements varies from segment to segment, ranging over 6 per cent for construction jobs to 30 per cent for oil and gas extraction and over 50 per cent for banks and financial institutions (for firms with under 500 employees) (KSA economic review 2012). This program divides the labour market into 41 activities and each activity is grouped under five sizes (Giant, Large, Medium, Small and Very Small) resulting in 205 categories in all. The performance of the establishment in the localisation of jobs is to be evaluated by comparing it with similar establishment to have fair standard for the evaluation. After the evaluation, Nitaqat classifies these establishments into ranges (Excellent, Green, Yellow and Red) based on the ratio of the citizens working in the establishment. The motive behind applying the Nitaqat system is to make the appointment of Saudi citizens a competitive advantage in the various establishments in the Kingdom.

The Ministry of Labour (MOL) in Saudi Arabia granted several advantages to Excellent and Green categories by giving them the eligibility to issue work visas for the development of new businesses. Furthermore, the MOL will give them the ability to contract with non-Saudi workers from the establishments of the Red and Yellow ranges. This will result in granting the establishments that have achieved high rates of localisation, the opportunity to appoint non-Saudi workers from among the available talent pool in the Kingdom. In contrast, the establishments in the Red and Yellow Ranges will be forced to speed up the localisation of the jobs or lose control over the non-Saudi workers in the establishment and not be allowed to obtain new work visas to appoint non-Saudi workers or set up subsidiaries or branches.

Alongside expulsion or deportation of undocumented workers after the grace period, it promises a system that will reliably identify those who are authorised to work in Saudi Arabia and that it will prevent identity theft/spurious visas and end the hiring of future unauthorised workers. It offers a 'path to legality' to illegally resident expatriates and mandates that all workers be accounted for on a public database. Overall, Nitaqat has the potential to introduce much-needed market-adjustments to enhance the efficiency of the private sector.

Naturalisation and immigration control is a high-ranking issue on the Saudi political agenda, which has considerably strained its relation with India and other South Asian sending countries. It is a commonly held belief that recent immigration policies have made the goals of better wages, improved working conditions and upward mobility even more distant for many expatriate workers in the Kingdom. On the other hand, we have seen past India–Saudi emigrations persist notwithstanding three decades of increasingly restrictive immigration policies and the financial crisis. Although the Saudi government is formally complying with Nitaqat it has opened avenues for 'legalisation' of workers and even shifting of workers from one sponsor to another.

Country case study: Europe

Originally a military propaganda term from the Second World War,[1] 'Fortress Europe' is today understood to be a reference to the state immigration policies in mainland Europe. It is today seen to comprise two main aspects – keeping out those who have no right to come and integrating those who do. As several experts have pointed out, there are several contradictory forces at play in Europe on account of the Eurozone crisis on the one hand, and ageing populations on the other. And even within these issues there is lack of consensus. As Barber (2012) points out, while the Eurozone's troubles on the one hand are driving European governments towards closer economic integration, the asylum-seekers and economic migrants arriving from outside the bloc threaten to create the opposite reaction, putting at risk the commitment to the free movement of people enshrined in the Schengen agreement.[2] Recent developments in EU neighbouring regions, in particular the Arab Spring, also sparked concerns about unmanageable migration pressures on Europe, mostly in the southern Member States. This led to some member states putting forward proposals on controls at internal borders. These developments raised questions over whether the measures were in line with the Schengen acquis (the legal guarantor of the free movement of people within the EU).

The twin economic and fiscal crises have led to increased unemployment, in some Member States as much as 20 per cent. This in turn has put a tremendous pressure on political leaders to create jobs, stimulate their economies and crack down on illegal migration. In a number of EU Member States xenophobic and protectionist parties have gained ground. This obviously goes against the advice of experts that the EU will need more immigrants in coming decades to compensate for ageing populations and low birth rates. EU Commissioner Malmström has admitted openly that European ministers of labour almost all speak of the need for immigrant workers but when the ministers go and speak in front of their national public, this message is not to be heard at all.[3]

Any move on EU-level harmonisation of migration policies must begin with a recognition that Member States have very different histories on immigration and have chosen thus unique systems for regulating immigration. Some have chosen varying forms of quotas, while others have chosen more general rules. Recent pronouncements make it clear that Member States find it very important to be able to control the number of labour immigrants entering. A clear focus of many national-level policies has been on highly skilled immigrants. Today many Member States are introducing measures to attract (skilled) labour from third countries. These efforts are to a large degree not being done in a coordinated manner. Given the political context, it is probably not feasible to aim towards a high level of harmonisation at this time.[4]

India–EU migration

Literature on migration shows that migration is the result of interplay of various historical, political, economic and cultural factors. For instance, the characteristics of migration between India and the United Kingdom are extensively related to the colonial history of the countries. Obviously this does not hold generally for the Indian Diaspora in mainland Europe. Very interestingly, there are some important historical links; for example, the Portugal connection with Goa (the former Portuguese colony in India); the French connection with Pondicherry, and the Indian indentured labour origin of the Persons of Indian Origin (PIO) in Le Reunion and Guadeloupe; and the largest of PIO in mainland Europe, the Surinamese Indians in the Netherlands. Other than that, most of the Indian Diaspora in mainland Europe is of recent origin. (Since there is a plethora of literature on the Indian Diaspora in the United Kingdom, in this chapter we would concentrate on mainland Europe and specifically on the five European countries with the largest concentration of overseas Indians.)

India–Europe migration is fast becoming a central element of international relations between India and the EU, both at the bilateral and multilateral levels. Interestingly, both sides have a common stated agenda and view migration similarly from the three-pronged approach of promoting legal migration, discouraging illegal migration and working together in the area of migration and development. In this age of globalisation and the strategic relationship between India and EU, it is time the dialogue be reframed so as to transcend migration and address mobility of human capital in general. It can reasonably be expected that this dialogue will go further and a mutually beneficial partnership would result.

Indian Diaspora in some key European countries

As mentioned earlier, it is important to point out here that as in the sub-continent of India, the Indian Diaspora cannot be seen as or projected as a homogeneous phenomenon; not only were such emigration waves at different periods of time, they also represent different Indian communities and geographies. However, as Esman (2009) points out, the multifacetedness of dissimilar Diaspora communities 'simultaneously highlights the multitudinousness and dynamism of their collectivities'.[5] In this context we must see the break-up between PIO (with European citizenship) and non-resident Indians (NRIs – Indian Passport holders) as depicted in graph of Figure 3.1. Of the five-focus countries we

60 Politics in countries of destination

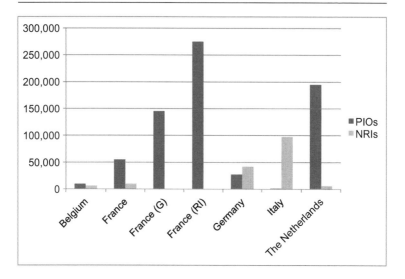

Figure 3.1 Bar graph representing estimated population of Indian Diaspora (PIOs and NRIs) in five European countries in the year 2011.
Source: HLC on Indian Diaspora.

have portrayed here, France (especially the territories of Reunion Island and Guadeloupe) and the Netherlands have substantial indenture-origin PIOs. However, even if one were to take all of Indian Diaspora in each of these countries, they do not account for even 1 per cent of the population (except the Netherlands at 1.2 per cent). In the overall scheme of things obviously their impact and clout in their host countries is at best limited.

Estimate of the size of the Indian Diaspora in all of Europe as per the *Report of the High Level Committee on Indian Diaspora*, 2001 (Ministry of External Affairs, 2001) was almost 2 million (1,984,957 as totalled from the country estimates of the report). Estimate of the Ministry of Overseas Indian Affairs in 2011, based on figures provided by Indian Missions in the same countries, put this at 2.5 million (estimates of all the countries totalling to 2,502,701).[6] This indicates a growth of 26 per cent in the last ten years. If one were to take the five focus countries, it can be seen from the graph of Figure 3.2 that there is substantial increase in all of them (ranging from 25 to over 125 per cent), except the Netherlands (at just over 2 per cent). This empirical evidence of steady growth in numbers clearly shows the pull factor operating in Europe as also is a comment on the stability of the Indo–EU Diaspora.

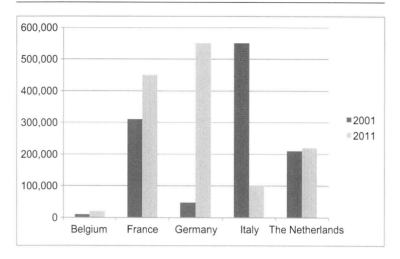

Figure 3.2 Bar graph representing increase in the number of Indian Diaspora in five European countries from 2001 to 2011.

Source: Same as Figure 3.1.

Notes:
(1) The population includes PIOs and NRIs in all the five countries in years 2001 and 2011.
(2) The population of France also covers population of France (Guadeloupe) and France (Reunion Island).

This section focuses on five countries in mainland Europe which have significant overseas Indian population; status of the Indian Diaspora in each of these and their immigration policies are outlined.

A) Indian Diaspora in France

Relations between India and France have traditionally been close and friendly and therefore the Indian presence in France has a long history. Migrants from Pondicherry in India constitute the most prominent Indian community in France, both numerically and in terms of social importance. They comprise people from the former French colonies in India[7] who were given the option of French nationality when the subcontinent became independent. Also during the nineteenth century, 'indentured' labour was taken from India to the French colonies of Le Reunion and Guadeloupe. Today they continue to be French-administered territories. Other Indians have also subsequently arrived in France in small numbers, mainly Sikhs.

During the nineteenth century, many from the Indian elite in French areas went to study in Europe. Besides students, a number of Indian merchants, predominantly pearl traders, came to settle in France in the nineteenth century (Lal et al., 2006). The beginning of the twentieth century saw the growth of nationalism and the freedom movement in India. This also influenced some sections of the Indian community in Britain, French territory in India and Europe to move to France which became a place of refuge for anti-British activities. From 1905 onwards, important personalities linked to the Indian nationalism movement settled in France. Among them were Madam Cama and Vinayak Damodar 'Sawarkar' (Lal et al., 2006). After independence, few of these people (only 2 per cent) opted for French nationality.

Today, PIO in France comprises recent settlers and the old indenture origin French citizens. It is estimated that there are 90,000 PIOs in France and some 30,000 NRIs. In French Guadeloupe, there are 57,000 PIOs and only some 20 NRIs, and in French Reunion Island, 2,75,000 PIOs and 200 NRIs. Together this amounts to fairly substantial 4,52,200 overseas Indians in France and a 39 per cent increase in the last ten years. Today the relations between the two countries are growing rapidly in important areas; with wide-ranging cooperation in political, economic and cultural fields and on defence, space, science and technology and education. The overseas Indians have a firm platform for furthering their and the two countries' relations.

B) Indian Diaspora in Germany

There are about 70,500 overseas Indians in Germany. Of these, about 40,000 hold Indian passports, while the rest have acquired German citizenship over the years. The Indian Diaspora mainly comprises technocrats, small-time businessmen/traders and nurses. There are a number of Indian organisations and associations active on the business/cultural front, cementing ties between India and Germany at the people-to-people level.

Soon after the end of the Second World War, students and workers began to arrive in the Federal Republic of Germany (West Germany) and in the German Democratic Republic (East Germany). In the West, the post-war economic miracle had created need for qualified workers, the universities were open to foreign students and Indians could enter the country without a visa (Lal et al., 2006). The Indian migrants entered the labour market in the highly skilled sector, were able to get good jobs and were socially and economically well integrated into the middle class, to which they belonged in India. East Germany was similar, though at a lesser scale. Due to the economic recession in 1970s, German states stopped extending the work permits of Indian workers. Many migrants had to come back to India; others moved into the less restricted areas of Germany. Several Indian nurses from Kerala lost their jobs. The increasingly restrictive immigration policy from 1970s onwards resulted in considerable decrease in the numbers of Indians arriving in West Germany. Only spouses and some students were allowed to enter legally.

The end of 1990s once again saw the change in the immigration rules of now unified Germany. Due to the re-emergence of scarcity of health care workers, Malayali nurses, whose work permit had not been extended in 1970s, were allowed to return to Germany. The major change, however, came in 2000, when the German chancellor announced a 'Green Card' for IT specialists, which encouraged the migration of many young Indian IT professionals, who also brought their families with them. Hence, the number of Indian citizens living in Germany increased from about 35,000 at the end of 1990s to more than 43,000 in 2003 (Lal et al., 2006). The new migrants lived mainly in the urban centres as Munich, and have developed their own networks. As they are allowed to stay only for five years, their residence is not permanent. The advent of IT professionals has changed the image of India in Germany, which was one of poverty, suppressed women and spiritual superiority. The new emerged image was one of technologically advanced Indians. This was obviously a positive development.

However, the second-generation migrants have now developed into new groups of Indians in Germany. Some of them have retained Indian citizenship but their links to and knowledge of India differ considerably. They live, like their parents, in Germany with difference in terms of skin colour, family name and traditions but they also differ from their parents in that Germany is their first home. More than their parents, they are part of the German society. The PIOs in Germany have founded many associations in Germany; members obviously are few and geographically scattered. Political participation is also limited. Many Indo-Germans are rich businessman but have not yet moved into the political arena. German immigration rules have influenced greatly the migratory process from India as well as the segment of population who migrate.

C) Indian Diaspora in the Netherlands

Most PIO in the Netherlands are the descendent of indentured labourers of the Dutch colony of Suriname, who went there during 1873–1914, to primarily work on plantations. Most of the immigrants were recruited from Uttar Pradesh and Bihar. During their integration into the Surinamese society, they began referring to themselves and their language as Hindustani. Hindustani migration to the Netherlands started in the early 1960s and peaked around transfer of sovereignty to Suriname in 1975.[8]

At present, the Netherlands has the second largest population of people of Indian origin in Europe (next only to the United Kingdom). It is home to about 220,000 Indian and Surinami Hindustani Diaspora, wholly integrated into Dutch society. Although their forebears left India nearly 150 years ago, the Hindustani–Surinami community has deep cultural links with India and is active in promoting cultural cooperation through well-established institutions. There has been a Member of Parliament from the community. Prominent Surinamese are members of municipal councils, like the current deputy mayor of the Hague Municipality – Mr. Rabin Baldew Singh. Mahatma Gandhi was honoured in the Netherlands in a special way through opening of an Indian Cultural Centre named 'Gandhi Centre' in The Hague on occasion of his birth anniversary on 2 October 2011. Opening of the Centre fulfilled the long-standing aspirations of Indian and Surinami Hindustani community in the Netherlands.

NRIs and PIOs from the Netherlands regularly participate in Pravasi Bharatiya Divas conventions. The Regional Pravasi Bharatiya Divas (PBD) Europe – the third edition in the series of regional mini-PBDs – was held in The Hague on 19 September 2009, in partnership with Indian Embassy, the Hague Municipality and Indian Diaspora organisations in the Netherlands. It is unprecedented that two prominent PIOs based in the Netherlands have been awarded the prestigious overseas Indian award Pravasi Bharatiya Samman (in 2009 and 2011) for their contribution to Diaspora-related issues.[9]

D) Indian Diaspora in Italy

According to the Ministry of Overseas Indian Affairs' statistics, the total number of Indian Diaspora in Italy in the year 2001 was 71,500, of which 36,000 were PIOs and 35,500 were NRIs. The number grew significantly over the years and in the year 2011 the total number is shown as 99,127. (Unofficially the number is quoted to be nearer 1,40,000 including irregulars.)

Indian migration to Italy started during 1960s, consequent to establishment of economic links between India and Italy, with the Italian auto-industry. There were some Indians who went to Italy as theology students in early 1960s; however, significant numbers only are seen in the 1990s. It is estimated that 70 per cent of Diaspora is from the state of Punjab, most of them employed in the agriculture, dairy and leather industry. The number of professionals would be 'less than 1 per cent' and Indians owning business is abysmally low. There is a smattering of Indians from the states of Kerala, Haryana and Rajasthan. Indians are largely concentrated in rural areas in Northern Italy.

Like other European countries, Italy's immigration policy has also been fluctuating according to the demand and supply of labour. While Italy's legal immigrants make up less than 5 per cent of the total population, far fewer than in many other EU countries, several amnesties and regularisation programmes in the last decade have done little to reduce the sizeable undocumented population that plays an important role in the informal economy. From another angle, the debate over undocumented immigration is shaped by the Italian private sector's desperate need to replenish a workforce depleted by the rapid ageing and shrinking of the native-born population. Italy's business community continues to be a powerful voice for increased legal migration, and the government has responded with some revisions to Italian labour laws.

E) Indian Diaspora in Belgium

Belgium is one of the most multicultural and multiracial country of the EU. Today, the immigrant-origin population represents about 12 per cent of the total population (Martiniello, 2003). The Indian Diaspora however is very small, being just around 0.7 per cent, but very influential and rich representing the highest percentile of the rich.

According to the Ministry of Overseas Indian Affairs' statistics, the total number of Indian Diaspora in Belgium in the year 2001 was 7000, which increased up to 16,000 in the year 2011, of whom nearly 10,000 had obtained Belgian citizenship. Around 2500 NRIs/PIOs are based in Antwerp, mainly from Gujarat, and are involved in the diamond trade. Indians are employed mainly in the software and diamond industries as well as other local industries in major cities. For example, the Gujaratis from Palanpur district in Gujarat, India, initially arrived in Antwerp to work in the diamond industry. Antwerp in Belgium with Surat in Gujarat, India, formed one of the world's most successful 'Diaspora corridors of business'. Not only are there backward and forward linkages in the diamond trade visible here, but it also involves migrant populations, networks and circular mobility. Software companies like HCL, TCS and Infosys also have a presence in Belgium and employ several people of Indian origin. There are around 500–1000 Indian students pursuing studies in educational institutions of Belgium.

Country case study: The United States

This particular section of the chapter discusses the position in the United States. Considered as the biggest economic power of the world, the United States has always been a most attractive destination for migrants. It is believed that Paleo-Indians from the Asian subcontinent had migrated to the country some 15,000 years ago and since then America is known for its multicultural and diverse background.

The flavour of the United States that has been portrayed in this chapter mostly concentrates on the issue of migration, more precisely on the policies of immigration. It describes the history of immigration laws that has been initiated in the United States. This section starts with a narrow focus of Indian migrants to the United States, their emergence in the country, fight for their inclusion and their journey of integration into civic life. This section will be followed by available statistics on the numbers, nature and characteristics of the migrants to the United States from all the countries taken together. The last section deals with the policies undertaken by the government of the United States to regulate or handle the issue of migration. This section has taken a more general approach in establishing a chronological development of the major events regarding immigration of the country.

Overseas Indians' emergence in the United States

The Indian Diaspora in the United States can be studied or identified roughly into two different phases. Their foray into the country started some hundred years ago during the colonisation of India by the British; Indians learned about the opportunities to migrate while serving in the British military. Since most of the Indian troops in the military hailed from Punjab, we also do find the initial immigrants to the United States basically from the Sikh community. They first marked their presence as agricultural labours working in the agricultural fields of California. This was a period when India was still under the colonial British rule in their home country and they by their background were a highly ignorant, dejected and discriminated community in the destination country. However, despite these Indians fought for their rights, against the social discrimination that they faced.

Indian Diaspora: Fight for freedom

Initially, the then British officials in India had no fear of Indians going to the United States, until the foundation of Ghadar (or 'revolutionary')

Party in 1913 in San Francisco. This for the first time revealed the fact that Indians were seeking support and getting unified to overthrow the colonial power. The central role in this movement for freedom was played by Tarak Nath, an activist who had fought many times against the anti-Asian laws in the United States. The political upheaval that followed thereafter put the host country in an embarrassing position which drove the then US government to initiate steps against the Ghadrites. The formation of the Ghadar Party was believed to be the first step of the Indians in establishing a political movement in the country. But soon in 1917 with the Immigration Act coming in, Asians were restricted from entering the United States with the fear that they would support independence or demand better conditions – overseas or for their own society in the country. Further the existing Indians were denied citizenship which prevented them from owning or leasing land under the Alien Land Law of 1920. This series of regulations resulted in a sharp decline of the Indian population from that time. Later with some concerted efforts of the influential Indians like Sikh merchant J. J. Singh and Dilip Singh Saund, Indians again revived their position in the economy. Initiatives like India Welfare League and India League of America were instrumental in bringing forward efforts for providing citizenship to the Indians.

Towards achieving nationality

A pathway to achieving political power came through the Atlantic Charter Act of 1941, agreed upon by the Allies, which promoted the idea, including for Indians, the right to self-government. For immigrants, however, things changed with the Immigration and Nationality Act of 1965, signed by President Lyndon Johnson. This is also known as the Hart-Celler Act. According to this Act, more individuals from third-world countries were allowed to enter the United States (including Asians, who had traditionally been hindered from entering the United States). It also entailed a separate quota for refugees. The main motive behind such a step was to promote and welcome the skill and not the origin in particular. According to the Immigration and Naturalisation Act of 1965, a quota of 20,000 immigrants was allowed from each country. This marks the commencement of the formal political history of Indians in America (Lal, 1999).

Indian immigration was again seen to surge by the end of 1975, but this time the composition of Indians entering the United States was different in comparison to the initial flock of Indians. These were new emigrants from a composition of different provinces of India unlike the earlier Punjabi immigrants, and also distinguished by way of education and economic prosperity. By the time of the 1990 census, Indians represented the most educated community in the United States, with 87.5 per cent having completed high school, and 58 per cent having a bachelor's degree. These migrants started claiming the legal procedures in the United States to fight for their rights. The first victory in this context came in 1990 when a federal court pronounced Indians to be the descendants of the Aryan race and advised that they should not be subjected or discriminated against because of their race (a rather blinkered ruling but significant nevertheless) By this time, educated Indians started showing up in various government sectors of the United States. Be it in the area of medicine or technology, Indians started emerging as entrepreneurs in businesses, computer programmers and entering other important sectors. These qualities and the professional efficiency of Indians slowly got translated into political ambition. These immigrants had understood the importance of collective power and began to get organised to strengthen their voice.

Historically, the first step behind the formation of collective power probably came through the establishment of a Gurudwara in Stockton, California, in 1912, to be followed up by many more Gurudwaras and temples that today thrive all across the United States. These religious institutions were not only places of worship, but also acted as a meeting place for discussing political affairs. Later on they became more organised and took the shape of associations. (Some of those collective efforts that took the shape of associations are outlined in Appendix IV.)

Empirical evidence of the estimates of migration

Outlined below are some statistics, provided to have a glimpse of the importance of the immigration issue to the country. The presence of migrants in all the states of the United States and the ever-increasing trend is an indication of its significance. Figure 3.3 estimates the number of immigrants to the country between 1995 and 2007 which has seen a continuous surge.

Figure 3.3 has been improved upon in the next section to include the percentage increase in the number of immigrants to the country over the stipulated time period (Figure 3.4). Though the number of immigrants has increased in absolute numbers, the rate of immigrants coming in has seen a decrease until 1970 which again soars up in the last decade.

Table 3.1 gives a list of the top 25 countries according to their presence in the United States. The figure describes a time period of 30 years,

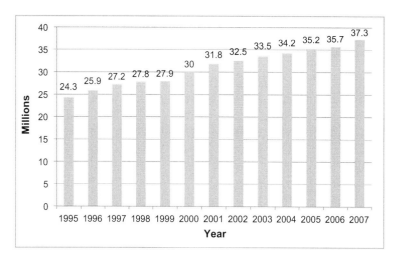

Figure 3.3 Immigrants in the United States, 1995–2007.

Source: Camarota (2007), Immigrants in the United States, 2007, Center for Immigration Studies.

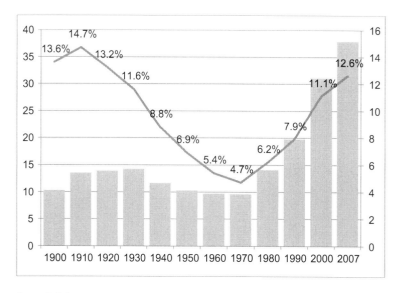

Figure 3.4 Immigrants in the United States, numbers and per cent, 1900–2007.

Source: Camarota (2007), Immigrants in the United States, 2007, Center for Immigration Studies.

Table 3.1 Top 25 countries of birth in 2007

	Total	Share who are citizens (%)	Year of entry[1] Pre-1980	1980–89	1990–99	2000–07
Mexico[2]	11,671	19.8	1,788	2,408	3,890	3,583
China	2,007	52.3	336	492	610	568
India	1,704	38.5	222	314	539	629
Philippines	1,665	60.3	346	450	473	396
Vietnam	999	68.8	188	288	368	155
El Salvador	998	25.8	84	323	336	249
Cuba	980	47.6	362	120	237	261
Former USSR	973	54.7	119	90	471	292
Korea	906	43.4	177	264	210	255
Dominican Republic	856	40.1	146	190	296	224
Canada	699	43.2	309	90	184	116
Guatemala	681	17.4	45	145	188	303
Columbia	669	42.7	135	154	188	192
United Kingdom	590	41.0	236	92	112	150
Jamaica	550	60.4	148	175	126	101
Germany	514	62.6	357	41	45	71
Haiti	514	54.0	88	138	166	122
Honduras	439	20.3	36	56	136	211
Poland	427	51.1	121	77	159	70
Italy	418	76.3	328	34	27	29
Ecuador	411	37.2	72	102	147	90
Iran	371	75.8	109	130	88	44
Peru	354	39.0	58	74	109	113
Brazil	338	24.9	41	53	120	124
Japan	286	28.0	91	26	56	113
World Total	**37,280**	**39.0**	**7,873**	**7,854**	**11,292**	**10,258**

Source: Center for Immigration Studies analysis of March 2007 Current Population Survey cited Camarota (2007), Immigrants in the United States, 2007.

1. Indicates the year that immigrants said they came to the United States. Included in totals are a tiny number of persons who did not indicate a year of arrival.
2. Includes 100,000 persons who indicated they are foreign-born, Hispanic, and Mexican, but who did not indicate a country of birth.

where each span of years has reported the entry of migrants in correspondence to the respective countries. The total number of migrants of the countries and their respective share to the total population are also described in detail. As per the statistics of the Current Population Survey, 2007, Mexico topped the list with the maximum number of migrants coming to the United States until the year 2007. India stands third after Mexico and China in the number of migrants with a share of 40 per cent of them with citizenship status.

Indians in the United States

Indian immigrants appeared to have a considerable share of the total immigrant population in the United States. Hence it is imperative to look at the available statistics of the Indian population in the United States, the size and distribution of the population, demographic and social characteristics of the population and their legal status.

Size and distribution

There were about 1.6 million foreign-born populations from India residing in the United States in 2008. Nearly half of all Indian immigrants resided in California, New Jersey, New York and Texas. The

Table 3.2 Total and Indian foreign-born populations, 1960–2008

Year	Foreign born	Indian born Number	Share of all foreign born (%)	Rank (a)
1960	9,738,091	12,296	0.10	42
1970	9,619,302	51,000	0.50	30
1980	14,079,906	206,087	1.50	16
1990	19,797,316	450,406	2.30	12
2000	31,107,889	1,022,552	3.30	4
2008	37,960,773	1,622,522	4.30	3

Source: Data for 2000 from the 2000 census; data for 2008 from the American Community Survey 2008. Data for earlier decades from Campbell Gibson and Emily Lennon, 'Historical Census Statistics on the Foreign-Born Population of the United States: 1850 to 1990' (Working Paper No. 29, US Census Bureau, Washington, DC, 1999) cited from Terrazas and Batog (2010): Migration Policy Institute.

Notes: A Rank refers to the position of the Indian-born relative to other immigrant groups in terms of size of the population residing in the United States in a given census year.

Indian-born people accounted for about one in ten immigrants in six states. Between 2000 and 2008, the size of the Indian immigrant population more than doubled in ten states. Over one in six Indian immigrants resided in the New York metropolitan area. Indian immigrants made up at least 10 per cent of the immigrant population in ten metropolitan areas. There were 2.3 million members of the Indian Diaspora residing in the United States in 2008, including 455,000 native-born US citizens of Indian ancestry.

Demographic and socio-economic overview

Over 40 per cent of the foreign-born Indian arrived in the United States in 2000 or later. Nearly three-quarters of Indian immigrants in 2008 were adults of working age. Indian immigrant men outnumbered women in 2008. Indian immigrants were as likely as the foreign born overall to be naturalised US citizens. Three of every ten Indian immigrants in 2008 were limited English proficient. About two-thirds of limited English-proficient Indian immigrants spoke Hindi, Guajarati or Punjabi. Nearly three-quarters of Indian foreign-born adults had a bachelor's degree or higher. Indian immigrant men were more likely to participate in the civilian labour force than foreign-born men overall. Over one-quarter of employed Indian-born men worked in IT. One-third of employed Indian-born women worked in management, business and finance, and in IT. Indian immigrants were less likely to live in poverty than natives. Indian immigrants were as likely as other immigrants to own their own home. About one in eight Indian immigrants did not have health insurance in 2008. More than 550,000 children under age 18 resided in a household with an Indian immigrant parent.

Legal and unauthorised Indian immigrant population

There were over than half a million Indian-born lawful permanent residents in 2008. Between 2000 and 2009, more than 635,000 foreign-born Indian gained lawful permanent residence in the United States. Three out of five Indian immigrants receiving lawful permanent residence in 2009 were admitted as family-based immigrants. In 2009, the foreign-born Indian made up 9 per cent of all foreign academic student admissions to the United States. About 400 Indian immigrants were granted asylum in 2009. As of 2008, 220,000 Indian-born lawful permanent residents were eligible to naturalise. In 2009, roughly 2 per cent of all unauthorised immigrants in the United States were from India.[10] The number of unauthorised immigrants from India rose 64 per cent between 2000 and 2009.

Immigration policy

The section on immigration policies has been divided broadly into two parts. The first part highlights the debate on the need of the migrants for the economic development of the United States. The history of migration policies of the United States is provided in Appendix III.

Debate on immigration

Immigration has been a highly debated issue as far as the national policies of the United States are concerned. There are two issues as far as the discussions on immigrations are concerned. These are broadly the economy and the national identity of the United States. Supporters of flexible immigration policies believe that migrants bring with them skills which help the economy towards its economic growth, whereas opponents are of the opinion that migrants are very weakly connected with the culture of the country and are not assimilated properly with the social system.

Issues on migration are mainly discussed on the following lines:

- Whether the government should place further restrictions on legal immigration.
- Whether the government should deny social services to illegal immigrants.
- Whether English shall be the official language of the United States.

Since the late nineteenth century, the government of the United States has taken steps from time to time to implement policies related to immigration. Outlined next is a brief overview of the notable events related to immigration policy of the United States.

From 1790 to 1929

1790: In the early years of migration, Congress passed a law which allowed naturalisation only for 'free white persons'. The law was based on racial discrimination which was in existence until 1940, when immigrants from some Asian countries were allowed naturalisation.

1882: Immigration policies that evolved during this phase of time period were largely aimed to preserve the European racial and religious composition of the United States and expelled non-whites. This was the time when a federal law put a bar on the Chinese immigrants by denying them citizenship and suspending their entry into the United States.

1906: The Naturalisation Act of 1906 was a tricky policy of the United States Congress which stated that the ability to speak and understand English was a requirement for naturalisation.

1917: Asia was designated to be 'a barred zone'. Congress prohibited immigration from all Asian countries except from Japan and the Philippines.

1921: This year showed an encouraged immigration from Northern and Western European countries and discouraged immigrants from Eastern and Southern Europe who were 'ineligible to citizenship'. This is policy which affected the Japanese the most.

1929: An annual quota of 150,000 immigrants of which 30 per cent are allowed from Southern and Eastern Europe. The US economy hit the Great Depression in 1929–30 which naturally reduced immigration and encouraged emigration from the United States.

1965: The civil rights movement of 1960 has significant contribution to the migration history of the country. It overthrew the race-based admission criteria and abolished the quota that discriminated against nationality. The overall limit of migration from the Eastern and Western Hemisphere was 170,000 and 120,000, respectively.

1975: A legislation permitting the Southeast Asian refugees to enter the United States was passed by the Congress in the aftermath of the Vietnam War.

1995: Efforts to prohibit undocumented immigrants from accessing public services like education, health services and general welfare, though the proposition was later considered to be unconstitutional.

1996: This year was marked by a significant reduction to immigrants' access to social – net programs, lack of adequate opportunities for the illegal immigrants to legalise their status.

The three reforms – welfare reform, immigration reform and anti-terrorism legislation – were the main proponents behind the significant changes in the services to the migrants. Apart from the lack of these social services to the migrants, legal rights to the migrants also reduced through their lack of access to the courts and increased grounds for deportation.

2001: Shortly after the 9/11 incident, the country gives the federal government the power to identify suspected terrorists and detain them. More than a thousand men were detained without charges and denied any due process rights.

2002: The Department of Homeland Security introduced 'Special Registration' for 24 countries specially focusing on the immigrants of Muslim countries of age 16 and older to report in person, be registered and be fingerprinted. In the first year of this program, almost 13,000 men were placed in deportation proceedings, though it was subsequently terminated; this was a special program conceived to detain members of specific ethnic groups.

2005: In this year, Congress raised the standard for political asylum seekers, created additional grounds for deporting immigrants and limited the issuance of driver's license and state ID documents to certain categories of immigrants. This was the time which saw more than 150 anti-immigrant bills. States like Arizona, Virginia and Arkansas adopted anti-immigrant laws which target the undocumented immigrants, day labourers and low-income families. Even laws in certain states like Arizona required the state and local government employees to report undocumented immigrants seeking publicly funded health and social services to federal immigration authorities.

2006: The State of Georgia required their employers to verify their worker's immigration status which should include a proper documentation of those employees who are receiving state benefits that includes welfare and Medicaid. The employer should also document their workers with social security number, if they do not possess this identification number; they are subject to a 6 per cent state tax. Undocumented immigrants are required to be reported to federal authorities.

2011: For President Barak Obama, his deepest commitment to the immigration system has been to lay out a vision for a twenty-first century immigration policy. The policy says as follows:

a. It is the responsibility of the federal government to secure the borders of the country. Enforcement forces should be targeted to prevent those who can possibly do harm to the country.
b. The employers are accountable if they deliberately hire undocumented workers. They are required by the law to collect and document all the necessary details about their employees.
c. The vision calls for strengthening the economic competiveness of the country by creating a legal immigration system which can reflect

their values and diverse needs. The immigration policy should be liberal to those undocumented migrants whose parents brought them illegally into the country. The vision calls for reunifying families and encouraging the young people to develop new technologies and industries in the United States. The laws should improve the procedure for employers who seek to hire foreign workers if US workers are inadequate.

d. The law also invokes the responsibility of the illegal people living in the United States. They must abide by the law by registering and undergoing national security and criminal background check. They must pay taxes and a penalty for delay and must learn English to be eligible for citizenship.

But, in the context of human rights, it has been said that though international law permits states to frame their own immigration policies and deportation procedures, it does not grant them the discretion to violate human rights. The United States has regularly failed to uphold the international human rights law in its immigration laws and enforcement policies: by violating the rights of immigrants to fair treatment at the hands of government, to proportional sanctions, to freedom from arbitrary detention, to respect for the right to family unity and to protect from return to persecution. Such policies violate the International Covenant on Civil and Political Rights and the Refugee Convention, treaties to which the United States is party.[11]

Country case study: Australia

Overseas Indians' emergence in Australia

The history of Indians in Australia dates back to 1850s when Australia was also a British colony. The British rulers with the main motive of importing camels and their drivers to Australia directed the North-West Indians to migrate to Australia. This was the time when thousands of Afghans (Afghanistan was then part of the Indian subcontinent) arrived in Melbourne as camel drivers. These Afghan-Indians were brought to Australia for a three-year contract, but those who stayed back started working as labourers in Australia. The Afghans working in Australia made a significant presence in building up the Australian infrastructure presently known as 'Ghan Express' (Special Committee on Indian Diaspora, 2002). Anglo-Indians (predominantly Christians) made their entry into the country after the Indian Mutiny of 1857. Anglo-Indian

Table 3.3 Percentage per religion by country of birth, Western Australia, 2001

Religious composition	Bangladesh born (%)	India born (%)	Pakistan born (%)	Total WA population (%)
Christian	34.7	77.0	39.1	63.3
Hindu	1.7	10.9	–	0.3
Islam	56.3	1.5	51.3	1.1
Sikh	–	2.3	–	Negligible

Source: ABS, cited from Afsar (2004).

culture helped them integrate and in a sense better communicate with the Australians. It is on this account that presence of Anglo-Indians became more persistent in the country especially in the western part of Australia.

A snap shot of the Indian presence in Australia as categorised on the basis of religion is provided in Table 3.3.

The subcontinents of India and Australia share a historically strong relationship. The first ports of call were in the western parts of Australia and these networks, family ties and similarity of culture due to earlier migrants proved to be the magnet for more Indians being attracted to Western Australia. The inflow of the migrants in the next phase, after the Citizenship Act of 1948, saw a shift in the composition of Indians migrating to the country from labourers and camel drivers to Indian doctors, IT professionals and other categories of professionals. This was also the time when the Indians in Fiji, owing to the mass political upheaval, started migrating to other countries, especially Australia, which was one of their choice countries. Almost 35,000–40,000 overseas Indians in Fiji emigrated to Australia. These Indians were later given special seats in the Australian universities as an initiative to assist them in resettling and to support family members back home.

With the Citizenship Act coming in, the country saw an increasing surge of Indian students, majority of whom tended to stay back in search of employment to avail job opportunities. They started getting identified in different spheres of the economy. They played a significant role in building the health care system of the country and were partly the reason for the real estate boom that followed. Major Australian companies also started employing Indians in top positions. The Indian Diaspora transformed the very understanding of Australians about India and it is rightly said that these NRIs are 'able to provide a company with indispensable background knowledge, an intimate understanding of India, its culture and business environment, and are highly qualified in their chosen field' (Afsar, 2004).

Migration policy

Australia was initially a country with six different colonies with possibly little or no communication between them and was governed by the British rulers as six different countries. These colonies were New South Wales, South Australia, Victoria, Queensland and Western Australia that existed on the Australian continent and Tasmania the island colony. But following the drought of 1890 which resulted in industrial strikes, things started changing; they started unifying themselves against the potential influx of other European nations – Germany, France and Russia who too were making their foray into the Pacific. The gold rush in Australia saw Chinese immigrants flocking to the country leading to the colonies to act strongly against the economic competition of migrants from Asia. In a sense, the need of a migration policy emerged from the dominant presence of the South Asian emigrants too in the Australian mainland. By the end of the nineteenth century, the threat from the heavy influx of foreigners led to the introduction of policies to manage immigration. It was very difficult for the then six colonies to attain a consensus until a final draft of Australian Federal Constitution was drawn up. Finally, in 1900, there was a majority agreement for a Federation and the Commonwealth of Australia was proclaimed on 1 January 1901 at a grand ceremony in Sydney's Centennial Park. Australia always wanted to remain a country of white people who lived by British customs. In order to prevent the undercutting of wages due to labour competition from Chinese and Pacific Islanders, trade unions were also keen in drawing up a policy to restrict the immigrants from entering into the country. As a result of this, one of the first pieces of legislation which was passed into the new Federal Parliament was the Immigration Restriction Act, better known as White Australia Policy which made it very difficult for Asians and Pacific Islanders to immigrate to Australia.

Immigration Act (1901)

This was exactly what the preamble stated: An Act to place certain restrictions on Immigration and to provide for the removal from the Commonwealth of prohibited Immigrants (No.17 of 1901). In 1901, 98 per cent of people in Australia were white. One of the first pieces of legislation passed in the new Federal Parliament was the Immigration Restriction Act. The *Immigration Restriction Act* was the key part of a package of legislation passed by the new Federal Parliament in 1901, aimed at excluding all non-European migrants. This package included the *Pacific Islander Labourers Act* and Section 15 of the *1901 Post and Telegraph Act*, This *Immigration Restriction Act 1901* has historic value because it has direct links with the Federation and the drafting of the first Australian Constitution. This document put in place the law that was the cornerstone of Australia's 'White Australia' policy.[12] The Act restricts any person considered to be insane and anyone who is likely to become a threat to the public or any charitable institution. The Act also excludes any person who is suffering from infectious disease 'of a loathsome or dangerous character' and prostitutes, criminals and anyone under a contract or agreement to perform manual labour within Australia (with some limited exceptions).

The Naturalisation Act 1903

The federal government amended the Naturalisation Act through which aliens could be granted naturalisation by the Commonwealth and attain the rights and privileges of British subjects. This Act was amended in a way which made naturalisation very difficult for the immigrants of Asia, Africa or the Pacific Islands. According to this Act, applicants for naturalisation need to advertise their intent, renounce their own nationality and prove they could read and write in English.

The Nationality Act 1920

Assented on 2 December 1920, and enacted by the King's Most Excellent Majesty, the Senate, and the House of Representatives of the Commonwealth of Australia, the Act introduced the following connotations: 'natural-born' British subject and residence requirements for naturalisation. The nationality of most of 'Australians' as was referred by them was solely that of British subject until 1949.

Empire Settlement Act 1922

The federal government undertook the responsibility of selecting migrants and all the migration operations in the United Kingdom in 1920. Most migrants arriving from England were assisted under the Empire Settlement Act 1922.

Department of immigration 1945

Department of immigration was established in 1945 which delivers a diverse range of services in Australia and overseas. Its key outputs and responsibilities include the following:[13]

i. migration and temporary entry
ii. refugee and humanitarian entry and stay
iii. enforcement of immigration law, including effective border security
iv. safe haven
v. offshore asylum seeker management
vi. settlement services
vii. translating and interpreting services
viii. Australian citizenship
ix. promoting the benefits of diversity and social inclusion.

The department holds the following objectives:

- To maximise the economic and social benefits for Australia from all forms of temporary and permanent migration.
- Foster an Australian society that is cohesive, diverse and inclusive.
- Improve public confidence in national security, particularly through effective border management.
- Identify and deliver productivity and improved risk management capability in an environment of fiscal restraint.

Nationality and Citizenship Act 1948

The year saw the launch of Australia's national immigration program. The main objective behind launching the program was the increase in Australian population required to meet the workforce needs of a growing economy and to combat the declining birth rate. Following the setback in the Second World War, a vast increase in population was seen as a key to develop a defensive army and to strengthen the workforce that has severely affected by war. Migration was considered apart from natural birth as a potential mean to populate the country which was of ultimate need for the development of Australia as the first Minister of Immigration, Arthur Calwell, had said, 'populate or perish'.

In introducing the Nationality and Citizenship Bill 1948 to the Parliament, Calwell described its intended effect:

> It will symbolise not only our own pride in Australia, but also our willingness to offer a share in our future to the new Australians we

are seeking in such vast numbers. These people are sure of a warm welcome to our shores. They will no longer need to strive towards an intangible goal, but can aspire to the honour of Australian citizenship. . . . My aim, and that of the Government, is to make the word, 'Australian' mean all that it truly stands for to every member of our community. We shall try to teach the children that they are fortunate to be British, and even more fortunate to be Australian.

Non-discriminatory Australia 1949

The year 1949 saw the first step behind the non-discriminatory immigration policy. Minister Holt's decision to allow 800 non-European refugees to stay, and Japanese war brides to be admitted, marked the first step towards a non-discriminatory policy.[14]

Nationality and Citizenship Act 1955

The Act eased out the difficulties as faced by the potential applicants in obtaining citizenship. Declarations of Intention which were to be made two years before the application of citizenship has been curtailed down to six months prior to the end of the five-year residency qualifying period. Other changes like the advertisement requirement in the newspaper were also removed. These changes brought significant rise in the number of those becoming Australian citizens with naturalisations jumping from 4,770 in 1954 to 49,087 in 1959.

Migration Act 1958

This was a major move towards the immigration policies of the nation when non-Europeans with 15 years residence in Australia were allowed to become Australian citizens. The Act simplified the entry requirements, abolished any discrimination on the basis of race, and the controversial dictation test. Minister for Immigration, Sir Alexander Downer, supported the migration of 'distinguished and highly qualified Asians'. The review of the non-European policy in March 1966 was followed by the announcement of Immigration Minister Hubert Opperman for applications that would be accepted from well-qualified people on the basis of their suitability as settlers, their ability to integrate readily and their possession of qualifications positively useful to Australia. At the same time, the government decided a number of 'temporary resident' non-Europeans, who were not required to leave Australia, could become permanent residents and citizens after five years (the same as for

Europeans).[15] This move by the government allowed the migration of non-Europeans 'somewhat greater than previously'.[16]

- The objective of this Act is to regulate, in the national interest, the coming into and presence in, Australia of non-citizens.
- To advance its objective, this Act provides for visas permitting non-citizens to enter or remain in Australia and the Parliament intends that this Act be the only source of the right of non-citizens to so enter or remain.
- To advance its objective, this Act requires persons, whether citizens or non-citizens, entering Australia to identify themselves so that the Commonwealth government can know who are the non-citizens so entering.
- To advance its objective, this Act provides for the removal or deportation from Australia of non-citizens whose presence in Australia is not permitted by this Act.
- To advance its objective, this Act provides for the taking of offshore entry persons from Australia to a regional processing country.

The Citizenship Act 1969

The Act was to make it easier for non-British migrants to become citizens by reducing the residency requirement for aliens to two years if they could read, write, speak and understand English proficiently. The Act signifies the term 'Australian citizen' and changed the status of citizens from being British subjects to being Australian citizens with the status of a British subject.

International Convention for the Elimination of All Forms of Racial Discrimination 1972

In 1972, Gough Whitlam, the Labour Party representative, won government following 23 years in opposition. The party's election platform called for a non-racially based immigration policy. But following a declining economic situation which led to the decrease in the number of migration program from 140,000 in 1971–72 to 110,000 in 1972–73 to 80,000 in 1974–75, priority for admission went to immediate family and workers in occupations for which there remained a demand. Then Immigration Minister, Al Grassby, spoke in 1973 of the 'family of a nation' in order to describe his government's aim of achieving a multicultural Australia through changes to the citizenship legislation, renamed in that year as the Australian Citizenship Act 1948.

Multiculturalism of Australia

Multicultural Australia defines the cultural and linguistic diversity of the nation. It is the idea of a non-discriminatory Australia and a feature of the modern life of Australia. The word describes the openness of the country towards imbibing the culture of different thoughts of people. Since the 1970s, the immigration policy of Australia was termed multicultural policy. The following section described the developments of the term 'multicultural' in Australia.

By 1973, the term 'multiculturalism' was first introduced. Migrant groups started unifying and started forming national associations to promote and maintain their culture, heritage and survival of their languages in the community.

Multicultural policy

At the launch of the policy, Australian prime minister rightly said that we sing '"Australians all" because we are. Our country's story is the story of our people in this place'. The multicultural policy has the following principles:

- *Principle 1*: The Australian government celebrates and values the benefits of cultural diversity for all Australians, within the broader aims of national unity, community harmony and maintenance of our democratic values.
- *Principle 2*: The Australian government is committed to a just, inclusive, and socially cohesive society where everyone can participate in the opportunities that Australia offers and where government services are responsive to the needs of Australians from culturally and linguistically diverse backgrounds.
- *Principle 3*: The Australian government welcomes the economic, trade, and investment benefits which arise from our successful multicultural nation.
- *Principle 4*: The Australian government will act to promote understanding and acceptance while responding to expressions of intolerance and discrimination with strength, and where necessary, with the force of the law.

Finally, Australia firmly established itself as a country that welcomed and nurtured multiculturalism and established permanent structures such as the Australian Multicultural Council to ensure this.

- Support a commitment to innovation, effective communication and accountability in the development and implementation of social policy in this key area.

Indian political connections: foray into politics

We do not encounter much of Indian Diaspora into politics until very recently. Indian community started running for local elections and is getting reflected in mainstream politics only in the last decade. It is unlikely that we will find a huge cohort of Indians in the Australian political scenario as we would in the United States.

As is the case for most other countries, the first requirement of being in public offices of any foreign country is education. Since the second phase of migration of Indians to Australia was mostly a cohort of educated personalities, they started getting reflected in both public offices and the Australian corporate world. This education and income empowered them to form associations which worked as a platform to raise the demands of the community and worked towards maintaining the culture, heritage and the needs of different sections of the community. Some of the major Diaspora Associations have also played active roles for the community. A detailed list of all these Diaspora associations is provided in Annexure IV.

Other than these, the voices of Indians in the foreign mainland is also reflected through the print media like *The Indian Down Under*, *India Post*, *India Voice*, *The Indian Link*, *Bharat Times*, *Bharat Sanchar* among many others. It is through this path that eminent personalities raised their voices in public and stood for elected positions.

Given the increasing number of Indians in Australia, the Federation of Indian Association of Victoria (FIAV) launched an initiative to support the Indians in entering into the mainstream politics of Australia. A convention was organised to discuss the role of Indians in Australian politics. The convention was attended by various members of the community and was represented by the Liberal and Australian Labour Parties. They were helpful in defining the procedures of joining mainstream politics. This is regarded as an innovative way of creating awareness among the migrant community regarding the politics of the destination country. Such general awareness created amongst the community lead to representations for various council elections. In the local and state government elections of Victoria, for the first time more than 40 Indians entered the poll in 2013, in what was being dubbed as a positive change in Australian elections.

Subcontinent ministerial consultative committee

A recent initiative to address the issues of migrants has been initiated by the Minister for Immigration and Citizenship, Chris Bowen MP, the Minister for Multicultural Affairs and some others. The Australian government inaugurated a committee called Subcontinent Ministerial Consultative Committee. The committee was established to include all the leaders of various communities to advise on the issues related to migration, skill trade and education of the migrants so that they can contribute to the success and prosperity of Australia. More than ten Indian-origin people are the inaugural members of this key committee.

The 'Subcontinent Ministerial Consultative Committee' will work under the Minister for Immigration and Citizenship Chris Bowen and will advise them on various issues related to people from the subcontinent in Australia. The committee comprises 17 members drawn from different subcontinent community.

Conclusions

The story of Indian migration to the Gulf, Europe, the United States and Australia is different from the 'indenture' phase of Indian emigration. All of these forays for economic gain are mostly underscored by individual choice and voluntary migration. The movements to the Gulf are larger in not just numbers but trades and professions. It is across the whole economic spectrum and yet it is walled in by the local immigration laws that determine it to be controlled and temporary – even though this may involve being there for many years. Citizenship is just not granted, therefore preventing these overseas Indians from integrating into the local environment and certainly unable to enter local politics. The story in the other destinations has been different, initially coming across discrimination, both social and legal, but over time encountering several opportunities to integrate into the local society. Political forays were the next step and have been taken by several members of the overseas communities. We shall see in the rest of this book how that factor influences the process of migration itself.

Notes

1 Fortress Europe (German: Festung Europa) was a military term which referred to the areas of Continental Europe occupied by Nazi Germany, as opposed to the free United Kingdom across the Channel. The term was used by both sides but, due to their respective geographic locations, in a very different sense. Currently, within Europe, the most common use of the term is as a pejorative description of the state of immigration into the European Union. This can be in reference either to attitudes toward immigration, or to the system of border patrols and detention centres that are used to make illegal immigration into the European Union more difficult (Wikipedia.com, accessed on 9 April 2012).
2 *Financial Times*, 'Fortress Europe: Immigration', 14 June 2011, Barber, T., at FT.com, accessed on 9 April 2012.
3 Quoted Ibid.
4 World Economic Forum Global Agenda Council on Migration Report 2012 (Draft), WEF, Geneva.
5 Esman, Milton J. (2009). *Diasporas in the Contemporary World*, Polity Press, Cambridge, UK.
6 It is important to also note that data used here is mostly from Indian sources. Data on the ethnicity of residents including migrants is not easy to come by in several European states where such data collection is forbidden by law or tradition. There are also rather bewildering situations; for example, Belgium is caught somewhere in between the two traditions of reporting ethnicity or not (Jacobs and Rea, 2005) and finds itself in a stalemate position. The French-speaking part of Belgium tends to follow the French tradition of refusing ethnic categorisation, while the Flemish (the Dutch-speaking part) try to copy the Dutch model in distinguishing between locals and foreigners.
7 During the colonial period, the French East India Company established links between France and India, importing Indian commodities, mainly textiles, which were popular in Europe (Lal et al., 2006). The company was also instrumental in establishing a strategic base in India for the French. Consequently, Pondicherry, Karaikal, Mahe, Chandranagore were officially declared French territories. Most significantly, the establishment of a French base in India provided the foundation for the development of an Indian community in France.
8 Lal, Brij V., Peter Reeves and Rajesh Rai (eds). (2006). *The Encyclopaedia of the Indian Diaspora*, Oxford University Press, Singapore.
9 The last awardee, Mr. Wahid Saleh, is a social entrepreneur and a community leader based in Netherlands who has received the award for his contribution to activities supporting educational institutions in Assam and Northeast region in India.
10 Terrazas, A., Batog, C. 2010. http://www.migrationinformation.org/spotlight-library.cfm, accessed on 19 December 2012.
11 Human Rights Watch, http://www.hrw.org/node/8472 , on 15 January 2013.
12 http://www.migrationheritage.nsw.gov.au/exhibition/objectsthroughtime/immigration-restriction-act/, accessed on 16 January 2013.

13 National Communications Branch, Department of Immigration and Citizenship, Canberra, 2012, cited from http://www.immi.gov.au/media/fact-sheets/06australias-multicultural-policy.htm, accessed on 10 January 2013.
14 http://www.immi.gov.au/media/fact-sheets/21managing.htm, accessed on 20 January 2013.
15 http://www.immi.gov.au/media/fact-sheets/21managing.htm, accessed on 19 November 2012.
16 http://www.comlaw.gov.au/Details/C2012C00855, accessed on 9 December 2012.

Chapter 4

Political mainstreaming of the Indian Diaspora

Introduction

The Indian Diaspora may well be regarded as an international phenomenon – with a strong presence of 27 million people in over 150 countries globally (Ministry of Overseas Indian Affairs, 2011). It is so widespread that the 'Sun never sets on the Indian Diaspora' (*Report of the High Level Committee on Indian Diaspora,* 2001). Emerging in the ancient period and expanding in the medieval period – it exhibited a fascinating evolution in colonial and post-colonial times. Today, it constitutes a significant and successful economic, social and cultural force in the world. Its vastness and diversities, at the international level, grew out of a variety of causes – mercantilism, colonialism and globalisation – and over several hundreds of years of migration in different waves. The origins and roots of the various movements have been different and the routes and patterns of the migration and settlement have been divergent. The level of their interaction with the new country of settlement and the emergence of new identities make the Indian Diaspora unique. The Diaspora reflects a growing self-consciousness that has been further strengthened by the development of new communication technologies. With increasing globalisation, the Indian Diaspora is growing and becoming more visible and influential worldwide. Yet, it is difficult to speak of one great 'Indian Diaspora' (Ministry of Overseas Indian Affairs, 2007). There are communities within communities and their bond with India, the manner and the extent of engagement is marked by their own experience.

Indian Diaspora is not a homogenous group. Its diversity is based on language, religion and geographical locations and the destination to which they have migrated (Dubey, 2000). As outlined earlier, migration in contemporary history is traced to emigration of indentured labourers during the colonial times. This phase was followed by a wave of voluntary migration just after the emergence of a nascent nation. This phase of migration was not conditioned by economic desperation and colonial manipulations, which were the predominant factors in the case of the former. The historical and contemporary locations of the Indian Diaspora may be seen in the various regions of the world such as South Asia, Europe, North America, South America, Middle-East, Caribbean countries, Africa, Central Asian region, South East Asia and the Far Eastern region. The contemporary fascination with the Diaspora arises mainly because of their economic potential to radically transform the fortunes of the Indian economy (Parekh et al., 2003). They have also transformed the economies and have come to occupy a significant place in the life of their countries of settlement, ranging from the unskilled, semi-skilled and skilled workers to farmers, scientists, administrators, professors, students, entrepreneurs, traders, doctors, engineers and IT experts. Their activities range from trade, investment, education, health, science and technology to culture and philanthropy. In several countries, they have surpassed the per capita income of the indigenous population. It is rightly said by Rabindranath Tagore that 'to study a banyan tree, you not only must know its main stem in its own soil but also must trace the growth of its greatness in the further soil, for then you can know the true nature of its vitality' (cited in Tinker, 1977). This applies aptly in the case of the Indian Diaspora.

The present chapter focuses on all countries of significant Diaspora populations: Canada, the United States, Trinidad and Tobago and Mauritius. In this focus in these key destination countries, we will seek to analyse the changing role the Indian Diaspora communities have been through in these countries. Not only will the chapter comment on the political role that the Indian Diaspora has had in these destination nations, but also on the need to bring a strategic dimension into the relationship between India and its overseas community in these focus countries as also between India and these select countries.

Country case study – Canada

Canada is home to the highest proportion of foreign-born population among the G8 countries (20.6 per cent) as compared to Germany (13 per cent in 2010) and the United States (12.9 per cent in 2010). Ahead of Canada, it is only Australia with 26.8 per cent of the total population belonging to foreign countries (Statistics Canada, 2001). The composition of Canadian immigrants ranges across some 200 countries primarily from the Asian and European regions, though the share of immigrants from Africa, Caribbean, Central and South America have increased in recent years. The Indian Diaspora commands the highest per capita income among all the racial or ethnic groups there.

In the estimates of NHS 2011, 78 per cent of the migrants who reportedly came to Canada prior to 1970 were from Europe, mostly from United Kingdom, Italy, Germany and the Netherlands. But this trend has shifted with Asia mapping the colour of the population with around 60 per cent of the immigrants coming from the region between 2001 and 2011, pushing Europe into second place. The Asian upsurge has been contributed mainly by three countries: the Philippines (13.1 per cent), China (10.5 per cent) and India (10.4 per cent) (as in the year 2011). The other countries which come in the top ten countries of immigrants' source countries are the United States, Pakistan, the United Kingdom, Iran, South Korea, Colombia and Mexico. Given below is the account of immigrants as coming to Canada from different regions across the world (Figure 4.1) over the period of forty years. The pictorial representation has shown a shift in the share of migrants from Europe to Asia.

The concentration of immigrants is highest in Ontario, British Columbia, Quebec and Alberta. With most of the immigrants preferring to live in metropolitan areas of Canada (91 per cent), Toronto, Vancouver and Montreal shelter 63.4 per cent of the country's immigration population

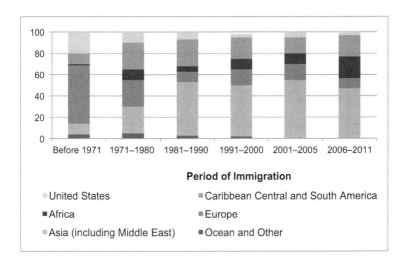

Figure 4.1 Region of birth of immigrants by period of immigration, Canada, 2011.

Table 4.1 Inflow of the immigrants in Canada, 2011

	Total population		Total immigrant		Recent immigrants	
	Number	Percentage	Number	Percentage	Number	Percentage
Canada	32,852,320	100.0	6,775,765	100.0	1,162,915	100.0
Toronto	5,521,235	16.8	2,537,405	37.4	381,745	32.8
Montréal	3,752,475	11.4	846,645	12.5	189,730	16.3
Vancouver	2,280,700	6.9	913,310	13.5	155,125	13.3
The Rest	21,297,910	65.0	2,478,405	37.0	436,315	38.0

Source: NHS, Canada, 2011.

Note: Recent immigrants are those immigrated to Canada during 2006–01.

(see Table 4.1). The following table has mapped the three most important metropolises of Canada against the rest taken together as far as the immigration is concerned.

India and Canada: Relations

In Canada, liberalised immigration laws led to increase in Indian immigration starting in the 1960s. The rural origins of the early Punjabi settlers and the racism they encountered led to a great deal of insecurity and alienation but the newer arrivals were much more educated and urbanised (Ember et al., 2005). At present, they constitute 1.8 per cent of Canadian population with the numerical estimate of 1,000,000. As per the 2006 census, 962,670 persons of Indian origin live in Canada. Of them, 50 per cent are Sikhs, 39 per cent Hindus and the rest comprises Muslims, Christians, Jains and Buddhists. The political representation of Indo-Canadian MPs in the House of Commons is nine with one in the Senate. Two Ministers of State in the federal government and one Parliamentary Secretary to the foreign minister belonging to Indian origin.

Before 1945, India was not counted as a major source country of migrants to Canada, but the significance was felt after 1946 when Indian migrants represented around 2 per cent of the total immigrants to the country. Table 4.2 illustrates this.

The statistics of Canada, Census of Canada 2011, came up with the list of languages that are spoken by the immigrants. This analysis is helpful to understand the composition of migrants and their origin in terms

Table 4.2 Total number of immigrants, 1946–80

	Countries	Immigrants	Percentages
1	Great Britain	11,07,362	23.1
2	Italy	4,85,191	10.1
3	United States	4,70,991	9.8
4	West Germany	3,28,646	6.8
5	The Netherlands	1,85,006	3.8
6	West Indies	1,83,998	3.8
7	Portugal	1,47,327	3.0
8	Greece	1,31,452	2.7
9	France	1,26,199	2.6
10	Poland	1,13,323	2.3
11	India	88,873	1.8
12	Austria	70,321	1.4
13	Yugoslavia	60,098	1.2
14	Hungary	57,001	1.19
15	Australia	55,533	1.15
16	Ireland	46,151	0.9
17	Belgium	45,780	0.9
18	Switzerland	42,905	0.89
19	Denmark	40,302	0.84
	Total	4,787,845	100.00

Source: Data calculated from Alan B. Andeson and James S. Frideres, *Ethnicity in Canada. Theoretical Perspectives*, Toronto, Butterworth, 1981, 334p, pp. 140–55. http://faculty.marianopolis.edu/c.belanger/QuebecHistory/readings/SourceofCanadianImmigrtants1921–1945.html, accessed on 10 May 2013.

of home country. In this Table 4.3, we can see that the highest percentage of the immigrants speak Italian, Spanish and Portuguese which are as high as the number speaking Punjabi, Urdu, Persian, Gujarati and Hindi taken together. The profound presence of Indo-Iranian languages as mother tongue among the Canadian migrant families reflects the outspread of Indians in Canada.

Disaggregating further the family of languages to have an estimate of those languages spoken by over 100,000 Canadians, it is seen that Punjabi is the highest spoken language. Among the other Indian languages, Tamil, Hindi and Gujarati position themselves in the top 22 widely spoken languages (Figure 4.2).

Table 4.3 Immigrant population by languages family speak

Language family	Main languages	Number	Percentage
Niger-Congo languages	Akan, Swahili, Rundi	81,135	1.2
Cushitic languages	Somali, Oromo	45,880	0.7
Semitic languages	Arabic, Hebrew, Amharic	449,580	6.6
Turkic languages	Turkish, Azerbaijani	36,750	0.5
Armenian	Armenian	31.680	0.5
Indo-Iranian languages	Punjabi, Urdu, Persian, Gujarati, Hindi	1,179,990	17.3
Dravidian languages	Tamil, Malayalam, Telugu	175,280	2.6
Chinese languages	Chinese (n.o.s.[2]), Cantonese, Mandarin	1,112,610	16.3
Tibeto-Burman languages	Tibetan, Burmese	8,210	0.1
Korean	Korean	142,880	2.1
Japanese	Japanese	43,040	0.6
Malayo-Polynesian languages	Tagalog, Ilocano, Malay	443,750	6.5
Tai-Kadai languages	Lao, Thai	22,615	0.3
Austro-Asiatic languages	Vietnamese, Khmer	174,455	2.6
Romance languages	Spanish, Italian, Portuguese	1,196,390	17.5
Germanic languages	German, Dutch, Yiddish	611,165	8.9
Slavic languages	Polish, Russian, Ukrainian	721,605	10.6
Baltic languages	Lithuanian, Latvian	14,055	0.2
Finno-Ugric languages	Hungarian, Finnish, Estonian	96,200	1.4
Celtic languages	Walsh	3,885	0.1
Greek	Greek	117,890	1.7
Albanian	Albanian	25,010	0.4
Creole languages	Haitian Creole	75,255	1.1
Other languages	Kabyle, Georgian, Mongol	29,410	0.4
All immigrant languages		6,838,705	100

Source: Statistics Canada, Census of Canada 2011.

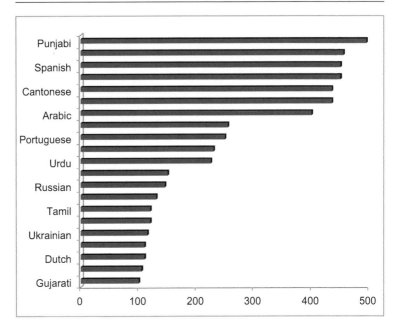

Figure 4.2 Number of Canadians whose mother tongue is one of the twenty-two immigrant languages reported by more than 100,000 persons in Canada, 2011.

Source: Statistics Canada, Census of Population 2011

Political developments

It was the Sikh community which marked their first presence in Canada. The chronology of events as described in this section labels the history of Indians which is in other words the history of the first-generation Sikhs in Canada. According to local records one Kesar Singh is recorded as the first Indian to visit Canada in 1897.[1]

The first Sikhs to come to Canada were from among those who had served in the British Army. Soldiers of the Sikh Lancers and Infantry were travelling through Canada on account of an official commitment. On their way back to India, they happened to meet Indian soldiers in Hong Kong, Shanghai and Singapore to whom they narrated about the opportunities in Canada.

A major step towards the Sikhs accepting Canada as a place for settlement came in the form of arrival of the holy book of the Sikh, Guru Granth Sahib Ji, to Vancouver in 1902, which resulted in the foundation of the Khalsa Diwan Society. The Khalsa Diwan Society, formally established in 1906, took the initiative in establishing the first Gurudwara in 1908 which was the first of its kind in the whole American continent.[2]

In order to placate the white population of Canada and to please the Asiatic Exclusion League which had earlier taken out a protest march in the form of 'Anti-Asiatic Parade' in 1906–07 against the Asian immigrants, the then Government of Canada passed an order in the Vancouver Council in 1908 as a step to ban Indians in Canada. Indians were asked to enter the city through the formal route only through a continuous journey after buying tickets from their home country. As a next step, the Canadian government took the initiative to send the Indians out of Canada to another British Colony – British Honduras. A report done by some Sikh delegates on the poor conditions in the Honduras was publically read in the Gurudwara in front of the huge congregation of Indians present. This marked a watershed the political rise of the community, where the Gurudwara originally set up only with the motive of worship emerged as a common meeting point of all Indians irrespective of their religion to discuss important issues. This incident was followed by strengthening the Khalsa Diwan Society in 1909 through the following lines:[3]

- To appoint ministers of the Sikh Religion to officiate in the Province of British Columbia and elsewhere.
- To appoint missionaries of the Sikh Religion for the purpose of attending to scattered communities of Sikhs both in the Province of British Columbia and elsewhere.
- To manage the affairs of the Sikh Temple now situated at 1866 Second Ave West, Vancouver.

Important decisions like these have been taken over different periods at the Sikh Gurudwara of Vancouver and have been applauded by fellow Indians. These initiatives led to a cohesion and cooperation between not just Sikhs but also all other Indians. In the 1900s when the huge influx of Punjabis made their entry into Canada and were establishing their foothold in the continent, the Canadian government responded with an exclusionist policy to stop the 'Brown Invasion'. These laws included a stipulation that all arriving Indian immigrants are bound by law to have an amount of $200 with them to enter Canada and they must come through a direct route. It was this stipulation that led to the famous *Komagata Maru* incident.

Gurudit Singh, an affluent businessman chartered *Komagata Maru*, a Japanese streamliner to carry Indians to Canada. The ship departed from Hong Kong, took the route through Japan to Canada. The ship carried 376 Indian Punjabi passengers. When the news of *Komagata Maru* heading towards Canada reached the continent, the Vancouver daily *Province* carried a story with the heading 'Boat Loads of Hindus on Way to Vancouver'. While on the one hand Indians made preparations to welcome *Komagata Maru*, the Canadian authorities took steps to prevent it from docking. On 23rd of March 1914, the ship anchored at Burrad Inlet, and a heated legal battle between Indian lawyers and the authorities ensued which finally ended with *Komagata Maru* being forced back from Canada on 23rd of July 1914 with only 24 passengers allowed to stay back in the country. Upon their arrival back in Calcutta, the passengers were taken some miles out of Calcutta and Punjabi passengers were forced to leave for Punjab to their native land. Several protested and started marching towards the city. This resulted in a confrontation between these passengers and British officials which ultimately led to firing by the army and to the death of 20 passengers. It is this incident which has gone down in history as a major rebellion by natives against their foreign rulers.

In the same year, the War Measures Act was passed which allowed the Canadian government to arrest and deport 'enemy aliens' which resulted in more than 5,000 immigrants detained in the country. Later in 1917, the Wartime Elections Act ratified after the commencement of the First World War, was the first Act which gave the right to vote for women in federal elections, yet at the same time prohibiting the immigrant citizens who were naturalised to vote unless their relatives were serving in the British Army!

In spite of such profound discrimination against Sikhs in Canada, they continued to emerge as a strong power in the local milieu of Canada. The Gurudwaras played the most important role in coordinating the activities of Sikhs in Canada and served as a place for gathering support for the Sikhs in their struggle against the immigration ban for Indians. This finally resulted in the immigration ban being overturned and the families of the legal migrants were allowed to enter the country. Despite this step they were not given the right to vote. As a result of this, Indians were barred from taking government jobs or entering into contracts with government agencies. They were also not allowed to buy properties in certain areas and had no representation in the politics of the country. Finally, it was in 1947 that the ban on voting rights for the legal migrants was withdrawn and immigrants then could contribute to the social and political scene. Canada, in adopting the UN's Universal Declaration of Human Rights in 1948, also declared that race could no longer be considered a reason to deny voting rights. The policies of Canadian government to address the immigration issues were made more proactive and a Department of Citizenship and Immigration was established. In 1951, a government-to-government agreement was signed between Canada and India which allowed a fixed number of Indian citizens into Canada.

The 1962 immigration policy however introduced the most drastic regulatory changes which upturned all the racial rules of the immigration laws of Canada. The composition of Indian migrants changed as a point system was introduced in 1967 which would determine the eligibility of the immigrants to enter into the country.[4] This led to the changing composition of Indian immigrants to Canada. Many Indians who were emigrants in the countries of Caribbean, Africa and Oceania made their way to Canada. (Much of these movements of Indians from the African region can be traced to a 'forced migration' as a result of the political upheaval in the African countries.) In 1971, the federal government announced its policy of multiculturalism followed by the Immigration Act of 1976 constructed mainly on three clauses of admission: on the basis of points system to assess the employment skills, education and language abilities rather than national or 'racial' origin; sponsorship by close family members; and refugee status. All these steps towards admitting immigrants into Canada were backed by the evolving interest of Canada as a country. Later as per the 1976 policy, new types of immigrants who belonged to the business class were encouraged. Finally the Immigration and Refugee Protection Act 2001 emphasised education, training and language adaptability of the migrants as necessary requirements to enter the country. Under this Act, few new categories of immigrant visas were introduced to strengthen the creation of global human capital. These are Federal Skilled Worker Program, Temporary Workers Program, Arranged Employer Opinion and Provincial Nominee Program.

Foray into politics

It is believed that 'people who first come into a community are likely to have fewer associational ties, information on community affairs, fewer political contacts, and fewer emotional and material stakes in the group tensions that express themselves in politics'. This changes over time as emigrants get more and more integrated into the local society and realise the importance of political positions in a democratic society. Such realisation and progress of Indian immigrants resulted in a situation where today there are nine Indo-Canadian MPs in the House of Commons and one in the Senate. Two PIO MPs are Ministers of State in the federal government and one PIO MP is Parliamentary Secretary to the Foreign Minister!

Besides politics, the growing importance of Indian-origin Canadian businessmen also finds expression in the establishment and involvement in business bodies. Among the prominent Indo-Canadian bodies are the Canada India Business Council (CIBC), the India Canada Chamber of Commerce (ICCC) and Canada India Foundation (CIF) along with other local chambers and associations.[5]

Country case study – The United States

Indian-American community: A background

The Indian-American community is considered a model community and one that has grown rapidly in the last decade. It now numbers approximately 1.7 million people, making it the most rapidly growing Asian-American group (Seth, 2001: 9). For a long time, however, Indian-Americans were an almost invisible community. It had not assimilated as much and disappeared into American society. It was a community with a low political profile and its cultural impact on the United States was also low. Americans ate at Indian restaurants, occasionally visited a Hindu temple out of curiosity and, despite the prosperity of the Indian community, saw the average Indian as an *Apu*, a character who ran a convenience store. An additional contribution to this state of being, as opined by some, was that the Indians in America had (and continue to have) a weak sense of national identity, choosing instead to identify with their different regional, linguistic and religious groupings (Prashad, 2002).

Thus there are overseas Indian Muslims, Indian Christians and Indian Hindu community organisations with umbrella organisations called the Indian American Christian Association and the Federation of Indian Muslim Associations etc. Similarly, different ethnic and linguistic groups have set up their own national associations, for example, the Federation of Kerala Associations in North America, Federation of Gujarati Associations in North America, Telugu Association of North America; and the Bengali Association of North America. In some cities there are Tamil Brahmin, Sri Lankan Tamil and general

Tamil organisations. Caste-based organisations have also been set up; for example, there exists a Brahmin Society of New York that comprises Gujarati Brahmins (Prashad, 2002). The pull of religious and ethno-linguistic ties leads to a diffusion of mobilisation efforts as groups tend to focus their resources on parochial as opposed to national or Diaspora interests. Coupled with this is the phenomenon of 'cultural freeze' (Prashad, 2004). This is a situation where immigrants retain the traditions, culture and values of their home country dating back to when they emigrated, even though these may have been significantly modified in their country of origin.

The second major wave of Indian immigrants came in the 1960s and, once in the United States, froze part of their culture and attitudes. Cultural freezes may not be conducive to the modern national identity that India projects. A young Indian woman, for example, was told at some Indian-American meetings that she was not an Indian because she was a Christian. Similarly, the excessive emphasis on caste and religion among the Diaspora works against modern India's portrayal of itself as a secular state as well as against ongoing trends in Indian society. An Indian Diaspora that is living and working with attitudes that do not fit into modern India can only be viewed as hindering the relationship with the host state. The growth of the Vishwa Hindu Parishad America is a case in point (Prashad, 2004).

Causes for political mobilisation

In the 1990s, however, there was a growing political mobilisation by the Indian-American community as well as a move by the Indian government to try and woo its expatriate groups. As Robert Hathaway argues, the Indian community had by the 1990s grown in size and started to make its influence felt among congressional members and their staffs. By 2004, the India caucus in Congress had the largest membership (186) of any such political group (Seth, 2001: 68). Congressmen, who in the past had supported cutting foreign aid to India, now strenuously opposed such moves. When India carried out a series of nuclear tests in 1998, American non-proliferation laws were automatically enforced and India was subject to both economic and military sanctions. Yet, within a year, legislators had given the Clinton administration the authority to waive all the sanctions. The lobbying efforts of the Indian-American community were obviously significant in bringing about this shift in Congressional attitude, although other factors did play a role in revoking of the sanctions.

The Indian government's attitude

Coupled with rise of Indian-American activism has been a shift in the policies of the Indian government towards its greater Diaspora community. In the past, India had typically adopted a hands-off approach towards its Diaspora. As mentioned earlier, Jawaharlal Nehru said that these communities should not call themselves Indian and, instead, identify with, and assimilate into, their host countries. It was only in the early 1990s, when India dropped its socialist pattern of economic development and initiated market reforms, that there was a drive to encourage NRI investments in the country due to so-called policy change despite the fact that for two decades prior to this decision NRIs in the Persian Gulf countries (and elsewhere) had been repatriating large amounts of money to their families in India. Monies were used not just for local consumption expenses of the families, but also for investments. Since then, both the Indian central government and Indian state governments have consciously started developing ties with the Indian Diaspora and particularly with the Indian-American community, in order to invite investments.

The Indian-American community has 'arrived' in that its political participation has shifted from symbolic to tactical-strategic goals. The objectives of the Indian-Americans were usually symbolic for they aimed at such gestures as getting a local politician to attend cultural events or to sign a photograph. As one Indian-American activist commented, 'Indians tend to sell themselves cheaply and American politicians know it. Sometimes giving a contribution just to get a photo with your Senator is considered a great accomplishment' (Kanjilal, 2004: 109). In part, such a lack of political awareness also came from the community's transplantation into a political milieu that they were unfamiliar with. Indian immigrants were unfamiliar, for example, with a political system that required lobbying efforts to achieve goals. For several reasons, however, the community has become more politically active. It has reached critical mass with a concentrated population in certain major metropolitan areas – the community's population also doubled from 1990 to 2000, touching approximately 1.7 million (Kanjilal, 2004: 6).

The Indian-American community is prosperous and can therefore, potentially, organise fairly effectively. Second, it is digitally connected both within the United States and to the home nation. One of the consequences of the Indian information technology boom has been a growing web presence of both official and unofficial organisations in India that can be tapped into by the Diaspora community. At the same time,

India's print media has also recognised the importance of establishing a web presence and is now readily available to those interested in following local India news in their own region. As Deepika Bahri points out, 'Since these new technologies of representation became available, the relative isolation of expatriate South Asians in their discrete locations in Northern countries (Canada and the United States) has been effectively offset by the presence of a large, virtual, instant community that may be geographically scattered but is electronically – and sometimes epistemologically and ideologically – connected and contiguous' (cited in Gupta, 2009).

Thus, the Gujarati-American community was able to respond rapidly and effectively to the 2001 Bhuj earthquake. Similarly, the 2002 sectarian riots in Gujarat gained international attention because they were the first riots that the digital age was able to transmit globally. Secular Indian groups, both in India and living abroad, were able to mobilise and use the web to highlight the tragedy and the perceived incompetence of the Indian and Gujarat governments in dealing with the upsurge of violence. Third, in the past decade, a new generation of Indian-Americans has attained political maturity. They are organised, are politically savvy, understand the process in Washington, and have a range of interests that they seek to promote. Thus, Desist Rising Up and Moving (DRUM) fights for the rights of working-class South Asians along the East Coast and has sought to organise taxi drivers in New York and northern Virginia (Kanjilal, 2004: 113).

The Indian-American Leadership Initiative Public Action Committee (IALIPAC) seeks to train young Indians in political activism and hopes to have a dozen Indian-Americans in elected office by the end of the decade. Fourth, a portion of the Indian Diaspora now comprises the children and siblings of the Indian elite. Increasingly, Indian businessmen, bureaucrats, military personnel and, to a lesser extent, politicians have their children studying or living in the United States. This elite group has the ability to reach the most relevant sectors of Indian decision making with their complaints and concerns. It is also an elite group that for practical reasons – particularly business reasons – maintains a strong connection with the home country. Lastly, Diaspora groups may be passive in terms of their identity, as Scandinavian groups in the United States are, or they may be proactive (Sahay, 2009: 124).

What influences this attitude and makes a Diaspora conscious of its identity is a critical event that signals discrimination or conflict either within the host country or in the homeland. In the Indian case two major events worked to raise political consciousness and mobilise the Diaspora. The first event was the growing tensions between India and Pakistan that was exacerbated with India's 1998 decision to test nuclear weapons. The second was the terrorist attacks of 11 September 2001 in the United States. The tests were followed by an automatic imposition of economic and military sanctions by the US government (Gopal, 2003: 73). Consequently, Indian groups worked actively to have these sanctions rolled back. Since then, the same groups have been active in attempting to increase United States–India cooperation, in helping forge a strategic relationship with Jewish groups in the United States, and in working to counter Pakistani lobbying efforts in the United States. Of these, the link with Jewish groups is the most interesting since it is an attempt to piggyback on the lobbying skills of these groups to achieve certain political ends – most notably the sale of defence technologies like Israel's Phalcon airborne warning system and the Arrow anti-ballistic missile (Sahay, 2009: 33). Indian groups have been working with pro-Israeli groups to have the US government remove its objections to the proposed sale.

Another factor has been the increasing business and investment between the two countries. These investments by the overseas Indians especially have been, as the Reserve Bank of India states, a major source of capital inflows during the 1990s and helped boost India's hard currency reserves. Unfortunately, however, the Indian-American Diaspora was not very successful in emerging as a major supplier of technology. Most of the sensitive and high-end technologies that India needs require congressional approval and there is little that the Indian-American community could do to facilitate such transfers. The reluctance of the American strategic community to transfer the Arrow anti-ballistic missile and the continued US insistence that India, ideally, sign the Nuclear Non-Proliferation Treaty are examples of the continued resistance in American governmental circles to open the technological cupboard to India and to treat it as an equal partner (Kapur, 2010: 174). Perhaps the best way to understand the political mobilisation efforts of the Indian-American community is to recognise that from being a group in themselves they have become a group for themselves. A great deal of the political mobilisation that is taking place is to enhance the economic standing of the community, to secure legal protection for it and to develop the networking ties that would promote the careers of the next generation of Indian-Americans.

In India, the Indian-American community is now viewed as helping further Indian foreign policy and security goals as well as contributing towards its economic development. The Government of India's High Level Committee Report on the Indian Diaspora states: 'A section of financially powerful and politically well-connected Indo-Americans has emerged during the last decade. They have effectively mobilized on issues ranging from the nuclear tests in 1998 to Kargil, played a crucial role in generating a favourable climate of opinion in Congress and defeating anti-India legislation there, and lobbied effectively on other issues of concern to the Indian community. They have also demonstrated willingness to contribute financially to Indian causes, such as relief for the Orissa cyclone and the Latur and Gujarat earthquakes, higher technical education and innumerable charitable causes' (High Level Committee Report, 2001). Thus, their political influence due to their increased status in the United States has certainly attracted the attention of Indian political leadership. But there are several challenges within India, to include Diaspora in its development programme.

American politics is going through a transformation with the increasing number of Indian-Americans conquering political heights along with other leaders. These Indian-Americans are making an ever big impact in the American politics by their influential personality and have set a benchmark in this domain with their hard work and willingness. Success stories such as that of Bobby Jindal, the current governor of Louisiana; Nikki Haley, the current governor of South Carolina; and Kamala Harris, the current attorney general of California, underscore the point.

Country case study: Trinidad and Tobago

Unlike most of the English-speaking Caribbean, Trinidad and Tobago is a primarily industrialised country whose economy is based on petroleum and petrochemicals. People of Indian and African descent make up almost 80 per cent of the population, while the remainder are mostly mixed race with small European, Chinese and Syrian-Lebanese minorities.[6] Trinidad and Tobago is famous for its pre-Lenten Carnival and as the birthplace of 'steel-pan' and limbo.

Trinidad's East Indian culture came to the island with indentured labour brought to fill a labour shortage created by the emancipation of the African slaves in 1833.[7] Most remained on the land, and they still dominate the agricultural sector, but many have become prominent in business and the professions. East Indians have retained much of their own way of life, including Hindu and Muslim religious festivals and practices.

Demographic features of the Indian Diaspora

A majority of Indians (PIO) in Trinidad are Hindus. Major minorities are Muslims and various denominations of Christians. Though all of them have retained their distinctive culture, generally they function in a multiracial milieu. The Bhojpuri-Hindi, Urdu and Tamil languages of their ancestors have largely been lost, although a number of these words have entered the Trinidadian vernacular. Bollywood movies, Indian music and Indian cooking have entered the mainstream culture of Trinidad and Tobago.

The abolition of slavery in the early 1830s in the British, French and Dutch colonies of the West Indies/Caribbean led to a severe shortage of labour in the sugarcane plantations. The ex-slaves had exercised their right of freedom of choice to discontinue working on the sugarcane even for a wage. The subsequent shortage of labour served as a catalyst for the introduction of a system of imported contract labour. The British first introduced labourers from India to the Caribbean through a semi-slave system of contract labour, lasting five to ten years, described earlier too as 'Indentureship'.[8] In 1838, Britain sent the first Indian labourers from the port of Calcutta to British Guiana (now Guyana) based on the success of the system in Mauritius.

The first Indians arrived in Trinidad on 30 May 1845. The immigration of indentured Indians continued until 1917 when it was banned by the Government of India. Most of these immigrants came from places in the United Provinces where Bhojpuri is spoken. A significant minority came from Madras Presidency or present-day Tamil Nadu where Tamil and Telugu were spoken. A substantial minority of Indo-Trinidadians trace their ancestry to indentured labourers who immigrated to Guyana, Jamaica, St. Vincent, Grenada or other islands in the Caribbean. A few are descendants of later immigrants from India, Pakistan, Bangladesh or Sri Lanka, predominantly doctors and Gujarati businessmen.

In the early days of indenture, when the passage from India to the Caribbean took at least three to four months, conditions on the ships were deplorable. Many Indians did not make it to their destinations, but died on the ships as a result of disease and lack of medical care. Apart from physical discomfort, Indians also faced psychological and emotional distress on board the ships which traversed the Middle Passage. Many Indians regarded departing from India with horror and referred to the passage from India to the West Indies as the dreaded *kalapani* or dark waters. Caste endogamy broke down on the ships as well as on the plantations on the New World. Due to the harsh conditions that Indians faced, they became united in their struggle for survival. Despite these cruel living conditions, Indians eventually produced a middle class of small farmers and shop owners.

By the time Indentureship ended in 1917, many Indians did not exercise their option to return to India. They chose, instead, to remain as permanent settlers in the Caribbean where they got, bought or rented land to do agriculture and rear cows. By the end of First World War, those who chose to settle in the colonies easily constituted about half the population of Guyana, Suriname and Trinidad (and Tobago). They also formed the largest minority in Jamaica, Grenada, St. Vincent, St. Lucia and St. Kitts. Today, they constitute over 1.5 million in the region, settling in the territories of the Caribbean from Cuba and Jamaica in the North West to Guyana and Suriname in the South East. They form a visible ethnic group that has changed the face and form of culture, religion, music, food, architecture, politics and the economy in the Caribbean.

The social circumstances of the early years were exceedingly difficult. Not only were Indians thousands of miles from the land of their birth, they also faced an apprehensive and sometimes hostile host community of non-Indians and non-Hindus. Despite the loss of many valuable traditions through the death of their elders and the inability to resist the dominant Afro-European culture, several aspects of Indian cultural heritage have survived. The growing presence of Indians saw the rise of racial, cultural and religious trends that have contributed to the creation of a uniquely cosmopolitan Caribbean society at the beginning of the twenty-first century. Notwithstanding their impoverished means and limited opportunities, the Indian presence has demonstrated steady social advancement in every field of endeavour, including agriculture, literature, music, art, sports, business and the media.

The early Indian immigrants and the first generation of their children had been mainly interested in their economic advancement. They had gradually overtaken the Afro-Caribbean emigrants in the economic sector. They had little craving for political power. In fact, they had the intention of returning back to their homeland. However, in later years, they gradually began to move into the forefronts of the country's politics, which was until then dominated by the People's National Movement, an Afro-centric party. But with the advent of the charismatic Basdeo Pandey, the PIOs have catapulted themselves into political power.

The Right Honourable George F. Fitzpatrick (1875–1920) was a prominent barrister of East Indian descent and member of Trinidad and Tobago's Legislative Council.[9] He played an early role in helping bring to light malpractices carried out under the system of Indian indentured labour. In 1909, George Fitzpatrick provided testimony before a British parliamentary investigation, led by Lord Sanderson, regarding alleged mistreatment of East Indian labourers living in Trinidad. The Sanderson Committee, however, failed to bring about the immediate abolition of the indentured system, only its postponement, which was further deferred by the onset of the First World War. It was not until 2 January 1920 that the system of indentured labour would come to an end.[10]

Diaspora associations

- A major Hindu organisation in Trinidad is the Sanatan Dharma Maha Sabha led by Satnarayan Maharaj.
- The major Muslim organisation is the Anjuman Sunnat-ul-Jamaat Association (ASJA) led by Yacoob Ali. Although these organisations were once seen to speak for the vast majority of Hindus and Muslims in Trinidad, their membership has gradually eroded.
- GOPIO chapter

Basdeo Panday (born 25 May 1933) was the fifth prime minister of Trinidad and Tobago from 1995 to 2001 and has served as Leader of the Opposition from 1976 to 1977, 1978 to 1986, 1989 to 1995 and 2001 to 2010. He was first elected to Parliament in 1976 as the Member for Couva North. He is the former chairman and party leader of the opposition United National Congress. However, he lost the party's internal elections on 24 January 2010 to Deputy Leader Kamala Persad-Bissessar by a large margin. In 2006, he was awarded the Pravasi Bharatiya Samman by the Ministry of Overseas Indian Affairs. Kamla Persad-Bissessar SC, MP, is the seventh prime minister of the Republic of Trinidad and Tobago, the sixth person to hold this position. She was sworn in as prime minister on 26 May 2010 and is the country's first female prime minister. Persad-Bissessar is the political leader of the United National Congress and leads the People's Partnership, a coalition of four parties, formed for the general election of 24 May 2010. She was the first woman to serve as attorney general, acting prime minister and Leader of the Opposition of Trinidad and Tobago. She became Political Leader of the United National Congress and Opposition in 2010.

Country case study – Mauritius

India–Mauritius relations refer to the historical, political, economic, military, social and cultural connections between the Republic of India and the Republic of Mauritius. Connections between these two countries date back to 1730, when artisans were brought from Pondicherry and Tamil Nadu. However, diplomatic relations were established in 1948, before Mauritius became an independent state. The cultural affinities and long historical ties between the two nations have contributed to strong and cordial relations between the two nations. More than 68 per cent of the Mauritian population is of Indian origin, most commonly known as Indo-Mauritians.

Indians constitute the single largest ethnic community in Mauritius which is more than 60 per cent of the total population (Ember et al., 2005: 289). The population is estimated to be 8,82,220 which is almost entirely represented by PIOs with NRIs having population of only 15,000. Among this community, Hindus make up the largest group at 50 per cent, and Muslims at 17 per cent (Lal et al., 2006: 271). Under the French colony, Indians played a key role in the development of the island and since independence; the socio-political life of Mauritius has in large measure been determined by people of Indian origin. Indians also constitute 31 per cent and 6.1 per cent of populations of Reunion Island and Seychelles, respectively (Lal et al., 2006).

History and political mobilisation

Indians came to Mauritius originally as slaves, then indentured labour, free workers, traders, sailors, soldiers; and even as women spouses provided for European settlers by the French East India Company. Indian soldiers took part with the British Army in the conquest of Mauritius in 1810. They came in more massive numbers from 1834 to 1835 as indentured labourers and also as traders, jewellers etc. who followed this massive movement induced by the sugar oligarchy (which itself comprised some rich Indian owners) and the British colonial government. Those of them who were not slaves during the French Revolution started struggling for some freedoms like wearing their traditional attire in the newly created revolutionary militia for Coloured persons alongside white militias and were admitted to the elected Colonial Assembly (a revolutionary organ that broke away from France when slavery was abolished by the French revolution). Napoleon reinstated in 1803 the discrimination against the Coloured Indians and Creoles (the latter mixed origins).

The coolies who came mostly in 1834–35 started opposing their oppressive landlords who were backed by the colonial administration by various forms of resistance and those Indian workers and small planters were even helped by legendary historical leaders from the white community like Thomi Hugon, a white Mauritian employed by the Indian administration in the nineteenth century, and Adolphe de Plevitz, a Frenchman owning a sugar plantation.

The working masses of Indian small planters and labourers and Creoles (mainly descendants of slaves) under the guidance of Manilall Doctor (sent by Gandhi) and Dr. Eugene Laurent (a Creole of Indian origin) in the early 1900s, then Dr. Maurice Curé (a Coloured Creole), the founder of the Mauritius Labour Party who developed links with the pro-independence Indian Congress in India from 1930s to 1940s. Dr. Curé appointed Pandit Basdeo Bissoondoyal, during his studies in India, as representative of the Labour Party and his brother Sookdeo Bissoondoyal, the politician, formed the Jan Andolan allied with the Labour Party which they left in disagreement with Dr. Seewoosagur Ramgoolam when the latter became the leader of the Labour Party.

Labour and the Independent Forward Bloc of the Bissoondoyal brothers, albeit virulently opposed to each other, helped the working masses of Indians and Creoles to obtain political freedom with the right to vote from 1948, then universal suffrage in 1959 and the country's independence in 1968. From then on, the democratic and a strong welfare state (free universal education, free universal health care, later a National Pension etc.) has helped the emergence of the masses who now decide who will constitute Parliament, and there has also been the emergence of a non-Oligarchy political leadership, though a White Plantocracy still controls much of the economy today, albeit with emerging, yet less economically powerful groups from other communities.

The ethnic communities are delicately balanced and ethnic politics is now rife with communalism and casteism, today's scourges. Yet, the political leaders, despite practicing ethnic politics, also officially appeal to the notion of 'One People, One Nation' to rally the biggest multiethnic vote banks and their elected members in Parliament represent all segments of the population ethnically. The economy is as neo-liberal as it can be. Socialism has crumbled; consumerism has taken huge proportions.

The political game is one of alliances today; where everybody is seen courting everybody. The leader of government is Navin Ramgoolam, son of the first prime minister, and the Leader of the Opposition is Paul Bérenger, a white man but not an Oligarch, leader of the Mouvement

Militant Mauricien (temporarily replaced by Alan Ganoo, a Hindu) and both parties are multiethnic in composition and each rally nearly half of the national electorate. The MMM and former president and PM Sir Anerood Jugnauth's Mouvement Socialiste Mauricien, who led the country as prime minister to an economic miracle in the 1980s and 1990s, has allied itself to Bérenger's MMM as they did in 2000 to form now the Remake 2000 alliance party to contest the next elections due early 2015, if not before. The MSM is itself an offshoot of the MMM party in which Jugnauth and Bérenger ousted former PM Sir Seewoosagur Ramgoolam from power in 1982 when they won all parliamentary seats (before attribution of best loser seats). Jugnauth and Bérenger will share power as they did in 2000–05 as PM if they win again.

Today, issues have changed from those of the old days when the struggle was for basic political freedoms, which are now all enshrined in the Constitution. The struggle for power is no more ideological or for independence or for the emancipation of oppressed ethnic groups. Class struggle has receded. Ethnic/religious fundamentalists are few even if some lobby actively wherever they can do it. All the three major parties want now to remove from the Constitution reference to ethnic groups for elections as part of a vast electoral reform project. This is targeted at promoting 'Mauritianism' and abolishing the 'Best Loser System' that refers to communities specifically and meant in the old days to reassure non-Hindu minorities of parliamentary representation by nomination of best losers at general elections. The major parties think that the time is ripe to get rid of this 'communal system' as no community is believed to be threatened by under-representation.

The best description of the ethnic situation was once given by Labour politician Sir Kher Jagatsingh who said, 'We are all minorities!' which explains this desire to do away with communities in the Constitution once and for all. Yet other political matters having nothing to do with the communal factor may prevent this for the time being.

Bilateral investment treaty

India and Mauritius have signed a wide range of bilateral agreements. Some of the important agreements are the Double Taxation Avoidance Convention (1982), Bilateral Investment Promotion and Protection Agreement (1998), Agreement on Cooperation in Information and Technology (2000), Extradition Treaty (2003), MoU on Cooperation against Terrorism (2005), MoU on Sports and Youth Affairs (2012) and Educational Exchange Programme (2012).[11] In addition, cultural exchange programmes have been regularly concluded since 1971. India is Mauritius' largest trading partner and has been the largest exporter of goods and services to Mauritius since 2007.

Conclusions

This chapter has focused on the Indian Diaspora in Canada, the United States, Trinidad and Tobago and Mauritius. All these countries have significant Indian Diaspora populations. Two of these countries represent the old colonial era emigrants or indenture emigrants, that is, Trinidad and Mauritius and the other two represent the later or modern migrant experience that in fact is still playing out in both Canada and the United States. In both Mauritius and Trinidad and Tobago, the persons of Indian origin represent a significant and very large portion of the total population as these are countries where economic compulsions of the Empire led to first slaves being taken to work the plantations and then the indentured workers. Since many of the Indian labourers stayed back and made these colonies their home, it was but natural that they would play an important role in the political governance of these countries, once the colonial masters departed. It has been a struggle, especially in Trinidad, where the Indian origin population is not in a majority; but the community has produced leaders to take on the mantle of democratic governance. In doing so, they have also established strong political and economic bonds with the home country of India.

The experience in Canada and the United States has been different. Their numbers have been small and in the earlier years they faced much discrimination. As they gained in commercial and economic spheres, the overseas Indian realised that entering the political space was an important factor of both the community's maturing as also of participating in the democratic framework of these countries. Their story in this domain is far from over, and the future holds promise of both their successes in the political opportunities in their adopted nations as also of further links with their homeland.

Notes

1 Source: Khalsa Diwan Society – Canada cited from http://www.sikhpioneers.org/chrono.html#1897, accessed on 17 May 2013.
2 As the influx of the Sikhs increased, the society built a new gurudwara in 1970 on the 500th birthday occasion of Guru Nanak.
3 Source: *MEHFIL*, 'The magazine for today's Indo-Canadian', December 1997, pages 29 and 76. Cited from http://www.sikhpioneers.org/chrono.html#1913a, accessed on 25 February 2013.

4 Among the new eligibility conditions, priority was given to those who knew English or French; those who were not too old to take regular jobs in Canada and had arranged for employment in the country; someone who had a relative in Canada and had undertaken a proper education and training before emigrating to a region of high employment. Based on these eligibility conditions, they were assigned a point system of 0–15; the more points the migrants could secure, the higher their chance of entering into the country.
5 http://www.mea.gov.in/Portal/ForeignRelation/India_Canada_Bilateral.pdf, accessed on 3 June 2013.
6 Ministry of Overseas Indian Affairs, official website, http://moia.gov.in/accessories.aspx?aid=11, accessed in November 2013.
7 Ibid.
8 Local socio-economic conditions prevailing during the colonial days served as push factors to encourage migrants to depart their homeland in search of a better future. Several exploitative and seemingly arbitrary taxes such as dhururai or dust cess, for dust raised as cattle passed the landlord's estate; and payment of presents, called nazar, in festivals such as Dusshera, Holi and Eid; neota or invitation cess, when villagers were asked to join in celebrations. So severe was the system of taxation that the practice of kanya vikray (sale of daughters, typically very young girls, to be married to much older men) developed to enable peasants to withstand conditions of extreme deprivation.
9 Campbell, Carl C. (2000). *The Young Colonials: A Social History of Education in Trinidad and Tobago, 1834–1939*, University of West Indies Press, pp. p168. ISBN 978-976-640-011-8.
10 Takravarty, L. (1978). 'Emergence of an industrial labour force in a dual economy-British India, 1880–1920', *Indian Economic Social History Review*, 15: 249–327.
11 http://mea.gov.in/Portal/ForeignRelation/India-Mauritius_Relations.pdf, accessed on 20 February 2014.

Chapter 5
The political economy of migration in Indian states

This chapter seeks to analyse the role of the Indian Diaspora in home politics. What are the legal and political frameworks that exist in India, especially at the level of the states, which present the possibility of the Diaspora influencing domestic politics? Is this involvement limited to the political sphere? Does this involvement go deeper – leading to the Diaspora's participation in socio-economic issues? We often hear of remittances and philanthropy, when we talk of Diaspora participation. There is hardly any mention of the social capital that the Diaspora brings to their home state. Do adequate official frameworks exist that provide the structure for such participation? Do Diaspora organisations exist at the state level and what role do they play, as 'friend, philosopher and guide' of the Diaspora? How does the state engage with its Diaspora? Is there a permanent structure for interaction? Are there gaps between commitment and delivery? How are these measured and deficiencies, if any, addressed? All of these are pertinent questions that the research will focus on, in three key states – Gujarat, Punjab and Kerala.

In this chapter, an attempt is made to contextualise such Diaspora engagement in the political economy of the state, seeing it as an inter-disciplinary study encompassing the socio-economic environment in the context of domestic politics and seeking to understand what role the Diaspora could play in the local environment.

Overall parameters

To start with, it would be essential to understand what role has been envisaged for the states under the Indian Constitution. Theoretically speaking, migration is a central subject and therefore, any migration-related activity falls under the umbrella of the central government. At the centre, therefore, the Ministry of Overseas Indian Affairs (MOIA), which was set up in 2004, looks after all the policy relating to migration and it engages with Diaspora, as stated in earlier chapters. At the centre, one piece of legislation – Emigration Act of 1983, whose purpose is to protect the migrants and regulate emigration from India. In practice, it is, however, the states that are required to play this role, as all political and economic activities take place there. Furthermore, the states get involved with all matters relating to the protection of personal life and property, which are the main concerns of the Diaspora.

With a view to ensuring better connectivity with the states, the centre has evolved certain guidelines, which the states are expected to follow. Given the importance of the Diaspora, each state has been requested to set up a Department of NRI Affairs. (NRI is used as a generic term, which embraces the Diaspora, comprising NRIs and PIOs.) Further, the centre has entered into MOUs with the leading emigrant sending states focusing on areas which are of interest to a particular state. An annual state-level consultation mechanism has been created which connects officials from the centre with the states and other stakeholders as they engage in migratory process and Diaspora-related issues. Each state has also created its own Diaspora-related structures to meet its specific needs. In this chapter, we analyse the setting for each of the three states under the following heads:

- Profile of the Diaspora from the state of Punjab/Gujarat/Kerala
- Framework for the centre's engagement with the state
- Supplementary policies of the state government and Diaspora-related state structures
- Diaspora organisations in the state and their role
- Role of foreign Diaspora bodies in the state
- Diaspora engagement with the state: issues and politics

State case study 1: Punjab

Nature and profile of the Diaspora from the state

Punjab has emerged as an important state in India for out-migration.[1] While migration of workers to the Gulf is a post-1980s phenomenon, Punjabis have been lead players in voluntary migration to the developed countries. Punjabis have been part of virtually all the migratory streams from India. Among the Indians, Punjabis were pioneers, as voluntary migrants to Canada and United States in the 1890s. Migrants from

Punjab comprise unskilled, semi-skilled, highly skilled professionals. In the colonial times, Punjabis had answered the call for carpenters, technicians and white-collar workers from East Africa; for police officials from Malaysia and Singapore and for farmers and ex-soldiers from Australia, Canada, United Kingdom and the United States.

Presently too, Punjab continues to remain an important source of migration to the developed countries. As recently as the period 2004–08, Canada had issued over 10,000 permanent resident visas annually from Punjab accounting for 30 per cent of the visas issued to Indians. Canada, in fact, is the only country that maintains a Consulate General in Chandigarh, the capital of Punjab, indicative of its strong connect with the region. Punjabis also accounted for 50 per cent of the visas issued to Indians by New Zealand. Punjabis have also emerged as a predominant community in Italy, accounting for approximately 80 per cent of the total Indian residents; estimated to number around 120,000. Punjabis have enjoyed a dominant migrant status in the United Kingdom and have acquired dominance in Canada too. They are also emerging as an important community in the United States. Presently, there are around 3 million Punjabis spread all over the globe. As the saying goes, 'Punjabis and Potatoes are found everywhere!'

A significant feature of migration from Punjab is the need to recognise that as if it is in every Punjabi's DNA to migrate. Every third family has a migrant. It is considered fashionable, almost compulsive to migrate abroad. They are, therefore, prepared to adopt any means that is possible, be it legal or illegal, to go abroad. Punjabis have also taken advantage of the asylum facilities, post 1984. They are also in the forefront whenever an amnesty is granted by the host state. In 1999, when Malaysia granted amnesty, the then high commissioner had to make contingency arrangements to issue as many as 1,000 passports on a daily basis. Similarly, they took advantage when Italy and Spain offered amnesty in 2009–10. It is here in these contingencies that the politics of migration enters, about which we will discuss in the subsequent parts.

The salient features of Punjabi migration, which predominantly comprises of Sikhs, are as follows:

- It has maintained links with the homeland, as 'Des' (home) has always remained an integral part of a Punjabi, even in 'Pardes' (foreign land).
- It is self-contained but has also maintained its diversity, based on religion and regions, including caste, even though the Sikhs subscribe to equality based social structure and society. At times, this

became a source of conflict amongst different groups.
- It has been deeply committed to its faith and maintains its identity which sometimes leads to identity politics, resulting in its bearing the brunt of hate crimes, even when it may have been a case of mistaken identity.
- It has been politically alive and has actively participated in the political structures of the host society. Dilip Singh Saund was the first Indian to be elected to the Legislature Assembly of California (the United States) in 1920 – Dosanjh was the first Indian to become Premier of British Columbia. It has had a sizeable number of members in the Canadian Parliament.
- It is resourceful and has successfully met challenges faced by it in maintaining its identity; be it the United Kingdom, France, the United States or any other country. In fact, most recently, it has been reported that Sikhs are fighting misdirected hate crimes in the United States through aggressive awareness campaigns.[2]
- It has adapted itself well in the host states and has earned the distinction of a model community.

Some of the above features would, however, result in its entering into the arena of domestic politics of the home as well as the host states, as it negotiates its place and role.

Framework for centre's engagement with the state

Punjab acquired the distinction of becoming the first state in signing a MOU with the MOIA on 26 May 2008, with focus on involving the government in Diaspora-related issues. The objectives included generating awareness on safe and legal migration and employment opportunities overseas; up gradation of skills of migrants, and attending to socio-economic issues relating to NRI marriages and illegal migration.

To achieve the above objectives, the state government was expected to set up a migration resource centre (MRC) which was to act as a single window of information on migration and thus facilitate safe and legal migration. It was also to provide 24 × 7 services to migrants and their families on other migration-related issues and facilitate information on relief measures to the Diaspora stranded abroad. Unfortunately the proposed MRC has not still become operational. A debate is still going on, on whether to locate this centre in Jalandhar or Chandigarh, as the Haryana government has already established an MRC at Panchkula,

Chandigarh. Punjab, however, has a mixed record in implementing other programmes initiated by the centre. Punjab's progress has been rather limited on the upgradation of skills component and a very small number of persons have availed of this facility, as against the position in other states. Punjab has so far received two groups of NRI youth under the MOIA 'Know India Programme' (KIP) of the Overseas Indian Ministry. Punjab is also one of the states that have joined as a member of the Overseas Indian Facilitation Centre (OIFC). Punjab, however, has not been actively involved in other programmes of the Ministry like 'Tracing the Roots' and the PIO University.

Punjab has however been an active participant, along with other migrant sending states at the Annual State Consultative Meeting, organised by MOIA. Fourteen states attended the first Consultative Meet, held in Delhi on 8–9 July 2008. In his inaugural address, Minister, MOIA, urged the states to attract investments as well as ensure rigorous enforcement of emigration laws. He also wanted them to take steps to upgrade skills of Indian workers to meet the requirements of international labour standards. So far, five such consultations have been held and these have been viewed as an opportunity for promoting and nurturing a sustainable and mutually beneficial partnership with the overseas Indian community. Overall, this format has been found useful as it provides for essential connectivity between the centre and the state.

At such consultations, the Punjab government has expressed its concerns over rising illegal migration from the state, which had been largely due to various factors like unemployment and desire to fulfil the dream to go abroad and to improve one's life style. The state government has at such interactions outlined the steps taken to promote awareness on safe and legal migration and to handle other migration-related issues, such as NRI marriages etc. The state has already passed an act on human trafficking that aims at curbing the activities of recruiting agents, through provision of stiffer penalties.

Supplementary policies of the state government and Diaspora-related state structures

As stated earlier, migration is in the DNA of every Punjabi. It was, therefore, not surprising to find that NRI-related issues finding a mention in the 2007 election manifesto of the two major political parties. The manifesto of the Congress Party struck a note on making more effective laws and establishing new structures like 'Fast Track Revenue Courts' to help NRIs get their rented or occupied property vacated. It took credit for Punjab becoming the only state in 2002 to set up a separate Department for NRIs at the state level and the steps taken to restructure the NRI sabha. The Akali manifesto repeated the commitment to create a new minister of NRIs and setting up of fast track courts. It also talked of enhancing matching grants by the government to encourage NRIs' participation in development projects, proposing to enhance the share of the state to 75 per cent from the existing 50 per cent of development projects funded by the Diaspora, as well as special arrangements to contain cheating by travel agents.

These commitments were again reiterated in the election manifesto for the 2012 Assembly elections. The government has lived up to its commitments made in the election manifesto and other fora to promote better engagement with the Diaspora and to look after their interests. In this part we would look at some of the policy steps taken by the government to set up Diaspora-related structures at the state level and the manner and the level of its engagement with the Diaspora.

Diaspora policies of the state: At the policy level, the state has taken a number of initiatives; some of these have already resulted into laws/regulations, while the others are at various stages of implementation. Some of the important measures are as under:

- *Mera Pind* (My village) Initiative:
  This is primarily meant to encourage NRIs' participation in the adoption and development of their home villages. This scheme works on the principle of matching grant by the state government and its share has gone up from 25 per cent to 75 per cent of the project cost. The government's subsidy is only for the initial cost and no provision exists for the maintenance of projects. Diaspora involvement in the state-funded projects has grown over the years, but it has still not reached the level that the state can be proud of.
- Amendments have been made to the existing legislation to help the NRIs get back their encroached agricultural lands as well as get their urban property vacated. Despite such steps, relief still gets tied down to the decision in the courts as in many cases the control of the property in is the hands of relatives or friends.
- Review of the list of Proclaimed Offenders (POs) or asylum seekers in the United States and Europe (ostensibly from the time of the Khalistan troubles in Punjab) with a view to facilitating the return of these persons to India. Political overtones have resulted in the slowing down of the procedures leading to removal of names.

- Assistance to Abandoned Wives: The deputy chief minister and his wife, Harsimrat Badal, Member of Parliament, have been paying special attention to this. A special conclave to generate awareness was organised by Inspector General Police (IGP) for NRIs at Jallandhar in August 2012. The state government is also taking necessary legislative steps towards compulsory registration of NRI marriages.
- Enactment of Human Smuggling Act. The state government has gone through various stages to enact this legislation to address the menace of fraudulent recruiting agents.

Diaspora structures in the state: Some of the Diaspora-related structures are as follows:

- An NRI department exists in the state government since June 2002, headed by a cabinet minister. At times, this was headed by the chief minister himself.
- An NRI commissioner heads the department at the official level.
- A dedicated post of IGP for NRIs was created and is now located at Jallandhar, which is the hub of NRIs.
- NRI lambardars have been created to speed up revenue-related cases.
- NRI police stations, dedicated to look after complaints of NRIs, have been created in important districts.
- NRI commission with judicial powers was set up in June 2011.

Forums for engagement: How does the state government engage with the Diaspora? These are listed below:

- **Punjab NRI Sammelans:** This is the most important forum and is held annually in conjunction with the Pravasi Bhartiya Divas. The last such sammelan was held in January 2014. It is a two-stage activity: firstly, the official component, which is held at Chandigarh, providing for interaction between the government and the Diaspora; the second part is held in Jallandhar, where NRI sabha performs the role of a coordinator in providing connectivity between the government and the Diaspora and among the Diaspora.
- **States' participation at the Pravasi Bhartiya Divas:** At this conference, slots are provided to state representatives, for the interaction with their respective Diaspora. In the case of Punjab, it has been the deputy chief minister/NRI minister, who had

spoken at this forum. This has been a good forum for interaction, as it provides for opportunity to the Diaspora to voice their concerns and seek redressal of their grievances. The main grievances of the Punjabi Diaspora had been on the law and order–related issues: protection of properties and maintenance of their identity like hurdles on wearing of turbans in France which has become an emotional issue.

- **Individual or group meetings with leaders:** The government provides for such windows of opportunity, knowing the importance of such meetings.

At the previously mentioned fora, the thrust of the message is that it is a two-way engagement, which is mutually beneficial. It is not the government that is seeking NRI investment only, but it is also willing and prepared to render assistance to NRIs.

Diaspora bodies in the state and their role

Punjab is one of the few states which have a state-created Diaspora body called the NRI sabha. This body was set up in 1996 and is located in Jallandhar. Under its Constitution, the chief minister is the patron. The NRI commissioner or commissioner of Jallandhar Division, the senior most official in the division, is the chairperson of this body. It has an elected president, with tenure of two years and is elected by the NRIs themselves. A provision for weighted voting exists, depending upon the contribution. There is an overlapping of functions between the chairperson and the president, with the power of the president getting emasculated, as the chairperson effectively dons the hat of CEO. It is interesting to note that NRI sabhas also operate at the district level, with the deputy commissioner as the chairperson in the district.

NRI sabha has been designed to act as a forum for the welfare and promotion of interests of NRIs, in general, and NRIs of Punjab, in particular. It also promotes ethnic bonds among Punjabis and Punjabi NRIs. It also aims at ensuring their welfare and assists their participation in the development of Punjab. In practice, the NRI sabha has not been able to play an effective role, mainly because of the controversy attached to the election of its president. The character of its membership got changed at the time of elections in February 2013 as a large number of NRIs from the Gulf joined as members adding another element of controversy. The election of the new president also stands challenged.[3]

The inherent structural weakness in the body has prevented it from playing any meaningful role. It is not perceived to be an apolitical body and finds its role restricted to two socio-economic problems faced by NRIs – NRI marriages and disputes over properties. With the induction of new members from the Gulf, it may change its focus. Theoretically speaking, it has a good mandate, but it still has a long way to go, before it can come up to the expectations of the Diaspora.

Besides NRI sabha, there are a number of other organisations and individuals which get involved in handling Diaspora-related issues. Some of these are as follows:

- Lok Bhilai Party: It is a political outfit headed by Balwant Singh Ramoowalia, and its focuses on NRI marriages and illegal migration.
- Real NRIs: A body set up by an NRI from the United Kingdom, Jassi Khangura, and a former MLA from the Congress Party. It organises conferences on an ad hoc basis.
- Malta Boat Tragedy Mission: It is headed by Balwant Singh Khera and is still pursuing the case of 187 Indians, who lost their lives in the tragedy in December 1996.

Role of foreign Diaspora bodies in the state

Several Indian Diaspora organisations and associations overseas are organised on the basis of religion and regions. It is, therefore, not surprising to see a plethora of such organisations in the host states. A large number of these organisations get indirectly involved, as they pursue certain human right issues, which have become global in character, giving the freedom to any organisation to pursue such matters. In this category fall organisations such as Sikhs for Justice, Sikh Coalition etc. which are based in the United States and other human rights organisations in the United Kingdom and the West. In this part, we are concentrating only on those foreign Diaspora bodies which have made their appearance in Punjab. We would, however, look at the role of one such organisation, which is of recent origin, having been established in 2010, but is more actively seen on the political horizon of Punjab. It is called the North American Punjabi Association (NAPA), with headquarters in California, the United States, and has been holding conferences in Punjab and commenting on Diaspora-related issues.

NAPA describes itself as 'a non-partisan, non-sectarian global organization'.[4] It has chapters in the United States, Canada and the United

Kingdom. Its aim is to promote the interests of people of Indian origin in North America, by monitoring and addressing current critical issues of concern. It has also assigned to itself to play an important role as a pressure group in the political system for the great interest, of our community in our back home in Punjab.[5] We are concerned with this part of the activities of NAPA. There are various ways in which NAPA has tried to fulfil its aims and objectives as stated above, resulting in its involvement in home politics. It has taken various forms as gleaned from its interventions. These are described below:

- **Policy input:** It has urged the government to consider the appointment of an NRI, as member of the NRI commission in Punjab. It has also spoken on the need of setting up fast track courts for NRI disputes.[6]
- **Endorsement of policy initiatives:** It has lent its weight through endorsement of government's decision on the setting up of NRI commission with judicial powers and other similar issues.
- **Protection of heritage:** It has voiced its concern over the sale of heritage buildings in the royal city of Patiala.
- **Protection of migrant workers:** It has urged the government to diplomatically intervene to protect Indian workers who would be affected by the implementation of Nitaqat (Naturalisation) programme of the Government of Saudi Arabia. However, no statement has been issued by the government, unlike the concerns enforced by Kerala.
- **Promoting the Sikh identity:** It has participated, directly or indirectly, in programmes and other activities to protect the community from the negative impact it has faced because of mistaken identity. Its activities, in this regard, have included support to Anti-bullying Bill and Anti-Gun Law in the United States.

Diaspora engagement with the Punjab state: issues and politics

This part is the crux of our subject, where we would comment on the interplay of politics, as the state of Punjab engages with the Diaspora. In a federal structure, the states play a fiduciary role, as it is the centre that is the main player. The Diaspora feels that it is empowered now; with the offer of the overseas citizenship of India and the conferment of voting rights at the General Elections to NRIs.[7] The interface takes place directly in the political arena and indirectly in other areas. For easier understanding, we would look at this phenomenon under following broad heads:

- Political engagement
- Icons and public relations
- Economic engagement
- Philanthropic engagement
- Migration-related issues
- Social issues
- Human and workers' rights
- Identity
- Cultural connectivity
- Social capital

Political: Punjab, like other states, has no role at the policy level. The Diaspora's engagement with the state, however, had political overtones, even prior to Operation Bluestar in June 1984. This was because of the demand for a Sikh Homeland by certain Diaspora groups, mainly from the United Kingdom (Jagjit Singh Chouhan), who was supported by other groups in the United States, Canada, and other countries in the West. In fact, Sikh Diaspora groups during mid-1980s became quite vocal and undermined India's national interests. The Diplomatic Missions, then, were faced with a peculiar situation, where they had to harness other Diaspora groups to neutralise the role of the Sikh Diaspora groups. Even though normalcy has returned, certain remnants still remain and these get manifested in the form of court cases against political leaders from Punjab and India or moves in Australia,[8] Canada and the United States to declare the 1984 riots against the Sikhs as genocide. A recent online petition to President Obama launched on 15 November 2012 managed to generate more than 25,000 supporters on the internet – a threshold forcing a response from the White House. The White House refused to declare the 1984 riots as genocide, but noted that grave human rights violation had occurred.[9] The pot is still simmering as concerns are raised over the foreign funds reaching India to support 'BKI sleeper cells in Punjab and other places'.[10] Controversies over the screening of the film 'Sadda Haq' (My Right), focusing on the extremists, with the Shiromani Gurdwara Parbandhak Committee (SGPC) taking an ambivalent stand, have again raised concerns over disturbing the normalcy and peace that had returned to Punjab. Such developments have seeds for disturbing the equilibrium between Punjab and its Diaspora.[11]

A side effect of the 1984 riots had been the ease with which Sikhs managed to get asylum in countries in the West; on the ground of alleged persecution, even though they were economic migrants. A consequential impact of this phenomenon was that these asylum seekers were declared POs by the government of India, practically barring their return. Many of these people want to return and their cases are being reviewed. To this category are also added other persons, who are involved in other cases. According to IGP (NRIs), the NRI Cell has managed to slash the list by 40 per cent in the last five years, by removing 556 persons from a list of 1,400 persons.[12] Removal of names of POs results in political controversies between the centre and the state, with one blaming the other, for the slowness of the process and expressing concerns over political motives.[13]

How have Government of India's recent initiatives on granting Overseas Citizens of India (OCI) to PIOs and voting rights to the NRIs have played out in Punjab. While the Punjabis in the United Kingdom, the United States and Canada, and Germany have availed of OCI cards, persons in other countries like Malaysia, Singapore etc. have been reluctant as these countries do not subscribe to dual citizenship. PIOs, however, have been seen participating indirectly in the election process. In the case of Punjabis from Canada, the presence of electoral representatives was highly visible. It is a debatable issue as to whether foreign citizens could be openly participating in the electoral process in India as OCI is not tantamount to dual citizenship. Indirect involvement of overseas outfits of Indian political parties cannot be ruled out.

Regarding NRI participation at the March 2012 elections, there was a lot of hype prior to the holding of the elections. There were talks of plane loads of Punjabis descending in Punjab and casting their votes. This, however, did not happen. In fact, as per the press reports, only 9 NRIs were reported to have voted in the Jallandhar district, which is the hub of Diaspora in Punjab.[14] There were reports over the decline of flows of funds from abroad as well. The only place where the NRI impact was seen was at the elections of the NRI sabha, as a large number of NRIs in Gulf became members of that body, prior to the February 2013 election for the president. Only one former NRI was elected and is currently a cabinet minister.

Icons and public relations: Punjabis are happily placed as they have a surfeit of icons. They are politically alive and are well represented in the legislative assemblies, compared to their demographic strength in the host states. They enjoy a large presentation in the Canadian Parliament and have their presence in the parliaments of the United States, the United Kingdom, Singapore, Malaysia and other countries. There are parliamentary forums in the United Kingdom and the United States, where Punjabis have found representation. At present, another Punjabi – Nikki Randhawa, is the governor of South Carolina. Punjabi icons are also spread across the world, in other professions, including business, like Sant Singh Chatwal, hotelier in the United States, Lord Dalip Rana in Northern Ireland and professionals like Kapany (father of fibre optics) and A. S. Marwah (renowned dental surgeon) in the United States, Kirpal Singh (parliamentarian and lawyer). Many young professionals have distinguished themselves in their respective countries.

India has been reluctant in using its Diaspora in promoting its interests. It was a first when the Indian Diaspora, which included a number of Punjabis, helped in lobbying for India–United States Civil Nuclear Cooperation Agreement. India has also done its part in recognising its Diaspora by conferring Pravasi Bharartiya Samman Awards and Padma Awards. At times, such awards have generated controversy as was the case of the Padma Bhushan Award to Sant Singh Chhatwal,[15] Diaspora, on its part, also uses their status in getting facilities in India, be it in the form of setting up schools, hospitals and higher educational institutions. So, there is no free lunch, as the Americans say. This equally applies to Diaspora. It may, however, be remembered that involving the Diaspora in public relations activities or as a tool for soft diplomacy requires careful handling and it should be selectively resorted to in those countries, where there is official acceptance of such a role.

Economic engagement: How has the Diaspora engaged with Punjab? It is minimal in the investment arena. Exhortations for investment[16] for over a decade by successive chief ministers have not borne any fruit over the years. At the Punjabi NRI Sammelan, the Diaspora has not been impressed by high tech presentations as it is still looking for commercially viable projects. There are, however, some singular exceptions, in the case of Mittals (Acelor-Mittal), becoming a part of the Refinery Complex at Bhatinda. It may, however, be added that in the past, the Diaspora had participated in agriculture through such schemes as NRI tractors. At present, some NRIs are involved in progressive farming and dairy industry but their number is small. Punjabis also are not the lead players in sending remittances, as there is a proportionately small share of Punjabi workers in the Gulf; a group which is the primary sources of remittances to India. In the case of Diaspora from the United Kingdom, there appears to be more interest in selling agriculture land and properties in India; generating reverse flow of funds abroad.[17] According to the estimates of Zachariah and Rajan (2014), Punjab received Rs 14,279 crore in 2011.

Philanthropic engagement: It is in this area where the Punjabi Diaspora is relatively well entrenched. It is both, a case of response from inner self for community involvement and a response to the policies of the state government, which encourages the Diaspora to adopt their home villages for development, under a scheme called *Mera Pind* (My village). The state government also facilitates participation in philanthropic projects, by providing matching grants, with the state's share having increased from 25 per cent to 75 per cent. The scheme has grown over the years, from a paltry amount of Rs 5 lakh (0.5 million) in 2002–03 to Rs 9 crore (90 million) in 2009 as the state's contribution for development projects. This is still a low-level involvement and miniscule in financial terms. It may be noted that a Member of Parliament's grant under the Member of Parliament Local Area Development Scheme (MPLADS) now stands enhanced to Rs 5 crore (50 million), from erstwhile Rs 2 crore (20 million) per annum. Punjab has 13 Members of Parliament.

NRI philanthropic projects are largely concentrated in the four main Diaspora districts – Nawanshahr, Jallandhar, Hoshiarpur and Kapurthala. '*Mera Pind*' concept is being applied in a few villages, like Kharaudi (Hoshiarpur), Patiala (Kapurthala) and Barhampur (Ludhiana). Greater emphasis is now given to sewerage treatment, apart from building schools and hospitals. All the philanthropic projects are individual NRI-driven, as there is a paucity of Home Town Associations (HTAs). The umbilical cord is stronger in the case of Diaspora from Canada. At the group level, two groups are predominantly involved – Village Life Improvement Foundation of Dr. Raghbir Bassi (the United States) and Indo-Canadian Village Improvement Trust of Dr. Gurdev Singh Gill (Canada). Apart from that, some other NRIs have set up hospitals and educational institutions which are outside the state's partnership framework as they preferred to go their own way. It may also be noted that the philanthropic projects are not linked with the district development plans and bureaucratic hurdles are experienced in the implementation of the projects on account of paucity of funds and procedural hurdles.

Migration-related issues: The states are involved in the migratory process at various stages. Punjab's role in some of these issues is discussed under various subheads:

- **Illegal migration:** The Government of Punjab has enacted a legislation – the Human Smuggling Act which is aimed at providing severe punishment to recruiting agents. Awareness campaigns on Safe and Legal Migration have been conducted in the state by the embassies of the United Kingdom and Canada. MOIA in collaboration with the IOM and the Government of Belgium had also conducted two such campaigns in 2009 and 2010–11, which were conceptualised and executed by CRRID, Chandigarh. These campaigns have been well received and need to be continued on a regular basis, as these help in sending the message directly at the grassroots level, where it matters the most.

- **Amnesty for regularisation of resident status:** This is a natural corollary to illegal migration. At regular intervals, host states announce plans to regularise the status of undocumented persons and bring them to the regular stream, to their socio-economic requirements. Many countries, including Italy, Spain, Malaysia, Qatar and UAE, had announced such amnesty schemes, which provided a window of opportunity for the regularisation of status. It is here that the role of the state is triggered as the administrative machinery is required to establish their status as citizens since they had conveniently lost their passports. At times, some countries also insist on a Police Clearance Certificate at the federal level (Spain). It requires a coordinated approach between the centre and states. At times, it is a smooth process, as happened in the case of Malaysia. On other occasions there are tough moments, when the parties indulge in blame game, as happened in the case of Italy[18] and Spain,[19] between Punjab and the Ministry of External Affairs. At the end of the day, each party takes the credit, to sub serve their political ends. There is a need to develop a drill to respond to such offers of amnesty in future.

- **Returnees:** Punjab faces two types of situations. Firstly, voluntary returnees, as we have seen trends in the return of IT Educationists or Agriculture Professional have made a smooth transition, without any support from the government. However, there is no data available on them, which would help in making an analytical study on such trends. The second category is that of illegal migrants who are deported. In their case also, the state does not provide for any facilities for rehabilitation. However, in one case of returnees from Iraq, the state was forced to evolve a scheme, under instructions from the High Court.[20] The government has to evolve a scheme to handle similar cases in the future.

Social issues: As far as Punjab is concerned, it is involved with marriage-related issues, both at the Indian and foreign ends. At the

Indian end, it is playing a pro-active role, while at the foreign end, it is a mute spectator. The two situations are briefly described below:

- **NRI marriages:** This is an important social issue, as it affects practically every family. MOIA[21] had taken certain steps, both in terms of generating awareness as well as facilitating legal assistance. In Punjab, this has become the pet project for the deputy chief minister and his wife Harsimrat Badal, Member of Parliament. A focused Conference on NRI marriages was held in August 2013, where both of them were present. The problem with this issue is that it is that we are looking at the symptoms as this has to be addressed at the family level; in a majority of cases, it is the parents who push their daughters into this situation. Another aspect of this is that there have been cases where some men have been the receiving end as they are also being duped by girls posing as potential brides. The Punjab government has enacted legislation providing for compulsory registration of NRI marriages. Being an emotionally charged issue, it attracts greater media and political attention; it becomes a public relations event for publicity of leaders. Dignitaries like the chief justice of India have also addressed this issue.[22] It is a personal matter that falls in the domain of the family but one that has to be addressed but with a change in mind-set. How do we address the real issue rather than continue tinkering with the symptoms?
- **Forced and proxy marriages:** While NRI marriages are of concern to India, Forced and Proxy Marriages are of concern to the host states. In the case of Forced Marriages, it is a judgmental issue of values, where an arranged marriage is invariably perceived as a forced marriage, viewed as against the wish of the girls. In the the United Kingdom, there is legislation to regulate such practices. Among the South Asians, the primary focus is on the Pakistanis,[23] although Indians, including Punjabis, have also fallen foul of the legislation. In the case of Proxy Marriages, the objective is to prevent the institution of marriage being used as a tool for getting visas. In these cases, Indian authorities are helpless, as the implementation is in the hands of the host states.

Human and workers rights: Here the state governments have a limited role to play, as these are handled by the Ministries of External Affairs (MEA) and MOIA. The states are forced to play the role of pressure groups, as leadership owes political responsibility to their constituents. The states can, however, play an important role in generating awareness in promoting legal and safe migration. It can also connect to migrants and their families through the Migrants Resource Centre (MRC). Punjab has been slow in this regard.

Identity: Migration is intrinsically linked with the issue of Identity, between 'us' and 'them'. It is how a migrant negotiates his place in the host state, as he adapts himself, while maintaining his identity. Many Punjabis hold the view that there have been dual identities.[24] It is not always a smooth transition, as he/she faces challenges, not from outside his group, but from within the group also, if it has greater diversity within the Group. Another element of complexity is added, if the Group, like the Sikhs, has a visible distinct identity. The Sikh Identity has faced a number of challenges in the host state, some of these are as follows:

- Mistaken Identity, being clubbed with the Muslims.
- Visible Nature of Identity.
- Diversity within the Group.

How have these situations played out in practice and what has been the nature of response from the Punjab government. Some Sikhs have lost their lives, in particular, in the United States, because of mistaken identity. In a recent case, several people were killed in a Gurudwara in Milwaukee in August 2012. This has resulted in the community garnering support at the level of government including support from President Obama. The Chief Minister of Punjab extended his moral support when he went to the United States on a private visit. The community has tackled this through awareness campaign/s in many countries. The level and the nature of assistance are not known.

In the case of visible symbols of its identity, the Diaspora has pursued them locally. At times, it has successfully negotiated these while in other cases it is still lingering on, in particular, ban on visible symbols in France. So are the concerns on frisking. Both the Government of India and Punjab had tried to intervene but without much success.[25] There is also the problem of Jats and Dalits, as witnessed in killings in a religious place of worship in Vienna, Austria, in 2011.

Culture connectivity: This is an important and central area, as it is this cultural connectivity that binds an individual to the home state and among themselves. In the case of Punjabi culture, it has gone global,[26] as 'Bhangra' dance and music have become a rage with the youth. Similarly, the community connects through sports and holding of exhibitions on Punjabis.[27] The Punjab government has launched an Annual

International Kabbadi Tournament in Punjab.[28] There is, however, no support from the Punjab government in the learning of the Punjabi language, despite requests received from countries like Malaysia. Steps have also been taken by organisations such as the World Punjabi Organisation (WPO) to connect the Diaspora to its roots.[29]

Social capital: This is an important area, where the Diaspora has an important role to play, as instruments of social change. At times, however, it plays the opposite role, when it transplants its social baggage to the host states. Areas of concern for both the home and host states are issues of gender bias that find themselves reflected in incidents of female foeticide, rape and even honour killings.

Despite the possibilities and opportunities for knowledge transfer, Punjab has not been able to benefit from its Diaspora. This is despite the interest shown by the United Kingdom and Canada for the upgradation of skills. At the same time, initiatives have been taken by some Diaspora groups in the area of environment. Eco-Sikh,[30] a US-based group, has shown interest in this area in Punjab. It is involving the religious places in the fulfilment of its objectives, to create 'awareness about Sikh teachings on nature preservation', to promote planting drive and minimise energy in community kitchens.

Concluding observations

How does Punjab find itself placed, as it gets involved in the politics of migration and Diaspora? It is a case, full of intricacies and complexity, as it woos its Diaspora to be a participant in Punjab's development story (Sukhbir Badal),[31] while avoiding pitfalls of the post-1984 development when the Diaspora had distanced itself from not only Punjab but India also. In this exercise, historical moorings of the Punjabi Diaspora, and inseparability of the Sikh religion from politics, have to be factored in. During pre-independence days, it fought not only for India's independence in the early twentieth century through the Ghadar Party in California (the United States) but also for the rights of migrants in Canada and the United States, consequent to the *Kamagata Maru* incident of 1914. The Diaspora has been in the forefront, in its fight against discriminatory immigration laws that were against the spirit of human rights. At the present juncture, it is a question of the protection of the Sikh religion and the Sikh Identity.

How has this translated at the ground level? It is a strange case of history that India's Diaspora policy to effectively engage Diaspora, owes its origin to neutralising the Sikh Diaspora from its anti-Indian policies in the United Kingdom, the United States, Canada and other developed countries, consequent to the 1984 Blue star Operation. It was a time when asylum was liberally granted to the Sikhs, even though they were economic migrants, as they were able to effectively use the plea of religious persecution to their personal advantage, resulting in their being declared POs by the Government of India. This had resulted in adversely impacting India's bilateral relations with many countries. Despite the situation now returning to normalcy, the issue of POs remains infested with politics even now, resulting in both the centre and the state taking jibes at each other. It is feared that there is a trend towards ascendency of extremists.[32] The most recent controversy (April 2013) over the banning of the film 'Sadda Haq', which deals with the extremists, was symptomatic of the strife re-emerging in the society.[33] Such concerns have resulted in government seeking assurance from countries like the United Kingdom and Canada on keeping a watch over these extremists.[34] This certainly is a new phenomenon where the state fights rather than protect its Diaspora in these days of international terrorism. India, however, is not alone in this regard.

Diaspora, on its part, also continues to put pressure; Diaspora groups abroad (Sikhs for Justice, the United States, Human Rights Group in the United Kingdom) continue pursuing GOI and are becoming vocal in seeking justice for the victims of the 1984 riots. This has got manifested in many forms. Firstly, it was the Diaspora pressure that forced the Indian government to remove Jagdish Tytler from the ministerial post, when he was appointed to head the newly created MOIA in 2004. Court cases are mounted against Chief Minister Prakash Singh Badal in the United States,[35] or against Cabinet Minister Kamal Nath in Switzerland for human rights violations[36] or when the Supreme Court upholds life sentence for perpetrators of riots.[37] Similarly, court cases are going on, even in India, against Jagdish Tytler[38] and Sajjan Kumar.[39] The case of clemency for Bhullar has added a new dimension and protests have been voiced in London and other capitals.[40] These result in creating uneasiness in the relationship between Diaspora, the state of Punjab, and India.[41]

There is also a positive note to Punjab's engagement with its Diaspora, which is more intense and relevant at this juncture. This engagement has its own political dimension, which varies from country to country, depending upon the strength and political involvement of Diaspora in a particular state and the openness of its Diaspora policies. It is, therefore, not surprising that Punjab's relations with its Diaspora in Canada are more intense, given the frequency and regularity of exchange of visits,[42] followed by the United Kingdom and the United States. Canadian and UK parliamentarians are seen in Punjab at the time of elections to the state assemblies in March 2012. The Canadian parliamentarians also use this closeness with Punjab to promote their electoral prospects back home in Canada. Occasionally this could go wrong, when Ruby Dhalla, a Canadian MP, who was the poster lady at the MOIA PBD and Punjab NRI Sammelan, lost her seat in the last elections in Canada.

What are the ways, in which Punjab connects with its Diaspora and how effectively can it stay connected? It is a twin-purpose pursuit; where the state not only seeks out Diaspora, but it also tries to reach out to them as it tries to address their concerns (Prakash Singh Badal, Chief Minister, NRI Sammelan, 2008). This was again reiterated by Deputy Chief Minister Sukhbir Singh Badal on 5 April 2013, when he announced government's plan to make a reservation of 10 per cent of quota in projects, industrial plots and residential plots all new colonies of PUDA, GMADA and other urban development agencies for NRIs.[43]

So far, the Punjabi Diaspora has not bitten the investment bullet, as it still does not feel that it has a business-friendly environment.[44] Its single point agenda is to seek protection for its agricultural lands and urban property and help from the state in protecting its identity abroad. Given the NRI-favourable amended legislation, there is some improvement over the protection of property, with renewed assurances from the chief minister.[45] The issue of identity still hurts, despite the fact that the state leadership has been vocal, in protecting their identity and promoting *Punjabiyat*.[46]

Ultimately, we have to accept that the role that states have to play may be a limited one, given the fact that emigration is a central Subject. Nonetheless, the states can make their contribution, as Punjab has done, by taking policy initiatives of its own. In some cases, it has been path breaking in enacting legislation, for compulsory registration of NRI marriages or preventing human smuggling; amending of existing legislation, to provide reprieve to require agricultural land or residential urban property and setting up institutional structures, like NRI 'Lambardars', NRI police stations and NRI courts. These, however, have only addressed the negative outcomes of the migratory process. These are in the nature of 'firefighting devices'. The development aspect, in the form of 'Connectivity' with the Diaspora, is missing.

India harps on the demographic strength of its young population, and Punjab boasts to become the Global Centre for Skills. It is, however, woefully behind, to convert this into a reality. The action is missing in implementing a workable plan, despite promises of financial and infrastructural support from the government of India and foreign countries, like Canada and the United Kingdom, to help in upgrading skills that are required abroad. Punjab has also not evolved any scheme which could make productive use of returnees, either as a 'Knowledge Hub' or facilitate reintegration in to society of those who are forced to return, when their dream to go abroad turns sour.

At another level, Punjab has failed to effectively connect with the Diaspora, in providing moorings to them, by meeting their requirements of promoting Punjabi culture and language, because of decline in numbers, despite the fact that some countries, like Canada, have declared Punjabi, as a second language. Mega sports events like 'World Kabbadi' provides fanfare with the participation of film stars, but connectivity with the real Diaspora is missing.

The focus in Punjab remains on the VIP Diaspora, as is the craze for cars with red lights. The so-called Inclusive Approach is missing that relates to all shades of Diaspora. At another level, greater visibility is lent to Punjab, by its Diaspora, when prime ministers from the United Kingdom and Canada include a visit to Punjab as an essential part of their itineraries or when President Obama lauds the progressive Punjabi spirit, when paying tribute to Dalip Singh Saund, the first Indian to be elected a member of the Californian Parliament in 1950.[47] The Punjabi Diaspora has reached a level of maturity and recognition in host states. This has to be converted into a positive force and not allowed to return to a level of mistrust that existed in the 1980s. The natural call for Punjab is to add a 'Developmental Agenda' to its 'Diaspora Approach', through a set of well meaning, attractive and workable schemes, as dishing out Punjabi Diaspora Cards, providing discounts, need to be discounted. The ethnic media, which was a potent force in pre-independence days, has to be involved. The focus has to be on the youth and make him connect with his heritage.[48] While Punjab would like to deliver to its Diaspora, as stated by Deputy Chief Minister Sukhbir Badal,[49] NRIs are the 'chosen children' who have to deliver and go beyond 'the warmth and bonhomie' of the NRI Sammelans.[50] Is this Diaspora politics or connectivity?

State case study 2: Kerala

Kerala

In Kerala, colonialism's plantation economy introduced ideas of migration as a virtuous form of social mobility and modernity (Varghese, 2009). International migration from Kerala became more pronounced with the rise of petroleum extraction in the Middle East and oil company dependence on Indian workers, and over the last twenty years Kerala has been one of the most significant source regions for Indian temporary workers mainly to the GCC[51] nations.

According to Zachariah and Rajan (2012), 'Kerala has a vibrant diasporic presence in several countries. They could have made vital contributions to Kerala's development but their re-sources and skills have not been properly channelised. Nevertheless, remittance transfers from overseas workers have boosted the economy. Of course, if someone travels from Thiruvananthapuram to Kasargode by road, we can see the visible changes in its landscape thanks to the Malayalis abroad. Today, Kerala has about 2 million migrants and they remit about Rs 60,000 crore, which is equivalent to 31 per cent of the state domestic product. The Diaspora, if channelled productively, can be game changers in Kerala's development path. Already we see return migrants as MLAs, ensuring that Non-resident Keralite concerns are also given equal consideration in the state policy agenda. NORKA has made seminal contributions towards analysing and utilising the NRK potential'.

In the wake of new labour policy in Saudi and few other GCC countries (Nitaqat), a recent study has indicated a decreasing trend in emigration from the state. The number of Kerala emigrants living abroad in 2011 is estimated to be 2.28 million, up from 2.19 million in 2008, 1.84 million in 2003 and 1.36 million in 1998, indicating that the increase during inter-survey periods shows a decreasing trend (Zachariah et al., 2014).

One out of every four households on an average in Kerala has a migrant, and if the total remittances from the migrants work out to be much more than what devolves to the state from the centre, the importance of migration in the economic and socio-cultural transformation of Kerala needs no exaggeration.

Centre's engagement with the state

With more than 5.5 million Indian workers abroad and migration of more than 8.5 lakh workers annually from the country, the central government has sought assistance from state governments through the five-point MoU agreement for protection of workers and dealing with any organised migration racket prevailing in the states in late 2000. To achieve the above objectives, the state governments were asked to set up MRCs, which were to act as a single window of information on migration and thus facilitate safe and legal migration. The first Migration Centre was set up in Panchkula, next to Chandigarh.[52] MOIA established its second MRC in Kochi/Cochin on 1 September 2008. The primary idea behind the establishment of MRC is to disseminate information on legal, organised and humane migration; risks involved in the illegal migration and diversify the emigration base by informing intending emigrants about the various opportunities available in the member states of the EU and the entry requirements for the same.

Kerala has also been an active participant, along with other migrant sending states, at the Annual State Consultative Meeting, being organised by MOIA. Fourteen states attended the first Consultative Meet, held in Delhi on 8–9 July 2008. The Kerala delegates in the meeting explained the difficulty in preventing illegal emigration as legal emigration was more difficult and expensive. Further, action against illegal migrants created human problems too as despite the difficulties and exploitation suffered by such illegal migrants, they prefer to continue as many of them faced worse situation at home. So far, five such consultations have been held and these have been viewed as an opportunity for promoting and nurturing a sustainable and mutually beneficial partnership with the overseas Indian community.

Kerala government also actively participates in Government of India's efforts of associating the younger generation of Indian Diaspora closely with India (and to clarify the stereotyped perceptions of India). As part of it, a selected 30 member team visited Kerala in December 2006 and stayed there and experienced the life style, socio-economic programmes of the state for almost a month. Kerala has also been actively participating in 'Know India programme'.

Diaspora structures in the state

Way back in 1996, the Kerala government launched a new department exclusively for matters relating to Non-Resident Keralites (NRKs), the Non-Resident Keralites Affairs Department or NORKA. It was the first-ever department in the country targeted at addressing the needs of the Non-Resident citizens of a state.

As proof of the value of this structural framework, successive governments have continued the activities of NORKA and expanded its activities to evolve into a whole range of activities for ensuring the welfare of NRKs. Taking these steps further, NORKA has taken an initiative for implementing a range of welfare and insurance schemes specifically catering to the NRKs. Its objectives are to

- Address complaints on illegal overseas recruitment agencies, non-recipient of salary, accommodation and of NRK housemaids and other women in distress.
- Address problems faced by the NRKs by interacting with the state government departments.
- Process enquires on investment opportunities in Kerala.
- Process enquires on *Pravasi Suraksha Arogya Scheme.*
- Provide assistance to stranded Keralites and also take steps for bringing back the mortal remains of NRKs to Kerala.

NORKA-ROOTS is the field agency of the Department of NORKA, set up in 2002. It acts as an interface between the NRKs and the Government of Kerala and a forum for addressing the NRKs' problems, safeguarding their rights and rehabilitating the returnees.

Forums for engagement

NORKA Department and NORKA-ROOTS are regularly conducting meets of NRK's spread across the Globe to discuss the various issues of NRKs working abroad, NRKs within India (outside the State of Kerala) and the NRK returnees in Kerala. The first meet was held in Kochi in 2001; followed by Germany in 2002; in Thiruvananthapuram in 2005; in Ernakulam in 2008 and the last meet was in Thiruvananthapuram in 2011. These meets have contributed remarkably to policy formulation of government in matters pertaining to NRKs and addressing the various issues related to NRK's of the state. The recently concluded Global NRK Meet, the meeting of NRKs from all over the world at Thiruvananthapuram, have recommended that the Union Government should take necessary steps for augmenting the staff strength of embassies in the Middle-East countries for taking care of the community and labour welfare issues of the NRK population in these countries. Further, the meet requested for the assistance of the Union Government for institutionalising legal aid cells in embassies of the gulf sector, which will benefit the expatriate population.

Kerala government also organised and hosted the Pravasi Bharathiya Divas in association with MOIA in January 2013. Kerala government set up an autonomous body, Malayalam Mission, to reach out to the Diaspora and to spread Malayalam language and culture especially in the United States and Middle East.

Diaspora engagement with the state

Diaspora engagement with the Kerala state has had very minimal political overtones compared to other states and their Diasporas. Though the major political parties in the state like Congress, Kerala Congress and Indian Union Muslim League have very active pravasi wings, the impact those groups make on day-to-day politics is very minimal or negligible. The recent state election held in 2011 – the first time NRIs were eligible to vote – was a litmus test for the Diaspora's interest in elections. The fact that a very small number of NRIs turned up to vote showed that overseas Keralites may not consider the voting right granted for NRIs to physically return for voting in their constituency, as the one they had wanted, and as had been projected by a minority among them to the government. It implies that the Election Commission has to walk the extra mile to make the change more NRI-friendly by possibly granting online voting. There are close to two million Malayalees working abroad. But the number of NRIs from the state who registered in the electoral roll for the 13 April election was just 8,820. Of these, only 4,639 had turned up to cast their votes (Statesmen, 2011).

At the same time, former Diaspora members are gradually reaching the Kerala Legislative Assembly and both houses of parliament. A prominent Dubai-based businessman Peevee Abdul Wahab was a member representing Kerala in Rajya Sabha until recently. In the Kerala Assembly, NRIs have made an entry with Thomas Chandy from Kuttanad constituency and Manjalamkuzhy Ali from Mankada in 2006 elections. Both of them again won in 2011 election, and Ali is currently serving as the Minister for Urban Affairs and Welfare of Minorities.

Though most of the Diaspora organisations in Kerala are not directly active in politics, their engagement as a pressure group in Kerala society for pressing various needs and requirements of both NRIs and general public has been very visible. Some of the issues for which Malayalee NRI organisations were active are new Integrated Emigration Act and Rules, utilisation of emigration deposits for the rehabilitation of Pravasees, development of international airports of Kerala state, for solving the citizenship issues of Pravasi Malayalees in Pakistan, compensation for the relatives of Pravasis dying in foreign countries, compensation for Kuwait War, Tsunami disaster, certificate attestation, Pravasis in foreign jails, bringing the dead bodies, excess air fare charges, safety and security for the families of Pravasis etc.

The shifting of Air India Express flight's headquarters to Cochin and constitution of Pravasi Welfare fund and loans for returnee emigrants have been viewed as a major policy impact due to the pressure from Diaspora organisations.

The Kerala Diaspora also actively influences the regional politics through electronic media. There are reportedly 14 Malayalam channels in the Gulf countries, a large number of them are in Dubai. The Indian National Congress has its own channel named 'Jaihind'. It claims a first as the only Malayalam station operating from Dubai studio city with big support from Dubai-based Malayali investors. The channel is targeting the overseas Malayali community concentrated in the UAE and other GCC countries, and operates under the slogan 'For the family and for the nation'. The CPM too has its Malayalam channel funded by NRI investors.

Economic engagement

Kerala has about 2 million migrants and they remit about Rs 60,000 crore, which is equivalent to 31 per cent of the state domestic product annually.

The impact of remittances on the domestic politics is quite visible. Since more than half of the migrants are Muslims and from poor families, their wealth has altered the socio-economic profile, which obviously has a bearing on the regional politics. The Muslim Gulf returnees do get influenced by the Islamic practices and ethos of the Gulf countries. Thus along with money they bring back Islamic political influence and sensitivity. In fact they come as part of larger Islamic community – Ummah. 'While a pan Islamic orientation is not new, it has been significantly strengthened over the last 30 years. Gulf migration brought thousands of Malayali Muslims close to what they consider the heartland of Islam and has exposed them to life in Muslim-majority countries. This has renewed a sense of participation to the wider *dar-ul-Islam* – which is of course open to different interpretations and expectations on the opposite shores of the Indian Ocean-while also enabling them to tap into the business opportunities it opens up' (Osella and Osella, 2006).

Above all it is none other than Kerala's dynamic Diaspora who have played a major role in getting key development and infrastructural projects to the state. It is they who played/play the pivotal role in the formation of Cochin International Airport, the Trivandrum Technopark, Cochin Smart city and now behind the much-hyped 'Air Kerala'.

Concluding remarks

While analysing the Malayali Diaspora's engagement in Kerala politics, it is clear that most of Diaspora bodies and organisation act as pressure groups in getting their demands approved rather than engaging in the day-to-day activities of the political parties. At the same time compared to other states, Kerala had the highest turn out of NRI voters in last state elections, though it was still very low compared to the number of people living outside the state.

Unlike the business classes and highly affluent Gujarati and Punjabi migrants, majority of Kerala Diaspora consists of low-/semi-skilled workers. Though Kerala has a long migration history, it was only in the late 1990s the state government started noticing about the inhumane practices prevails in the migration area and also the human rights violations that migrants face in destination countries and initiated measures to protect their rights. Despite the measures taken by Kerala government in protecting the rights of migrants there is still a great chasm between the expectations of the Diaspora and the de facto situation in the states. It is necessary to bridge this in order to fully engage the Diaspora with the state.

State case study 3: Gujarat

Gujarat

Gujarat has a very long history of migration. The ancient Gujaratis were known for their trading with other countries. The Mercantile caste of western India, including Gujarat, has participated in overseas trade for many centuries and, as new opportunities arose in different parts of the British Empire, they were among the first to emigrate. Significant migrant Gujarati communities exist around the world. The largest expatriate Gujarati population is the former British East African Asian community in the United Kingdom. Other major Gujarati communities exist in South and East Africa and South East Asia. Many Gujaratis live in the United States also. Approximately 40 per cent of Indo-Americans are Gujaratis. The Gujarati Diaspora community is well known for their legendary entrepreneurship. Gujaratis also have powerful contribution in the political leadership of host countries. Lord Dholakia in Britain's Liberal Democratic Party is the best example of the success of the Gujaratis Diaspora. The resilience of the Gujarati Diaspora is evident from the fact that even after facing total ruin during the regime of Idi Amin in Uganda, the Gujarati Diaspora has resurfaced there, and is financially well settled. In this section, an attempt is made to understand the major role played by Gujarati Diaspora in the political circles in Gujarat.

The state of Gujarat in western India has a population of over 60 million. Today, it is lauded and critiqued for its well-known right-leaning economic and social affinities. These propensities are deeply rooted in Gujarat's history and have shaped the Gujarati community even abroad in significant ways. For decades after independence the Indian National

Congress – India's first and largest political party – ruled Gujarat. In 1995, India's Hindu nationalist party – the Bharatiya Janata Party – won control of the state legislature and has been ruling the state since.

Since its formation in 1960, Gujarat's political leaders have pursued a rigorous agenda of rapid industrial development through public–private partnerships and export-led development (Agarwala, 2012). By the 1970s, Gujarat had become an 'image of progressive liberalism' according to the national Minister of Industries at the time (Agarwala, 2012; Sinha, 2005). Until the Government of India initiated its liberalisation reforms in 1991, Gujarat's economic policies were in line with the national government's strong commitment to Fabian Socialism. Though it is a highly debatable point, the state of Gujarat has one of the fastest growing economies in India.

Diaspora structures in the state

In the 1990s, the Gujarat government began to reach out to the Gujarati Diaspora – using transnational organisations as an entry point. Chief Minister Kheshubhai Patel (of BJP) institutionalised the effort. In 1998, he created the Non-Resident Gujarati (NRG) Foundation that comprised non-government advisors and channelled money towards NRG issues. While the NRG Division already existed under the Government of Gujarat, the Foundation strengthened the Divisions' activities with monetary support. Twenty seven NRG Committees were created at the district level (with the District Collector serving at the Chairman) to deal with NRG issues, such as inheritance or philanthropy. He also revived the NRG identity card that provides members with discounts on Gujarati businesses around the world and enables the government to retain a database of overseas Gujaratis. In a short time with active interaction with NRIs/NRGs the foundation has identified several areas and has initiated actions.

Objectives of NRG Foundation:

- To establish effective communication with NRGs in various parts of the world, prepare and maintain a comprehensive database about NRGs.
- To study from time to time social and culture issues of NRGs and takes steps to formulate schemes for meeting their requirements.
- To take effective steps to survey and assess the technical and professional skills of NRGs and to utilise the same into development effort of southern Gujarat.
- To tap the technological, managerial and financial resources of the state for the economic and industrial development.

- To channelise the savings and surplus financial resources of the NRG for development efforts of southern Gujarat.
- To monitor the general welfare of the NRG and in time of crisis, identify specific problems of NRG and to take up the same with Government of India.
- To take up other such activities as many be entrust by state Government.
- To do the Listing/Data Collection of NGO who are approved by the Charity Commissioners under the law.

NRG Foundation issues a 'Gujarat Card' to NRGs, regardless of current citizenship at nominal fees of US$5. Gujarat card holders would get special attention from Gujarat Government agencies and enjoy benefits like priority reservations in hotels run by the Tourism Development Corporation of Gujarat and in Gujarat Road Transport Corporation buses, plus concessional hotel rates and discounts in selected establishments and shops. The Foundation has also set up a NRG Bhavan in Ahmadabad near the International Airport – to provide residential accommodation with a 24-hour business information centre for non-resident Gujaratis.

In addition to the NRG Foundation, the government has also created an NRI Division – in the General Administration Department of the state government under the supervision of the chief minister in order to have a formal and organised link between the NRIs and the Government of Gujarat. The NRI Division and NRG Foundation act as a single window to facilitate the role of NRGs in development and to address their problems.

Apart from these state level programmes, the Gujarat government is also a regular participant of Ministry of Overseas Indian Affairs sponsored Pravasi Bharatiya Divas and other NRI welfare programmes. Every year, the Gujarat government also holds a 'Vibrant Gujarat' meeting that targets global investors – very successfully at that, both with foreign investors and Gujarati Diaspora.

Diaspora in Gujarat politics

Gujarat is one of the states where the two major political parties in India contest directly in electoral politics. Both the Indian National Congress and Bharatiya Janata Party have a deep support base among the Indian Diaspora. In organisational terms, while the INOS is promoting the association with the Congress party, OFBJP is the consistency of the BJP.

According to Ajay Mehra (2010), three factors play a major role in emanating the high visibility of the Diaspora in Gujarat polity and electoral processes. First, it is the high financial capacity of the Diaspora community. According to an estimate in 2006, there were over 800,000 NRI accounts in Gujarat with deposits well over US$40 billion. Second, the high salience to culture-religion among the community generates empathy with right-wing cultural ideology, where BJP provides a judicious mix. Third, the performance of the state government has further bolstered the economic rationale in favour of the BJP. Ajay Mehra (2010) also pointed out that the Gujarat Diaspora has for the most part been holding the fort for Chief Minister Narendra Modi even through years of an international boycott in the aftermath of 2002 riots by countries like the United States and until recently the United Kingdom. Aware of their support to ending a decade-long boycott by the UK government and the efforts in the United States to change its 'no visa policy for Modi', the chief minister made sure that he used his technology-savvy campaign to reach out to the Gujarati Diaspora and frequently through satellites and social forums likes Google hangout. In 2005, a group of Indian-Americans worked to have the US government deny Modi an entry visa to the United States on the grounds of human rights violation during the anti-Muslim riots in Gujarat (Agarwala, 2012).

Though they are very active in the political lobbying in the state, like in other states here also very few NRIs were part of the electoral process in the last state election. Political parties blamed high travel cost for the low NRI turn out in elections.

Apart from political activities, the Gujarati Diaspora has been actively present in the home state social circles through different religious and social organisations. Hindu organisations are especially prevalent among Gujaratis immigrants. The Swaminarayn and Vallabhacharya traditions of Hinduism both originated and developed in Gujarat. The Patidars, who occupy a predominant role within the Diaspora in the United States, played an important role in the Gandhian strand of the nationalist movement after independence, and they have since become a 'major powerbase' for the BJP in Gujarat (Bhatt and Mukta, 2000).

Gujarati Diaspora also plays a major role in Gujarat through various hometown associations. Because many Gujarati immigrants in the United States come from a farmer caste and grew up in rural areas, they are very active in providing contributions to their home villages. The villages have extremely organised, professional, and structured leaders and village bodies to elicit the contributions, manage them and judiciously spend them. With overseas contributions, these villages have built hospitals, schools, cardiac research centres, heart surgery facilities (that host international patients), yoga retreat centres, water filtration facilities, and biogas production plants. Most of the contributions are conducted on an individual basis. Some, however, are organised through hometown associations.

Non-resident Gujaratis have also successfully lobbied in the Western capitals for foreign direct investment in Gujarat. They have also been at the forefront in getting the latest technological innovations to India. Chief Minister Narendra Modi in his tenth Pravasi Bharatiya Divas address stated that despite the global financial crisis, Gujarat's economy was boosted by record-breaking investments made by the Indian Diaspora and companies. The chief minister said the state had moved beyond its 200 industrial estates and 60 special economic zones (SEZs) to special investment regions (SIRs) now.

Concluding remarks

Gujarat has the most entrepreneurial and risk-taking group of communities and individuals, with a Diaspora spread far and wide, in East Africa, Europe, the United States and East Indies (Vaidyanathan, 2008). The Gujarat government has been able to project Gujarat as well governed despite the partisan politics and this has led the wider Gujarati NRIs to build a niche in performance (Mehra, 2010). Though the number of NRIs participating in voting is very low, their participation in the local PR exercise and political think tank is very strong. In short, Gujarati Diaspora engagement in home state politics is likely to become more intensified in the future taking into account the growing polarisation of Indian polity and BJP is likely to continue having a stronger support.

Notes

1 CRRID Report on Punjab, 2011.
2 http://www.bbc.com/news/world-us-canada-28615701, accessed on 22 August 2014.
3 Malhotra, Jasdeep Singh, 'Gill's election as NRI Sabha Chief Challenged', *The Hindustan Times*, 5 April 2013.
4 NAPA website.
5 http:www.sikhiwiki.org/index.php/North_America_Punjabi_Association, assessed on 4 April 2013.
6 Singh, I.P., 'North American Punjabi Association seeks special fast track court for NRI's disputes', *The Times of India*, 3 January 2013.
7 http://www.punjabnewsline.com/content/north-american-punjab-association-welcomes-nri, assessed on 4 April 2013.
8 Resolution moved in Australian Parliament.

9 'US refused to declare 1984 riots as genocide', *The Hindustan Times*, 3 April 2013.
10 Barua, Sanjib Kr, 'Fresh foreign funds for Khalistan', *The Hindustan Times*, 7 April 2013.
11 'Backing "SaddaHaq" was a mistake', *The Hindustan Times*, 9 April 2013.
12 'Punjab slashes list of NRI proclaimed offenders by 40%', *The Tribune*, 6 January 2013.
13 Rattal, Mall, 'Punjab to re-examine Non-Resident Indian (NRI) proclaimed offenders' list that includes many names from Canada,' *The Indi-Canadian Voice*, 17 September 2014.
14 Press report.
15 'Controversy on Padma Award to Chhatwal'.
16 'NRI investment would benefit Punjab', *The Tribune*, 16 January 2008.
17 'UK-based professor delivers lecture on Punjabi diaspora', *The Chandigarh Tribune*, 12 April 2013.
18 Case of Italy: Interaction with MEA.
19 Case of Spain: Interaction with Mission.
20 Malhotra, Anil, 'Trapped abroad, without reason', *The Tribune*, 31 March, 2012.
21 Ministry of Overseas Indian Affairs, Government of India.
22 'Need to check antecedents of NRI grooms, says CJI', *The Tribune*, 17 December 2013.
23 Bhatia, Shyam, 'UK moves to out lawforced marriages', *The Tribune*, 16 June 2012.
24 Dosanjh, Ujjal, 'Punjabi NRI Sammelan', *Jallandhar*, 6 January 2008.
25 'Sukhbir objects to frisking of Sikh turbans', *The Tribune*, 8 November 2010.
26 Prabhjot Singh, 'Baisakhi gains global significance', *The Tribune*, 13 April 2013.
27 'Exhibition on Punjabis in California opens', *The Tribune*, 3 April 2012.
28 Randeep Wadehra, 'Kabbadi World Cup or a gimmick?' *The Sunday Tribune*, 9 April 2013.
29 'Punjabi diaspora get together to remember their roots', *The Tribune*, 11 February 2004.
30 'Eco-Sikh plans major green initiative', *The Tribune*, 24 February 2013.
31 'NRI's to be partners in progress: Sukhbir', *The Hindustan Times*, 6 April 2013.
32 Sanjib K. Barua, 'Fresh foreign funds for Khalistan', *The Hindustan Times*, 7 April 2013.
33 'Punjab Govt. bans militancy movie "Sadda Haq"', *The Hindustan Times*, 5 April 2013.
34 Statements by Canadian leaders.
35 Centre against CM.
36 'Case filed against Kamal Nath in Switzerland', *The Hindu*, 25 January 2013.
37 'SC upholds life sentence of four in 84 riots case', *The Tribune*, 9 April 2013.
38 '84 riots: court reserves orders in Tytler Case', *The Times of India*, 5 April 2013.

39 'Anti Sikh riots case: Delhi Court reserves judgement', *The Indian Express*, 4 April 2013.
40 Sinha Kounteya, 'Protest against verdict in London', *The Times of India*, 16 April, 2013.
41 'Keeps politics out of it', *The Hindustan Times*, 16 April 2013.
42 'Punjabi diaspora doing well, says Canadian MP', *The Tribune*, 18 January 2008.
43 '10% quota for Punjab NRIs in Projects, Plots', *The Times of India*, 6 April 2013.
44 Diaspora Interaction with Chief Minister, NRI Samellan, Chandigarh, January 2008.
45 http:/news/saanj.net/Punjab-news/badal-assures-punjabi-diaspora-to-address-all-their-genui, accessed on 4 April 2013).
46 'CM for promotion of Punjabiat in big way', *The Tribune*, 1 May 2008.
47 Sen, Ashish Kumar, 'Punjab-born Saund to laud Asian contribution in first India-American Congressman', *The Tribune*, 10 May 2012.
48 'Demand for Say in NRI Commission', *The Tribune*, 5 January 2013.
49 'NRIs seek, Sukhbir vows to deliver Punjab to NRI's, *The Tribune*, 5 January 2013.
50 'Chosen children', Help NRIs, but make them investor too' (ed.), *The Tribune*, 7 January, 2013.
51 Cooperation Council for the Arab States of the Gulf or Gulf Cooperation Council (GCC).
52 MRCs were established as a joint initiative by the International Organization for Migration and MOIA, as an institutional framework under the EC-funded project 'Regional Dialogue and Program on Facilitating Managed and Legal Migration between Asia and the European Union (EU)'.

Chapter 6
Conclusion
Migration in a globalised world

Migration is a natural and continuous phenomenon. Along with accelerated mobility, the very notion of migration has been changing. From ancient times, when migration for many communities was the lifestyle of people, sometimes forced and dependent on geographic and social conditions, to the modern era, when certain persons or peoples migrate willingly for the individual betterment of their life, the concept of migration has come to be seen as more positive and dynamic. We have traced some of the important emigration trends from India. Based on this analysis it would also be of use to comment on some of the existing beliefs, or we could even say 'myths of migration'. We mentioned these in the Introduction and it would be interesting to see if these actually hold good for Indian emigration.

The matrix below comments on the relevance of these myths or beliefs so far as Indian migration analysis has shown.

Myth # 1: People migrate mostly because of economic compulsion	The entire colonial emigration was driven by political compulsions of Empire
Myth # 2: Migration mostly takes place in South to North direction	Indian migration has gone in all directions including South–South
Myth # 3: Migration is a simple move from an origin to a destination	Much of Indian migration has been multi-country
Myth # 4: Migration hurts the economy of the Country of Origin	Indian migration has greatly benefited the local economies
Myth # 5: Migrants take away jobs of locals in the country of destination	Indian Diaspora and Indian corporates continue to create jobs for locals
Myth # 6: Migrants are a drain on public services	Indian migrants and Diaspora has contributed significantly through taxes and social security payments to the local economy

Myth # 7: Migrants cause unnecessary population growth in country of destination	Indian migrants in the GCC countries actually return to their country
Myth # 8: Undocumented migrants are criminals	Indian migrants and Diaspora have been proven to be most law abiding in the host countries
Myth # 9: Migrants do not integrate with the host societies	Several of the Indian Diaspora have not only integrated but also joined the political mainstream in host countries
Myth # 10: Migrants are caught in a time-warp in the context of their connect with home country	Several Indian emigrants and Diaspora do continue to engage with the changed and evolved modern India

Conclusion

This is a book on the politics of migration. We have attempted to trace the background and growth of the Indian Diaspora in different host countries and outlined their emergence and status as residents in those communities. Quite clearly, in democratic environments, true status and position flows directly from the political clout each group or community has. This is not just a reflection of the far-sightedness or strategy of any Diaspora community, but mostly a result of their response to the socio-economic and political environment that they react to. The earlier chapters clearly show that such reaction has been as varied and disparate as the migration itself, as also the host country they have emigrated to. Are there any generic lessons to be learned from this widely varied development? Are there any conclusions for the Indian Diaspora or for migration as a phenomenon? This chapter will try to sift through the chaff.

Migration is certainly not a new phenomenon; it has existed even in earlier times. What is new is its changed dynamics. It has created a network of relationship between countries of origin, settlement and other Diasporas of the same origin. They may be regarded as a tool of politics or economic assets, which the country of origin may be eager to exploit. A country often finds it useful to invest in the maintenance of close and friendly relations with migrant communities, fostering cultural ties, providing political propaganda supportive of its regime, facilitating financial remittances and neutralising dissidence within the Diaspora communities.

A country invests in its Diaspora not only for the economic and political support they may provide, but also to maintain sufficient influence to prevent them from acting counter to the interest of the country. On the other hand, the country of origin is not always a reliable champion or defender of the interests of its Diaspora communities. Governments in the country of origin are inclined by empathy or by domestic political pressures to speak out in defence of its Diaspora when they experience ill-treatment. However, sometimes, foreign policy interests of States supersede their commitment to the Diaspora. In international politics, the reasoning of states normally takes precedence over other claims including the status of Diaspora communities. A state will normally not risk security or economic interests for the sake of its Diaspora communities.

As brought out in the earlier chapters, migrants do not completely assimilate with the country of settlement. Through a combination of preferences, they maintain their distinct identity. Along with internal cohesion, migrant groups tend to maintain links with their country of origin. Communication with kinfolks and financial remittances to relatives are the most common form of contact. A migrant community may look to the home country for visits or for permanent repatriation, and perhaps to its government for cultural reinforcement. They may take a keen interest in the political development in the home country and even try to influence it. Thus, a Diaspora community not only tries to retain its group identity, but also maintains its links, both material and sentimental, with its country of origin. These links become a dimension of international politics.

As we have seen in earlier chapters, Indian migration is the result of an ongoing historical process. In the modern era, the rise and settlement of Indian Diaspora in different parts of the world is a distinctive feature having unique socio-cultural histories and both encountering and representing different economic and political situations. Indian communities abroad have evolved as distinct Diaspora entities. They are persisting or retaining several social patterns and cultural element, which are a part of the Indian way of life – or at least the way of life as they remember or were used to.

Demographically, the Indian Diaspora is omnipresent. They are spread over almost all parts of the world. They developed differently in their host societies due to different phases of migration. The time, mode and magnitude have contributed to their heterogeneous nature. They are skilled and professional in Western countries, leading an affluent life, whereas some others are unskilled doing manual labour to carry out their livelihood, as in the West Asian region. Whatever the reasons may be (and there are many), at present the Indian Diaspora keeps on expanding economically and demographically. Though they vary in their regional, religious, caste, occupational, linguistic and cultural backgrounds, they are sentimentally united through India, their ancestral home. Thus, the plurality and diversity of Indian Diaspora make it unique. Its nature to adapt in any situation without losing it owns culture and tradition has provided it with great level of advantage.

Further, emigration from the country not only helps reduce the situation of unemployment but also earns valuable foreign exchange. Labour migration (mostly to the Gulf) has certainly helped the country in stabilising its balance of payments situation by earning foreign exchange through remittances. So has emigration of professionals to the West. Even permanent long-term emigrants are seen to have continued their economic connect with the homeland, and many continue to remit monies home to either support their families or for making local investments in land and other assets.

On one hand, through the permanent settlement of Indians abroad the country is relieved of some population, and employment pressure, and on the other it is seen as a loss of skilled manpower and talent to the country. India of course has never made an issue of this so-called brain drain. After all the country gains much-needed foreign exchange through remittances sent by the emigrants. This helps in national productivity and local development of regions receiving such remittances and helps create a favourable position for India in terms of its balance of payment situation.

The foregoing analysis in the chapters of this book shows that India adopted no planned policy towards its Diaspora and its reaction was mostly based on specific instances. During the colonial period, the deplorable condition of the indenture labour in several colonies was a matter of concern for the Indian National Congress. Several attempts were made to raise the issue of improvement of their condition. Such pressures did result in the British Empire finally stopping this emigration system. In the pre-independence period, the Government of India and the nationalists included the Diaspora as part of the country. Nationalists, in fact, sought to utilise the strength of the Diaspora in the struggle of national independence. But soon after independence, Indian attitude towards its Diaspora changed. Nehru's policy of non-inclusion of the Diaspora in the Indian domestic and foreign policy formulation with a suggestion to integrate with the host society was based on both realist and idealistic principles. But Nehru's suggestion could not reduce the ties at family and private levels. These expatriates were always in one way or other tied to their country of origin. One of the reasons or justification for their exclusion from national policy was the perception that the expatriate community had left their home country and they were therefore seen as not loyal to their motherland. Even if they showed interest in the homeland, this was perceived as being only for the sake of financial gain. Those who returned were seen as returning for their own benefit and not for the benefit of the country.

India was economically weak at the time of independence; yet the new government did not think of using Diaspora resources to solve economic and developmental problems. Despite the low levels of economic and development growth that the country was facing, the nationalist fathers of the nation chose to follow the ideological path, which essentially excluded the possibly resource-rich Diaspora. As a natural corollary, India also did not stand up to raise the issue of its expatriates facing social, economic and political discrimination in other countries. In these early years *of* post-independence, Prime Minister Nehru was more concerned about the role India could play at the international level, and the Diaspora was something which could limit such a perceived role. As outlined earlier, Nehru chose to exclude Diaspora and their issues from domestic and foreign policy formulation. This Nehruvian policy continued for long, and the expatriate community was neglected by successive governments. What could have been a mutually beneficial relationship for both did not develop. This book has argued that the Diasporas are powerful non-state actors who can influence policies in both their home and host countries. India chose to not take advantage of such possibility. In doing so, the country lost a great opportunity.

It was only since the emergence of Indian elite in the Western world post the 1970s, especially in the United States, Canada and the United Kingdom, that India evinced keen interest in NRIs, the new Diaspora. Suddenly we evince a policy shift and interest in so far as to attract their investments for developmental programmes in India. During the 1990s, following the policy of liberalisation, half-hearted attempts were made to secure the involvement of affluent NRIs in setting up industries and to tide over the foreign exchange crises through attractive financial schemes. India's policy of foreign non-involvement slowly changed over the years to allow the overseas Indians to take part in the economic development of the country. But the barriers remained so high that the process remained slow. This shift in India's policy towards its Diaspora certainly has generous doses of pragmatism as it is trying to economically and politically harness the Indian network and resources that until now only existed in the cultural domain through familiar relations and the nostalgic search for roots.

The politics of migration

Politics of migration would tantamount to using migration as an instrument of policy to promote national interest, with a view to achieving certain political, social, economic and cultural objective. Migration under colonial times, to retain control of the economies of the British colonies or the All Whites Policy followed by the United States until 1965 or by Australia until early 1970s, to prevent the entry of non-whites to avoid any change in the demographic character of the polity, would fall in this category.

In the present-day context, this has taken many forms, as different countries use different approaches or strategies to promote their interests. Some of the obvious examples are listed here.

The United Kingdom and most of EU have seen immigration policies aimed at limiting migration only to the entry of the best and the brightest. Matched somewhat silently with subtle strategies to using their existing migrant or Diaspora communities in fighting terrorism – internally and overseas. In the United Kingdom, there have been attempts to send out negative messages on the United Kingdom, as a suitable destination to future migrants – not just for illegal or Asian/African migrants but even those from Bulgaria/Romania, consequent to their joining EU. This is in line with the United Kingdom's policy reforms since 2010 of reducing immigration to, 'tens, rather than the hundreds, of thousands'.[1]

In the United States, of course, several strategies are in inter-play. Many political in nature. There is the attempt to strike a balance between illegal migration required as cheap labour and the securing of borders. Also there are likely concerns over Spanish-speaking voters, with an increased inflow of Mexican migrants. The whole immigration policy and Immigration Bill continue to be a major political issue in both the Senate and the House.

In the Gulf we have seen a firmly entrenched political policy. Immigrants, ostensibly temporary, will be admitted to meet the manpower requirements but not to change the demographic character of the society by being swamped by foreigners. The simple solution is denial of citizenship (and many other) rights.

It is undeniable that there is politics, when it comes to immigration and Diaspora-related activities. This is despite the fact that migration is considered to be a win–win preposition in its totality, both for the home and the host states. Politics makes its appearance, as it responds to various domestic compulsions, be it socio-economic or cultural and international requirements to achieve foreign policy objectives. There are around 232 million migrants, forming 3 per cent of the total population, spread over the world. Migration is a natural phenomenon in the process of globalisation. However, the flow of persons is still not regulated by international convention, but by the diktats of sovereign states, in keeping with their national interests.

These national interests are not static but dynamic in nature, resulting in policy responses, to meet national requirements and international challenges. There are, however, some international conventions that govern the protection of migrants, workers and human rights. The world is in a constant spin, so are the policies that govern migration and the protection of migrants. It is here that the interplay of politics takes place. The politics could make their appearance in any of the following situations:

- **Formulation of migration policies:** This is the starting point where the home and host states and the Diaspora engage and grapple with the formulation of policy. It could be to ensure the availability of manpower in the host states, as the economies try to remain competitive, while the home states try to insulate the adverse impact of brain drain. Some examples would include: how could 'brain gain' be achieved as Indian President exhorts PIOs and NRIs to return to India, so that it does not lose intellectual capital?[2] What role do sending states play? How does the United Kingdom procure the 'best and the brightest', as it adopts a selective policy of 'cherry-picking'[3] and Saudi Arabia achieves 'Nitaqat' (naturalisation) through progressive localisation of jobs, causing concerns in India?[4] These are all politically over-charged issues.
- **Management of migration:** It is here that the skills of home and host states are tested, as they try to find answers on how to promote safe and legal migration, while ensuring that misplaced over-emphasis does not result in curbing migration.[5] How do the home states involve themselves in providing relief to their Diaspora when they are returned? What role is played by international organisations, like IOM, ILO? Does politics enter in when negotiating Mobility Management Agreements?[6]
- **To address the cultural milieu:** To maintain harmonious conditions where different cultures co-exist. The Diaspora has to adapt itself to differing models, like the British 'multiculturalism' and the French 'cultural exceptionalism'. What are the ground realities, as questions are raised on the viability of multi-cultural society by the British prime minister Cameron.[7]

- **To meet the socio-economic challenges:** What are the issues that confront the Diaspora, in the process of adaption in the home states? How is identity negotiated? What is the interface between the social, cultural and family values, as these prevail in the home and the host states, in matters relating to language, marriages[8] custody of children[9] etc.?
- **Formulation of Diaspora policy:** To what extent does the Diaspora policy become a component of a state's foreign policy? How to ensure that a national foreign policy is not buffeted by regional emotions?[10] (Cartoon) A case study of India's national policy dictated by compulsion of Tamil Nationalism?
- **Diaspora: An instrument of soft policy:** Could the Diaspora be trusted to play this role? If so, the extent and nature of such role. India used its Diaspora in lobbying for the India–USA Civil Nuclear Cooperation Agreement.[11] The Philippines sees the Diaspora as an instrument of its soft power.[12] Similarly, for Mexico, Diaspora has an all-embracing role.[13]
- **Diaspora and anti-nationalism:** What role do human rights, growth of transnationalism, ethnic and religious terrorism play on the mindset of Diaspora? Is it a case of perceptions or reality? How does a state protect its citizens in this global war on terrorism?

All of these questions and issues remain. This book has been a first attempt to flag the politics that lurk behind the usual socio-economic realities and rationale of migration. Of course there are multifarious issues of push and pulls in migration. Politics could be one of them. The treatise of this book has been that the politics of migration are on many occasions *the* central theme. Several questions remain that further research and debate will address. We have attempted to but place the arguments on the table.

The reality is that the Indian Diaspora by its sheer numbers and economic strength is a growing powerhouse in the global firmament. By the fact of the demographic dividend, India is emerging as the largest and youngest nation with a surplus workforce. The world needs this, especially as we have seen, in the large number of countries faced with the problem of greying populations. It continues to grow in numbers and clout. The world will have to accommodate this force across several countries.

The writing is clear. If the Indian Diaspora is to attain its rightful place in the various host countries they find themselves in, they have to aspire to and acquire political clout. In many of the environments, even to preserve their existing position, social and economic, they will need to slowly acquire political influence and position.

The obvious question that arises is: what role will India as a country play in this? Should the Indian government and diplomatic strategy begin to realign itself to such a strategy? The answer is an unequivocal yes.

Notes

1. http://blogs.lse.ac.uk/politicsandpolicy/immigration/?utm_content=buffera14da&utm_medium=social&utm_source=twitter.com&utm_campaign=buffer, accessed on 22 August 2014.
2. 'Nation for behind China, US in innovation, says Pranab', *The Hindu*, 10 April 2013.
3. Suroor, Hasan, 'UK plans to 'cherry-pick' immigrants', *The Hindu*, 30 January 2012.
4. 'Expatriate Worries' (ed.), *The Hindu*, 3 April 2013 and Balaji, J., 'Saudi Arabia defers Nitaqat enforcement by two months', *The Hindu*, 7 April 2013. The Saudi government subsequently agreed to provide some relief till 20 June 2013.
5. Suroor, Hasan, 'UK immigration norms kick in', *The Hindu*, 7 April 2013.
6. 'H-1B visa cap reached; lottery will decide fate', *The Sunday Tribune*, 7 April 2013.
7. 'Britain needs to abandon multiculturalism: Cameron', *The Tribune*, 2 June 2011.
8. Forced marriage.
9. Custody of children.
10. Cartoon, 'Foreign policy aeroplane buffeted by regional emotions', *The Hindu*.
11. PM's statement at PBD 2009.
12. Gonzalez III, Joaquin Jay (2012) *Diaspora Diplomacy: Philippine Migration and Its Soft Power Influence*, Mill City Press, Minneapolis, USA.
13. Delano, Alexandra (2011) *Mexico and Its Diaspora in the United States: Policies of Emigration since 1848*, Cambridge University Press, New York.

Appendix 1
Year of beginning of migration of Indians

Country	Year
Philippines	1762
USA	1790
Indonesia	1798
Mauritius	1834
Ceylon	1834
Uganda	1834
Nigeria	1834
Guyana	1838
New Zealand	1840
Hong Kong	1841
Trinidad and Tobago	1845
Martinique and Guadeloupe	1854
Grenada	1856
St. Lucia	1856
St. Vincent	1856
Natal (South Africa)	1860
Malay	1860
St. Kitts	1861
Japan	1872
Suriname	1872
Jamaica	1873
Fiji	1879
Burma	1885
Canada	1904
Thailand	1910

Source: Motwani (1994), Roberts and Byne (1966).

Appendix II

Population of Indian Diaspora: countrywise

Sl. No.	Country		Overseas Indians (total)	NRI	PIO
1.	Gulf	UAE	17,02,911	17,00,000	2,911
		Saudi Arabia	17,89,000	17,89,000	NA
2.	Europe	Belgium	16,000	6,500	9,500
		France	65,000	10,000	55,000
		France (Reunion Island)	2,75,200	200	2,75,000
		France (Guadeloupe, St. Martinique)	1,45,000	00	1,45,000
		Germany	70,500	42,500	28,000
		Italy	99,127	97,719	1408
		The Netherlands	2,01,000	6,000	1,95,000
		The Netherlands Antilles	4500	NA	NA
3.	USA		22,45,239	9,27,283	13,17,956
4.	Australia		4,48,430	2,13,710	2,34,720
5.	Sri Lanka		16,00,500	500	16,00,000
6.	Canada		10,00,000	2,00,000	8,00,000
7.	Trinidad and Tobago		5,51,500	1,500	5,50,000
8.	Mauritius		8,82,220	15,000	8,67,220

Source: Ministry of Overseas Indian Affairs, Documented Data (last updated on 25 May 2011).

Appendix III

History of migration and immigration laws in the United States[1]

The history of migration in the United States has been a phenomenon of distant past. A series of immigration laws have been passed in the late 1990s and mid-2000s. Specially laws are instituted to regulate the immigration specially after the 9/11 incident; the priority is to restrict migration to the United States to the maximum possible extent. The following section explains and jots down all the important laws pertaining to immigration that have evolved in the nation. This section is an historical account of the important moves that have been made by the government of the United States regarding immigration to the country. It describes the challenges faced by the nation to exercise the issue of migration since the eighteenth century which continues to be one of the unresolved issues of the present government. It describes the political shift that made migration as the issue of highest political priority, the amendments made to make the issue more feasible and solvable.

Naturalisation Act (1790)

'The Naturalization Act of 1790 passed by Congress employed explicitly racial criteria limiting citizenship to ëfree white personsí; after this act was successfully challenged on behalf of blacks after the Civil War, ëAsian immigrants became the most significant ëotherí in terms of citizenship eligibilityí (Lesser, 85)' (Wong 5). Cheryl I Harris argued that 'white identity conferred tangible and economically valuable benefits' and is 'central to national identity and to the republican project' (280, 285). She referred to the changing definitions of citizenship as defined by the Act: 'The franchise, for example, was broadened to extend voting rights to unpropertied white men at the same time that black voters were specifically disenfranchised, arguably shifting the property required for voting from land to whiteness' (286) (Harris, 'Whiteness as Property', from Critical Race Theory cited from http://www.umass.edu/complit/aclanet/USMigrat.html accessed on 12 December 2012).

National amendments or prohibitions to citizenship

> *Amendment 14:* Civil rights citizenship granted to free African Americans (ratified in 1868).
> *Amendment 15:* Black Suffrage Voting rights extended to African Americans (ratified in 1870).
> *Asian Exclusion Acts:* Barring immigrants from citizenship and ownership of property.

'Though Congress never enacted a law that specifically names "Asians" or "Orientals" as an Asiatic racial category, legal theorist Neil Gotanda has argued that the sequence of laws in 1882, 1917, 1924 and 1934 that excluded immigrants from China, Japan, India and the Philippines, combined with the series of repeal acts overturning these exclusions, construct a common racial categorization for Asians that depended on consistently racializing each national-origin group as "nonwhite"' (Lowe, 19, cited from http://www.umass.edu/complit/aclanet/USMigrat.html, accessed on 12 December 2012).

Chinese Exclusion Acts/Immigration Exclusion Act (1882)

The act was passed which prohibited citizenship for Chinese immigrants. Similar acts reinforcing the exclusion of Chinese immigrant were passed in 1884, 1886 and 1888. 'In 1882, 1884, 1886, and 1888, Congress passed Chinese exclusion acts, suspending immigration of Chinese laborers and barring reentry of all Chinese laborers who departed and did not return before the passage of the Act' (Lowe, 180–81fn14, cited from http://www.umass.edu/complit/aclanet/USMigrat.html, accessed on 12 December 2012).

Immigration Act of 1917: Exclusion of Asian Indians (1917)

'A geographical criterion was used to exclude Asian Indians, because their racial or ethnic status was unclear' (Lowe, 180–81fn14, cited from http://www.umass.edu/complit/aclanet/USMigrat.html, accessed on 12 December 2012).

'Asia barred zone' (1917)

'The 1917 immigration act denied entry to people from a "barred zone" that included South Asia through Southeast Asia and islands in the Indian and Pacific Oceans, but excluded American possessions of the Philippines and Guam' (Lowe, 180–81fn14, cited from http://www.umass.edu/complit/aclanet/USMigrat.html, accessed on 12 December 2012).

Alien land laws (1913, 1920 and 1923)

'Prohibited Asian immigrants from owning land and other forms of property through the legal construction of nonwhites as aliens are ineligible to citizenship' (Lisa Lowe, Immigrant Acts 13).

Ozawa v. United States (1922)

'In the Ozawa v. United States case (1922), the Supreme Court ruled against a Japan-born applicant to naturalization (who had lived most of his life in the United States), arguing that had these particular races [like the Japanese] been suggested, the language of the act would have been so varied as to include them in its privileges. To circumvent the question of color, the Court defined "white" as "Caucasian"' (Wong, 5, cited from http://www.umass.edu/complit/aclanet/USMigrat.html, accessed on 12 December 2012).

Supreme Court decision regarding South Asian immigrations (1923)

'However, when an immigrant from India, Bhagat Singh Thind, attempted to gain citizenship by arguing that he was Caucasian, the Supreme Court changed its definition again, brushing aside anthropological and historical issues and appealing to the more popular meaning of the term "white"' (Chan, 1991: 94). Furthermore, in its 1923 decision against Thind, the Court invoked the criterion of assimilability to separate the desirable immigrants from the undesirable ones: 'Asian Indians were distinguished from the swarthy European immigrants, who were deemed *'readily amalgamated'* (italics in original) with the immigrants "already here" (Lesser, 88)' (Wong, 5, http://www.umass.edu/complit/aclanet/USMigrat.html, accessed on 12 December 2012.

The Johnson-Reed Act (1924)

This Act created a new national-origins quota system, which favors the immigrants from Northern Europe and restricting immigrants who are 'ineligible to citizenship', a provision that primarily affected the Japanese.

Immigrant Act of 1924: Exclusion of Japanese

'The Immigration Act of 1924 barred entry of "aliens ineligible to citizenship"; because Japanese and other Asians were barred by the 1790 naturalization law stipulating that "whites only" could be naturalized as citizens, the 1924 act totally excluded them from immigration' (Lowe, 180–81fn14, cited from http://www.umass.edu/complit/aclanet/USMigrat.html, accessed on 12 December 2012).

Tydings-McDuffie Act (1934): Exclusion of Filipinos

'The Act cut Filipino immigration to a quota of fifty persons per year, and all Filipinos in the United States were reclassified as "aliens." The U.S. exclusion of Filipino immigration was continually connected with the issue of Philippine independence from U.S. colonization . . .' (Lowe, 181fn14 cited from http://www.umass.edu/complit/aclanet/USMigrat.html, accessed on 12 December 2012).

Magnuson Act (1943)

'The Magnuson Act had three significant parts: it repealed the Exclusion Act of 1882; it established a quota for Chinese immigrants; and it made Chinese eligible for citizenship, negating the 1790 racial bar' (Lowe 20, cited from http://www.umass.edu/complit/aclanet/USMigrat.html, accessed on 12 December 2012).

Displaced Persons Act of 1948

The Act allows some of the people who became homeless after the American Civil War to come to the United States.

Mc Carran-Walter Act (1952): Abolished the restrictions on Asian migrants and allowed for immigration into the United States on the basis on ethnic quotas.

'Quotas were not specified by national origin, but through racialized ethnic categories such as "Chinese." In other words, the McCarran-Walter Act provided that one hundred ethnic Chinese persons enter annually; these Chinese originated from diverse nations. Even laws that repealed exclusion acts continued to "racialize" Asians. . . .' (Lowe, 193fn53). 'The McCarran-Walter Act establishes the basic laws of U.S. citizenship and immigration. This act, also known as the Immigration and Nationality Act of 1952, has undergone several changes since its adoption. Originally, the law admitted only a certain number of immigrants of each nationality. But a law passed by Congress in 1965 gave preference to immigrants with skills needed in the United States and to close relatives of U.S. citizens. A 1990 law continued these preferences. Aliens must be admitted as legal immigrants to get U.S. citizenship. People who flee to the United States after being officially certified as refugees may receive immigrant status' (*World Book Encyclopedia*).

Immigrant Act (1965): Eliminated immigration quotas, establishing new criteria for immigrants.

'The 1965 immigration act removed "natural origins" as the basis of American immigration legislation and was framed as an amendment to the 1952 McCarran-Walter Act. The 1965 act abolished "national origin" quotas and specified seven preferences for Eastern Hemisphere quota immigrants: (1) unmarried adult sons and daughters of citizens; (2) spouses and unmarried sons and daughters of permanent residents; (3) professionals, scientists, and artists of exceptional ability; (4) married adult sons and daughters of U.S. citizens; (5) siblings of adult citizens; (6) workers, skilled and unskilled, in occupations for which labor was in short supply in the United States; and (7) refugees from Communist-dominated countries or those uprooted by natural catastrophe. [Ö] Since 1965, two million Asian quota immigrants, two million non quota immigrants, and one million refugees outside the seventh preference have arrived' (Lowe, 181–82fn16). 'In the period since 1965, legal regulations on immigration include Asians among a broad segment of racialised immigrants, while policing has refocused particularly on "alien" and "illegal" Mexican and Latino workers. Asian Americans, with the history of being constituted as "aliens," have the collective 'memory' to be critical of the notion of citizenship and the liberal democracy it upholds; Asian American culture is the site of "remembering," in which the recognition of Asian immigrant history in the present predicament of Mexican and Latino immigrants is possible' (Lowe, 21, http://www.umass.edu/complit/aclanet/USMigrat.html, accessed on 12 December 2012).

Indochina Migration and Refugee Assistance Act (1975)

'The Indochina Migration and Refugee Assistance Act of 1975' sets forth the allowance of provisions for those who fled from the Southeast Asian countries as well as those who cannot return to those countries due to the threat of violence or ill-treatment. This may include providing financial assistance with relocation and resettlement for refugees that meet these criteria (Derek Runnels and Quynh Nhu, http://library.uwb.edu/guides/usimmigration/1970s_indochina.html, accessed on 14 January 2013).

Appropriations for Vietnamese and Cambodian Refugees (1975)

This Act, passed at the same time as the Indochina Migration and Refugee Assistance Act, specifies some details about assistance for said refugees. $305,000,000 was allocated to refugees from Cambodia through 30 June 1976. $100,000,000 was available to assist said refugees who are living in the United States through June 1976. This Act also states that no funds will be used to assist the Vietnamese government (Derek Runnels and Quynh Nhu, http://library.uwb.edu/guides/usimmigration/1970s_indochina.html, accessed on 14 January 2013).

Refugee Act (1980)

The Refugee Act of 1980 created The Federal Refugee Resettlement Program to provide for the effective resettlement of refugees and to assist them to achieve economic self-sufficiency as quickly as possible after arrival in the United States (http://www.acf.hhs.gov/programs/orr/resource/the-refugee-act, accessed on 14 January 2013).

Amerasian Homecoming Act (1987)

'Another distinguishing feature of the post-1965 Asian immigration is the predominance of immigrants from South Korea, the Phillipines, South Vietnam, and Cambodia, countries deeply affected by U.S. colonialism, war and neocolonialism' (Lowe, 16). 'Despite the usual assumptions that Asians immigrate from stable, continuous, "traditional" cultures, most of the post-1965 Asian immigrants come from societies already disrupted by colonialism and distorted by the upheavals of neocolonial capitalism and war' (Lowe, 16).

Immigrant Reform and Control Act (1986)

The Immigration Reform and Control Act was passed and signed into law on 6 November 1986. The purpose of this legislation was to amend, revise and reform/re-assess the status of unauthorised immigrants set forth in the Immigration and Nationality Act. This bill gave unauthorised aliens the opportunity to apply and gain legal status if they met mandated requirements. This bill also outlined previsions for temporary residents' travel, employment, false statements, numerical limitations, adjustments for status and treatment of applications by 'Designated Entities' (http://library.uwb.edu/guides/usimmigration/1986_immigration_reform_and_control_act.html, accessed on 11 December 2012).

Immigration Act (1990)

'As the Immigrant Reform and Control Act of 1986 and the Immigration Act of 1990 attest, however, immigration legislation continues to be the site for the resurgence of contradiction between capital and the state, between economic and political imperatives, between the ëpush-pullí of markets and the maintenance of civil rights and is riddled with conflicts as the state attempts to control through law what is also an economically driven phenomenon. In the 1990s, recent immigration policies and de facto immigration policies express this contradiction around the ëcrisisí of illegal immigration, particularly from Mexico and Latin America (though Haitian and Chinese examples have also emerged)' (Lowe 20).

California's Proposition 187

'California's Proposition 187 passed in 1994, attempts to deny schooling and medical care to illegal immigrants; although the referendum does not specify immigrants from Mexico and Latin America, its execution would certainly be aimed at these groups' (Lowe 20). 'Since the 1950s, undocumented immigrants from Mexico and Latin America have provided much of the low-wage labor in agriculture, construction, hotels, restaurants and domestic services in the western and southwestern United States. The wages and working conditions of these jobs do not attract U.S. workers: state policy will not legislate the improvement of labor conditions, but neither does it declare officially that the U.S. economy systematically produces jobs that only third world workers find attractive. The result is an officially disavowed and yet unofficially mandated, clandestine movement of illegal immigration, which addresses the economy's need for low-wage labor but whose dehumanization of migrant workers is politically contradictory' (Lowe, 21).

Illegal Immigration Reform & Immigrant Responsibility Act (1996)

'This act is a very large and complex piece of legislation, enacted on September 30, 1996 (Clinton was president at this time), which addresses many aspects of immigration (both legal and illegal). It directly addresses border patrol and upgrades needed for border patrol enforcers, equipment, and the overall patrolling process. It also details an increase in interior enforcement and practices with regard to INS and investigators monitoring visa applications and visa abusers. Illegal activities were a central concern in this bill and penalties for racketeering, alien smuggling and the use or creation of fraudulent immigration-related documents are high on the priority list. Other crimes and immigration-related offenses committed by aliens and the consequences, including deportation, are addressed in the sections following. Employment programs and employment eligibility issues are incorporated into the bill. Some miscellaneous provisions mentioned relate to medical services, pilot programs, and reporting. Alien residence (housing) and financial issues regarding the same are addressed including a plethora of miscellaneous provisions' (Germain and Stevens, http://library.uwb.edu/guides/usimmigration/1996_illegal_immigration_reform_and_immigrant_responsibility_act.html, accessed on 14 January 2012).

Anti-Terrorism Act, 2001

Eight days after the 9/11 incident, the administration submitted to Congress the act which proposes broad new authority to gather domestic intelligence, combat money laundering used in the terrorists activities used in the terrorism activities and to initiate procedures to deport suspected terrorists. This Act is better known as the Patriot Act of the United States which comes with the purpose of deterring and punishing terrorist acts in the United States and around the world and to enhance law enforcement investigatory tools, and other purposes, some of which include the following:

- To strengthen U.S. measures to prevent, detect and prosecute international money laundering and financing of terrorism;

- To subject to special scrutiny foreign jurisdictions, foreign financial institutions, and classes of international transactions or types of accounts that are susceptible to criminal abuse;
- To require all appropriate elements of the financial services industry to report potential money laundering;
- To strengthen measures to prevent use of the U.S. financial system for personal gain by corrupt foreign officials and facilitate repatriation of stolen assets to the citizens of countries to whom such assets belong (http://www.fincen.gov/statutes_regs/patriot/, accessed on 14 January, 2013).

Enhanced Border Security and Visa Entry Reform Act of 2002

This is the Act which was implemented through the Justice Department's entry exit registration system and has the following laid out plans:

- It enhanced the review of visa applicants through authorization of appropriate hiring and training government personnel.
- It calls for an improvement in Technology and Infrastructure so as to improve and expand the use of technology. It would be used for the purpose of enhancing border security, and to facilitate the flow of people and commerce at ports of entry by improving and expanding programs for preenrollment and preclearance.
- It requires the Attorney General and the Secretary of State to begin issuing machine-readable, tamper-resistant, travel documents with biometric identifiers.
- Look out committees have been established so that they can use the resources of the consular officers to receive specific training in identifying inadmissible aliens especially any potential terrorists (Enhanced Border Security and Visa Entry Reform Act of 2002, http://www.ofr.harvard.edu/additional_resources/Summary_of_Enhanced_Border_Security_Reform_Act_HR3525.pdf, accessed on 10 January 2013).

Border Protection, Antiterrorism, and Illegal Immigration Control Act (2005)

This bill was introduced in a session of Congress and was passed by the House on 16 December 2005 but was never passed by the Senate. The main purpose of the bill was to amend the Immigration and Nationality Act to strengthen enforcement of the immigration laws, to enhance border security, and for other purposes (http://www.govtrack.us/congress/bills/109/hr4437, accessed on 15 January 2013).

Comprehensive Immigration Reform Act (CIRA) of 2006

This act gives illegal immigrants who have resided in the United States for more than five years the chance to apply for citizenship, after paying fines and taxes. Those in the country for two to five years, or less than two years, would be subject to different restrictions. The act also allows employers to bring foreign workers into the country with a "blue card", permitting a stay of six years after which the employee would return to their country of origin for one year. It increases the number of guest workers in the US through a new **"blue card" visa program** (http://www.cfr.org/mexico/comprehensive-immigration-reform-act-2006-s-2611/p10808, accessed on 12 January 2013).

Comprehensive Immigration Reform Act (2010)

A bill which provides comprehensive immigration reform has six titles underlying in it.

- It establishes border enforcement triggers which should be met before any unauthorized immigrants can apply for permanent residency. It has enhanced coordination and planning for border security.
- It strengthens the security of the Visa Waiver Program and Entry and Exit Requirements to secure America as a prevention of authorized entry and removals.
- The act protects the vulnerable populations and provides protection to children involved in immigration enforcement actions.
- It creates a mandatory employment verification system to prevent unlawful employment of aliens.
- It reforms America's Legal Immigration System through the establishment of Standing Commission on Immigration, Labor Markets, and the National Interest. It Reforms to Current Temporary Worker Programs and Expansion of Worker Protections which protects the temporary seasonal workers related to foreign recruitment, cost of travel and other related expenses.
- Under the Family and Employment Visa Reforms, it permits the roll-over of unused visas in the future. It recaptures immigrant visas

lost to bureaucratic delay. It exempts certain categories of applicants from visa caps, which includes persons who have earned an advanced degree in the sciences from a U.S. university, physicians working in shortage areas, and persons admitted under extraordinary ability visas.
- The act gives the provision to registration of undocumented individuals. They are also given the social security number and which would help them building a legal status for the undocumented immigrants in USA who are present in USA as of September 30, 2010 and have never committed any serious crime and otherwise admissible to United States.
- It strengthens the integration and other reforms by uniting the communities with civics education and English skills. It helps in building stronger communities and emergency relief for the certain population
(http://www.immigrationpolicy.org/just-facts/comprehensive-immigration-reform-act-2010-summary and
http://americasvoiceonline.org/research/summary_the_comprehensive_immigration_reform_act_of_2010/, accessed on 16 January, 2012).

Enhanced Border Security Act (2011)

The act was enacted to apply counterinsurgency tactics under a coordinated and targeted strategy to combat the terrorist insurgency in Mexico waged by transnational criminal organisations, and for other purposes.

- Outlines the transnational criminal organisations in Mexico.
- Assesses Mexico's capabilities to counter such organisations.
- Describes such organisations' operations in the United States and at the United States and international borders, and presents a plan to combat their operations and financial networks.
- Utilises all such information to combat the terrorist insurgency in Mexico.
- Requires the Secretary and the Office of Foreign Assets Control of the Department of the Treasury to update such strategy reports quarterly.

Appendix IV

List of Indian associations in the United States

(http://www.thokalath.com/North-America/Indo-American-Community.php, accessed on 22 November 2012)

Kerala associations

Greater Richmond Malayalee Association Virginia, USA

The association is formed by the Malayalam-speaking people from Kerala, India. GRAMAM promotes and propagates the culture of Kerala by conducting quality cultural programs and organising get-togethers and picnics.

Greater Carolina Kerala Association (GCKA), USA

Greater Carolina Kerala Association (GCKA) based in Raleigh, North Carolina, USA. It is a cultural association to promote and facilitate the cultural, educational, social and economic welfare of the Keralite community both among Keralites and the surrounding community at large.

Kerala Association of New England (KANE)

Kerala Association of New England (KANE) is a non-profit, non-political, non-religious cultural organisation working towards the betterment of the social lifestyle of the Malayalee in the New England area.

Malayalee Association of Northern California (MANCA)

MANCA is based in San Francisco Bay area.

Federation of Kerala Associations of North America, Fremont, CA, USA

FOKANA is an umbrella organisation of Kerala Malayalee associations in North America and Canada. It seeks to preserve the North

American Malayalee integrity and promotes the Kerala Cultural identity.

Greater Atlanta Malayalee Association (GAMA)
Malayalee Association of North Florida

Manofa emphasises the goal of preserving and promoting the moral, social, cultural, educational, literary and artistic heritage of Indian community in North Florida.

Kerala Association of Los Angeles (KALA)
Kerala Association of Washington

A non-profit, non-political, non-religious cultural organisation working towards the betterment of the social lifestyle of Keralites.

Malayalee Association of Greater Houston (MAGH)

Malayalee Association of Greater Houston (MAGH) is a non-profit, non-political, secular and cultural organisation, organised exclusively for charitable, educational and scientific purposes.

Kerala Association of Greater Washington (KAGW)

Greater Washington Metro area that includes Maryland, Virginia, Baltimore and Richmond.

Kerala Association of Dallas

The Kerala Association of Dallas was established in 1976 as a non-profit cultural association to promote and foster international relationship and goodwill.

The Oklahoma Malayalee Association (OMA)

The Oklahoma Malayalee Association, OMA, is a secular, non-partisan and non-profit making organisation to promote social and cultural integration of Malayalees in Oklahoma and foster and promote cultural heritage of India in general, Kerala, in particular.

Illinois Malayalee Association (IMA)

Illinois Malayalee Association (IMA) strives to provide best to the Malayalee community in the region.

Detroit Malayalee Association (DMA)

Detroit Malayalee Association (DMA) provides a forum for the Malayalees residing in Detroit and neighbouring areas to meet and exchange views and also to foster their friendship, goodwill, moral, social, educational, literary, artistic and cultural heritage.

Kerala Club

A non-profit cultural organisation of Malayalees in Metro Detroit.

Sacramento Regional Association of Malayalees (SARGAM)

Sacramento Regional Association of Malayalees (SARGAM) is a non-profit Malayalee cultural organisation.

Minnesota Malayalee Association (MMA)

Minnesota Malayalee Association (MMA) is a non-profit, non-political, secular and cultural organisation organised exclusively for charitable, educational and scientific purposes.

Kerala Samajam of South Florida

Kerala Samajam of South Florida was established to promote cultural, educational and social activities and to encourage and revitalize the traditional arts and crafts of Kerala, a state in Southern India. To provide a forum for the Keralites and their descendants residing in the United States to preserve and foster their moral, social, cultural, educational, literary and artistic heritage.

Kairali Arts Club of South Florida

The Kairali Arts Club of South Florida has established a very healthy tradition of public service and commitment to the communities where it operates.

Orlando Malayalee Association

Orlando Regional Malayalee Association's mission is to promote cooperation and understanding among Malayalees of Orlando and surrounding cities.

Capital District Malayalee Association

To develop, promote, increase and cultivate an appreciation of Malayalee heritage through cultural, recreational and social activities.

Mid-Hudson Kerala Association, New York

Mid-Hudson Kerala Association is the focal point of Dutchess, Putnam, Ulster and Orange County Malayalees.

New England Malayalee Association (NEMA)

Detroit Malayalee Association (NEMA) promotes a deeper understanding of Malayalam language, literature and art.

Palm Beach Malayalees

A community from God's Own Country Kerala. We are located in West Palm Beach, South Florida, United States.

Kerala Association of Palm Beach, Florida (KAPB)

Kerala Association of Palm Beach's (KAPB) main objective is to maintain and preserve the culture and heritage of Kerala. The association intends to conduct numerous programs and activities for the progression of our community.

Gujarati associations

Federation of Gujarati Associations of North America
Gujarati Cultural Association of Bay Area

Promotes Gujarati culture.

Gujarati Association of Tampa Bay area
Gujarati Association of North Carolina, USA
Gujarati Samaj of Minnesota

A cultural, charitable and educational non-profit organisation based in Minneapolis, Minnesota. The Samaj is one of the largest cultural organisations in the Midwest, with thousands of Gujarati-speaking members and supporters.

Vishwa Gujarati Samaj USA

Vishwa Gujarati Samaj USA provides platform for the interaction amongst Gujaratis residing in the United States. It works for the growth, prosperity and progress of Gujaratis settled in the United States and inspires them to cultivate the spirit of brotherhood, co-operation and to promote and preserve Gujarati language, its tradition, its culture and its cultural heritage.

Telugu associations

Telugu Association of North America
American Telugu Association
Bay Area Telugu Association
Telugu Association of Greater Boston
Tristate Telugu Association
Telugu Association of Greater Chicago
Telugu association of North Texas
Arizona Telugu Association
Colorado Telugu Association
Greater Washington Telugu Cultural Society

Non-profit organisation devoted to the awareness and promotion of Telugu Culture in the Greater Washington Area.

Telugu Association of Central Ohio
Telugu Association of Greater Delaware Valley
Telugu Association of Greater Kansas City
Telugu Association of Metro Atlanta
Telugu Association of Southern California
Houston Telugu Cultural Association
Telugu Cultural Association, Austin, TX
Telugu Fine Arts Society

Serving the Telugu-speaking people in New Jersey.

Telugu Association of Greater Cleveland

To promote Telugu culture in the Cleveland-Akron Metropolitan Area. To strengthen Telugu community ties through various cultural and social events.

Atlanta Telugu Christava Samavesam
Telangana NRI Association: TeNA

TeNA is formed to provide a platform for literary, cultural, educational, social and developmental activities in the United States and in Telangana.

Telangana Culture Association

Telangana Culture Association is formed to help preserve and promote Telangana culture and festivals worldwide.

Marathi associations

Brihan Maharashtra Mandal

Promote and nurture Marathi culture through its arts, literature and language.

Maharashtra Mandal Bay Area

Non-profit organisation serving the Northern California, Bay Area, to promote cultural ties among people interested in Maharashtrian culture.

Dallas-Fort Worth Maharashtra Mandal
Los Angeles – MAIYTRA
New England Marathi Mandal
Maharashtra Mandal, New York
New Jersey Marathi Vishwa

Marathi Vishwa, is a cultural, educational, social service and non-profit organisation which represents the Marathi-speaking people from India in New Jersey.

Pittsburgh Maharashtra Mandal
Triveni Mitra Mandal of Greater Cincinnati
Marathi Kala Mandal of Greater Washington
Maharashtra Foundation

Maharashtra Foundation has worked towards reducing poverty in India via technology, education entrepreneurship. Some of our prime concerns are providing better healthcare and education for the underprivileged, and empowering women and minority groups for their economic improvement.

Baltimore Marathi Mandal

A unique social community for area residents to make new friends, renew cultural ties and encourage children to learn about the Maharashtrian tradition and culture.

Maharashtra Mandal of Atlanta

Forum for people who claim 'Marathi' as their mother tongue; however, it is open to anyone who wants to join.

Goan associations

The Goan Association of New Jersey

Promotes social, cultural, educational and charitable activities, primarily for the good of its members and worthwhile causes in Goa, India.

Goan Association of Florida

Goan Association of Florida – Partly Under Construction.

Goan Association of Florida – Website??

New Year Dance Ball, Celebration of St. Francis Xavier Feast, Annual Easter beach picnic, Spring Beach Picnic.

List of World Goan Associations

G.O.A. (Goans of America) – Los Angeles, The Goan Association – New York, The Goan Association of the Washington Metropolitan Area, New England Goans of Boston Massachusetts, Konkani Association of California (KAOCA).

Goan Association of Hudson Valley

The Goan Association of Hudson Valley is a non-profit organisation promoting cultural, educational and charitable activities for its members.

Goan Overseas Association – DC – USA
Catholic Goan Network

Catholic Goan Network is a network of Catholic Goans who conduct services and programmes for the benefit and welfare of the Catholic Goan Community around the world.

Punjabi associations

Academy of the Punjab in North America (APNA)

A non-religious, non-political organisation of all Punjabis for the promotion of Punjabi language, literature and culture.

Punjabi Cultural Society of Chicago

Cultural-oriented organisation cultivating social, recreational and cultural activities for the Punjabi community.

Punjabi American Heritage Society, USA
Sikh Atlanta Organisation, USA
Sikh Religious Society of Arizona

Kannada Associations

Association of Kannada Kootas of America
Austin Kannada Sangha
Brindavana Karnataka Cultural Organization, New Jersey
Colorado Kannada Koota
Kannada Koota of Northern California (KKNC), USA
Kasturi Kannada Association of North East, Cleveland
Chandana Kannada Sangha, Kansas City, USA

Chandana Kannada Sangha (CKS) is a cultural organisation that serves to promote cultural and social activities of Kannadigas in the Kansas City Metro Area.

Kannada Association of North Texas
Kannada Vrinda – Houston
Louisville Abhimaana Kannada Sangha
Kannada Association of Indianapolis

Mallige is a cultural organisation representing the Kannada-speaking people (Kannidigaas) from the state of Karnataka in South India who have settled in Indiana, USA.

North American Sankethi Association
New York Kannada Koota

Cultural organisation representing the Kannada-speaking people from Karnataka state in India who have settled in the New York area.

New England Kannada Koota
Nrupathunga Kannada Koota
Pampa Kannada Koota, Michigan
Srigandha Kannada Koota of FL
Sampige – Triangle Kannada Association
Sahyadri Kannada Sangha

Cultural organisation representing Kannada-speaking people residing in the Greater Seattle area and the state of Washington.

Tri-State Kannada Cultural Association

A confluence of Kannadigas from Delaware, New Jersey, and Pennsylvania areas.

Tamil Associations
Bay Area Tamil Manram
Boston Thamil Association

Our goal is to foster the growth and development of Tamil culture and advance the learning of the rich cultural values by Sri Lankan Tamil residents in the New England area.

Chicago Tamil Sangam
Greater Atlanta Tamil Sangam
Federation of Tamil Sangams of North America
Houston Tamil Sangam
Ilankai Tamil Sangam

Association of Tamils of Sri Lanka in the USA

Lexington, Kentucky, Tamil Cultural Association
Nagarathar Sangam of North America
New Jersey Tamil Sangam
Seattle Tamil Sangam

Tamil Association of Colorado (TAC)
Tamil Association of Greater Delaware Valley
Tamil Sangam of Carolina

Bengali associations

Bay Area Prabasi

PRABASI is a non-profit socio-cultural organisation of the Bengalis of the San Francisco Bay area.

Bengali Association of Greater Rochester
Bengali Cultural Association of Arizona
Bichitra

Non-profit Bengali cultural and religious organisation located in Metro Detroit area.

Greater Richmond Bengali Association
Northern Virginia Bengali Association
The Bengali Cultural Association of Colorado, USA
Udayani Cultural Club

Association of Indians in Connecticut for Bengali Indians.

India associations

Asian American Hotel Owners Association
Dallas-Fort Worth Oriya Society

This society consists of all Oriyas living in and around Dallas Fort Worth Metroplex.

India Association of Colorado
India Association of Greater Boston (IAGB)
India Association of Northern Colorado
India Association of North Texas (IANT)
India Association of Western Washington
India Association Tallahassee, Florida
Indo American Association of Delaware

IAAD is the largest cultural non-profit organisation whose mission is to promote Indian Culture amongst non-Indians in Delaware area.

Jain Center of Northern California
Young Sindhi Adults Association
Kerala Hindus of North America

Kerala Hindus of North America is the organisation for all Hindu Malayalees of the North American continent.

Bihar Association of North America (BANA)

Bihar Association of North America (BANA) is an organisation of people of Bihar origin residing in North America. BANA was formed to preserve and promote social and cultural heritage of Bihar.

Note

1 http://www.govtrack.us/congress/bills/112/hr3401#summary/libraryofcongress, accessed on 16 January 2013.

Bibliography

Afsar, R. (2004) 'Migration from Indian sub-continent to Western Australia: some intriguing issues of religious composition and political integration', Australian Population Association, http://www.apa.org.au/upload/2004-6C_Afsar.pdf, accessed 9 December 2012.

Agrawal, B. (2001) 'Indian Diaspora', *World Focus*, March, Vol. 22, No. 3, pp. 3-4.

Agarwala, R. (2012) Tapping the Indian Diaspora for Indian Development. http://www.princeton.edu/cmd/working-papers/2012TransnationalMeeting/2012-India.pdf, accessed on 8 September 2013.

AIA website, http://aianational.com/, accessed on 29 November 2012.

Al Ali, J. (2008) 'Emiratization: drawing UAE nationals into their surging economy', *International Journal of Sociology and Social Policy*, Vol. 28, No. 9/10, pp. 365-79.

Al Dosary, A. S. and K. M. Nahiduzzaman (2010) 'A futuristic discourse of higher education system linkages with the labor markets in the Kingdom of Saudi Arabia', *International Journal of Arab Culture, Management and Sustainable Development*, Vol. 1, No. 4, pp. 326-39.

Al Munajjed, M. and, K. Sabbagh (2011) *Youth in GCC Countries – Meeting the Challenge*, Booz & Company Ideation Center, Riyadh.

Al Sheikh, S. A. (2001) 'Demography movement in the Kingdom of Saudi Arabia and its effect on the labour market and economic growth', *The Saudi Economic Journal*, Spring, No. 5, pp. 68-73.

Al-Tamimi and Company (2010) UAE Immigration Laws and Procedures in Dubai (pp. 1-21) http://www.dha.gov.ae/en/servicecatalogue/DHA%20ServiceForms %20List/UAEImmigrationLaw.pdf, accessed on 3 March 2013.

Anderson, A. B. and James S. Frideres (1981) *Ethnicity in Canada. Theoretical Perspectives*, Butterworth, Toronto, 1981, 334p, pp. 140-55. http://faculty.marianopolis.edu/c.belanger/QuebecHistory/readings/SourceofCanadianImmigrtants1921-1945.html, accessed on 10 May 2013.

Arab News (2011a) 'Half the firms in yellow or red Nitaqat band: labor ministry', *Arab News*, 9 December 2011.

Bibliography

Arab News (2011b) 'Saudization campaign gets fresh impetuses, *Arab News*, 9 May 2011.
Arab News (2012) 'Sponsorship system on its way out', *Jeddah*, 14 May 2012.
Barber, L. (2012) 'Lessons from the Euro crisis', *Financial Times*, 23 October.
Barua, S. Kr (2013) 'Fresh foreign funds for Khalistan', *The Hindustan Times*, 7 April 2013.
Bhagwati, J. (1999) *A Stream of Windows: Unsettling Reflections on Trade, Immigration, and Democracy*, Massachusetts Institute of Technology, Harvard.
Bhatia, P. (1971) *Indian Ordeal in Africa*, New Delhi. Building a 21st century immigration system, White House Government, www.whitehouse.gov/sites/default/files/ . . . /immigration_blueprint.pdf, accessed on 13 January 2013.
Bhatt, C. and P. Mukta (2000) 'Hindutva in the West: mapping the antinomies of globalization', *Ethnic and Racial Studies*, Vol. 23, No. 3, pp. 407–41.
Camarota, S. (2007) *Immigrants in the United States, 2007, A Profile of Americas Foreign-Born Population*, Center for Immigration Studies, Washington.
Campbell, C. C. (2000). *The Young Colonials: A Social History of Education in Trinidad and Tobago, 1834–1939*. University of West Indies Press, Kingston, Jamaica, p. 168. ISBN 978-976-640-011-8.
Chakravarti, N. R. (1946) *The Indian Minority in Burma: The Rise and Decline of Immigrant Community*, Oxford University Press, London.
Chan, S. (1991) *Asian Americans: An Interpretive History*, Twayne, New York.
Clark, C., et al. (1990) *South Asian Overseas: Migration and Ethnicity*, Cambridge University Press, Cambridge.
Consulate General of India, Dubai (2012) *India Matters*, December 2012. http://www.cgidubai.com/category/news-media/india-matters.
Davis, K. (1951) *Population of India and Pakistan*, Princeton University Press, New Jersey.
Department of Immigration and Citizenship, Canberra. www.immi.gov.au/media/fact-sheets/20planning.htm, accessed on 30 April 2012.
Diaspora Interaction with Chief Minister, NRI Samellan, Chandigarh, January 2008.
Dosanjh, U. 'Punjabi NRI Sammelan', *Jallandhar*, 6 January 2008.
Dubey, A. (2000) 'Indian and experience of Indian diaspora in Africa', *Africa Quarterly*, Vol. 40, No. 2, pp. 69–92.
Dubey, A. (ed.) (2003) *Indian Diaspora: The Global Identity*, Kalinga Publications, New Delhi.
Dutta, A. (2003) *Human Migration: A Social Phenomenon*, Mittal Publishers, New Delhi.
'Eco-Sikh plans major green initiative', *The Tribune*, 24 February 2013.
Eisenstadt, S. N. (2003) *The Absorption of Immigrants: A Comparative Study Based Mainly on Jewish Community in Palestine and the State of Israel*, 1954, p. 1, cited in *AmalDatta, Human Migration: A Social Phenomenon*, Mittal Publications, New Delhi.

Ember, M., Ember, C. R. and Skoggard, I. (eds.) (2005) *Encyclopedia of Diaspora: Immigrant and Refugee Cultures around the World*, Springer, New York.

Esman, M. J. (2009) *Diasporas in the Contemporary World*, Polity Press, Cambridge, UK.

'Exhibition on Punjabis in California opens', *The Tribune*, 3 April 2012.

Fargues, P. (2011) 'Immigration without inclusion: non-nationals in nation-building in the Gulf states', *Asian and Pacific Migration Journal*, Vol. 20, No. 3–4, pp. 273–92.

Forstenlechner, I. and, E. Rutledge (2010) 'Unemployment in the Gulf: time to update the social contract', *Middle East Policy*, Vol. 17, No. 2, pp. 38–51.

Fransi, B. S. (2011) 'Employment quandary', *Riyadh*, 17 February 2011.

Gangopadhyay, A. (2005) 'India's policy towards its diaspora: continuity and change', *India Quarterly*, October–December, Vol. LXI, No. 4, pp. 93–122.

Ghai, Y. and D. Ghai (1970) *Portrait of Minority Asians in East Africa*, Oxford University Press, Nairobi.

Gillion, K. L. (1971) *Fiji's Indian Migrants: A History of the End of Indentured in 1920*, Oxford University Press, Melbourne.

Gopal, R. (2003) 'Partnerships with defence firms — HAL buffeted by approval process', *Business Line*, November 5.

Gopal, S. (2014) *Jawaharlal Nehru: A Biography* (3 Volumes), Volume I (1889–1947), Volume II (1947–1956), Volume III (1956–1964), Oxford University Press, New Delhi.

Grover, V. (1992) *International Relations and Foreign Policy of India*, Deep & Deep Publications, New Delhi.

Gupta, A. (1987) 'Indian, Fiji and South Pacific', *Economic and Political Weekly (Bombay)*, June, Vol. 22, No. 25, pp. 979–80.

Gupta, A. (2009) 'Indian diaspora as a strategic asset', Jayanta Kumar Ray (ed.), *Interpreting the Indian Diaspora: Lessons from History and Contemporary Politics*, PHISPC, New Delhi.

Gupta, A. and J. Ferguson. (1992) 'Beyond culture: space, identity and the politics of difference', *Cultural Anthropology*. Vol. 7, No. 1: 6–23.

Harris, C. I. (1993) 'Whiteness as property', *Harvard Law Review*, Vol. 106, No. 8, pp. 1707–91.

Helweg, A. W. (1993) 'The Sikh Diaspora and Sikh studies', John Stratton Hawley and Gurinder Singh Mann (eds), *Studying the Sikhs: Issues for North America*, State University of New York Press, Albany, New York, pp. 69–94.

Helweg, A. W. and U. M. Helweg (1990) *An Emigrant Success Story: East Indians in America*, Oxford University Press, Delhi.

http://library.uwb.edu/guides/usimmigration/1970s_indochina.html, accessed on 14 January 2013.

http://www.aapiusa.org/about/mission.aspx, accessed on 22 November 2012.

Bibliography

http://www.acf.hhs.gov/programs/orr/resource/the-refugee-act, accessed on 14 January 2013.

http://www.fincen.gov/statutes_regs/patriot/, accessed on 14 January 2013.

http://www.gopio.net/news_101212.htm, accessed on 22nd November 2012.

http://www.govtrack.us/congress/bills/109/hr4437, accessed on 15 January 2013.

http://www.govtrack.us/congress/bills/112/hr3401#summary/libraryofcongress, accessed on 16 January 2013.

http://www.immigrationpolicy.org/just-facts/comprehensive-immigration-reform-act-2010-summary, accessed on 8 September 2013.

http://www.mea.gov.in/Portal/ForeignRelation/India_Canada_Bilateral.pdf, accessed on 3 June 2013.

http://www.ofr.harvard.edu/additional_resources/Summary_of_Enhanced_Border_Security_Reform_Act_HR3525.pdf, accessed on 10 January 2013.

http://www.punjabnewsline.com/content/north-american-punjab-association-welcomes-nri, accessed on 4 April 2013.

http://www.umass.edu/complit/aclanet/USMigrat.html, accessed on 12 December 2012.

http://news/saanj.net/Punjab-news/badal-assures-punjabi-diaspora-to-address-all-their-genui, accessed on 4 April 2013.

http://www.sikhiwiki.org/index.php/North_America_Punjabi_Association, accessed on 4 April 2013.

Human Rights Watch, http://www.hrw.org/node/8472, accessed on 10 December 2012.

Hussain, Z. (2011) 'Immigration policies of the GCC countries: implications and responses', S. Irudaya Rajan and Marie Percot (eds.), *Dynamics of Indian Migration – Historical and Current Perspectives*, Routledge, India.

ICOE (2009) *Impact Assessment of Global Recession on Indian Migrant Workers in Countries of the Gulf Cooperation Council and Malaysia*. Indian Council of Overseas Employment, New Delhi.

IOM (2010) *World Migration Report 2010: The Future of Migration: Building Capacities for Change*, International Organization of Migration, Switzerland.

Jacobs, D. and A. Rea (2005) 'Construction et importation des classements ethniques. Allochtones et immigrés aux Pays-Bas et en Belgique', *Revue Européenne des Migrations Internationales*, Vol. 21, No. 2, pp. 35–59.

Jain, P. C. (1989) 'Emigration and settlement of Indians abroad', *Sociological Bulletin*, Vol. 38, No. 1, pp. 155–68.

Jain, P. C. (1990) *Racial Discrimination Against Overseas Indians: A Class Analysis*, Concept, New Delhi.

Jain, R. K. (1993) *Indian Communities Abroad*, Manohar Publishers and Distributors, New Delhi.

Jayaram, N. (ed.) (2004) *The Indian Diaspora: Dynamics of Migration*, Sage Publication, New Delhi.

Jayaraman, R. (1975) *Caste Communities in Ceylon: A Study of Social Structure of Three Tea Plantations*, Popular Prakashan, Bombay.

Jureidini, R. (2003) *Migrant Workers and Xenophobia in the Middle East*. Program Paper No. 2, Identities, Conflict and Cohesion Program, United Nations Research Institute for Social Development (UNRISD), Geneva.

Kanjilal, T. (2004), *Indian Americans and India: An Analysis of Mutual Relations*, Kalinga Publications, New Delhi.

Kapiszewski, A. (2001) *Nationals and Expatriates, Population and Labor Dilemma of the Gulf Cooperation Council States*, Garner Publishing Limited, UK.

Kapur, D. (2010) *Diaspora, Development and Democracy: The Domestic Impact of International Migration from India*, Oxford University Press, New Delhi.

'Keeps politics out of it', *The Hindustan Times*, 16 April 2013.

Khadria, B. (ed.) (2009) *India Migration Report 2009, International Migration and Diaspora Studies Project*, Jawarhalal Nehru University, New Delhi.

Khalsa Diwan Society – Canada cited from http://www.sikhpioneers.org/chrono.html#1897, accessed on 17 May 2013.

Khilnani, S. (1997), *The Idea of India*, Hamish Hamilton, London.

Klapdor, Michael, Moira Coombs and Catherine Bohm (2009–10) *Australian Citizenship: A Chronology of Major Developments in Policy and Law: Background Note Parliament of Australia*, Department of Parliamentary Services, Canberra, Australia.

Knapman, C. (2012) *United Arab Emirates: Migration Profile*, American University in Cairo, Cairo, Egypt.

Knerr, B. (1990) 'South Asian countries as competitors on the world labour market', in Colin Clark, et al. (ed.), *South Asian Overseas: Migration and Ethnicity*, Cambridge University Press, Cambridge, p. 173.

Kondapai, C. (1951) *Indian Overseas 1838–1949*, Indian Council of World Affairs, New Delhi.

Kounteya, S. (2013) 'Protest against verdict in London', *The Times of India*, 16 April 2013.

Krishna, K. S. and S. I. Rajan (2014) *Emigration in 21st Century India: Governance, Legislation, Institutions*. Routledge, New Delhi.

Lal, B. V., Peter Reeves and Rajesh Rai (eds.) (2006) *The Encyclopaedia of the Indian Diaspora*, Oxford University Press, Singapore.

Lal, V. (1999) 'Establishing roots, engendering awareness: a political history of Asian Indians in the United States', Leela Prasad (ed.), *Live Like the Banyan Tree: Images of the Indian American Experience*, Balch Institute for Ethnic Studies, Philadelphia, pp. 42–8.

Lall, M. (2003) 'Mother India's forgotten children', Nielsen, Eva Qstergaard (ed.), *International Migration and Sending Countries: Perceptions, Policies and Transnational Relations*, Palgrave Macmillan, New York.

Lall, M. C. (2001) *India's Missed Opportunity*, Ashgate Publishing, England.

Lee, E. S. (1966) 'A theory of migration', *Demography*, Vol. 3, No. 1, pp. 47–57.

Leonard, K. (1989) 'Punjabi pioneers in California: political skills on a new frontier', *South Asia* (Armidel, New South Wales), December, Vol. 12, No. 2, pp. 69–81.

Longva, A. N. (1999) 'Keeping migrant workers in check: the Kafala system in the Gulf', *Middle East Report*, Vol. 29, No. 2, pp. 20–22.

Mahajani, U. (1976) 'India and the people of Indian origin abroad', Rajan, M. S. (ed.), *India's Foreign Relations during the Nehru Era: Some Studies*, Asia Publishing House, Bombay.

Malhotra, A. (2012) 'Trapped abroad, without reason', *The Tribune*, 31 March 2012.

Malhotra, J. S. (2013) 'Gill's election as NRI sabha chief challenged', *The Hindustan Times*, 5 April 2013.

Malit, F. T., Jr., and Ali Al Youha (2013) *Labour Migration in the United Arab Emirates: Challenges and Responses. Migration Policy Institute (MPI)*. http://www.migrationinformation.org/Feature/display.cfm?ID=965, accessed on 3 March 2013.

Martiniello, M. (2003) 'Belgium immigration policy', *International Migration Review*, Spring, Vol. 37, No. 1, pp. 225–32.

Massey, D. S. (2009) 'The political economy of migration in an era of globalization', Samuel Martínez (ed.), *International Migration and Human Rights: The Global Repercussions of U.S. Policy*, University of California Press, Berkeley, CA, pp. 25–43.

Massey, D. S., Jorge Durand and Nolan J. Malone (2002) *Beyond Smoke and Mirrors: Mexican Immigration in an Age of Economic Integration*, Russell Sage Foundation, New York.

'MEHFIL: the magazine for today's Indo-Canadian', December 1997, pp. 29, 76. Cited from http://www.sikhpioneers.org/chrono.html#1913a, accessed on 25 February 2013.

Mehra, A. (ed.) (2010) *Emerging Trends in Indian Politics: Fifteenth General Elections in India*, Routledge, New Delhi.

Meissner, D. (2010) 'Five myths about immigration', *The Cap Times*, http://host.madison.com/news/opinion/column/doris-meissner-five-myths-about-immigration/article_11f9aa4c-a6de-5b43-b755-e8f182a4a559.html, accessed on February 2013.

Ministry of External Affairs (1991) *Annual Report 1990–91*, Government of India, New Delhi.

Ministry of External Affairs (2001) *Report of the High Level Committee on the Indian Diaspora*, Government of India, New Delhi.

Ministry of Overseas Indian Affairs (2007) *Annual Report 2006–07*, Government of India, New Delhi.

Ministry of Overseas Indian Affairs (2010) *Annual Report 2010–2011*, Government of India, New Delhi.

Ministry of Overseas Indian Affairs (2011) *Annual Report 2010–2011*, Government of India, New Delhi.

Ministry of Overseas Indian Affairs official website, http://moia.gov.in/accessories.aspx?aid=11, accessed in November 2013.

Mishra, P. and Urmila Mohapatra (2002) *South Asian Diaspora in North America: An Annotated Bibliography*, Kalinga Publication, New Delhi.

Motwani, Jagat (1994) 'Twenty million global Indians: an overview', *Manorama Year Book 1994*, Kottayam, Kerala.

Naim, M. (2002) 'The new diaspora', *Foreign Policy*, Vol. 131, pp. 95–96.

National Communications Branch, Department of Immigration and Citizenship, Canberra (2012) http://www.immi.gov.au/media/fact-sheets/06australias-multicultural-policy.htm, accessed on 10 January 2013.

Narayana, D. and Vinoj Abraham (2012) 'The Dubai model and the impacts of the financial crisis on South Asian migrant workers in the United Arab Emirates', S. Irudaya Rajan (ed.), *India Migration Report 2012: Global Financial Crisis, Migration and Remittances*, Chapter 6, pp. 94–121, Routledge, New Delhi.

'Need to check antecedents of NRI grooms, says CJI', *The Tribune*, 17 December 2013.

Omvedt, G. (1980) 'Migration in colonial India: the articulation of feudalism and capitalism by the colonial state', *Journal of Peasant Studies*, Vol. 7, No. 2, pp. 185–212.

Pant, G. (1998) 'South Asian migration to the Arab gulf: issues and prospects', *South Asia* Journal (New Delhi), October–November, Vol. 2, No. 2, pp. 111–27.

Parekh, B. (1993) 'Some reflections on Indian diaspora', *Journal of Contemporary Thought* (Vadodara), Vol. 3, pp. 105–51.

Parekh, B., Gurharpal Singh and Steven Vertovee (2003) *Culture and Economy in Indian Diaspora*, Routledge, London.

Polak, H. S. L. (1909) *The Indians of South Africa: Helots within the Empire and How They Are Treated*, G. A. Natesan Publishing House, Madras.

Potts L. (1990) *The World Labour Market: A History of Migration*, London and New Jersey.

Prashad, V. (2002) 'Countering Yankee Hindutva', *Frontline*, December, Vol. 19, No. 25, pp. 07–20.

Prashad, V. (2004) 'Dusra Hindustan', *Seminar*, June, No. 538, http://www.india.seminar.com/2004/538/538%20vijay%20prashad.htm, accessed on 3 March 2013.

Rajan, S. I. (ed.) (2010) *India Migration Report 2010: Governance and Labour Migration*, Routledge

Rajan, S. I. (ed.) (2011) *India Migration Report 2011: Migration, Identity and Conflict*, Routledge, New Delhi.

Rajan, S. I. (ed.) (2012) *India Migration Report 2012: Global Financial Crisis, Migration and Remittances*, Routledge, New Delhi.

Rajan, S. I. (ed.) (2013) *India Migration Report 2013: Social Costs of Migration*, Routledge, New Delhi.
Rajan, S. I. and J. Joseph (2013) 'Adapting, adjusting and accommodating: social costs of migration to Saudi Arabia', S. Irudaya Rajan (ed.), *India Migration Report 2013: Social Costs of Migration*, Chapter 9, pp. 139–53, Routledge, New Delhi.
Rajan, S. I. and D Narayana (2010) *The Financial Crisis in the Gulf and its Impact on South Asian Migrant Workers*, Centre for Development Studies Working Paper No. 436, Thiruvananthapuram.
Rajan, S. I. and D. Narayana (2012) 'The financial crisis in the Gulf and its impact on South Asian migration and remittances', S. Irudaya Rajan (ed.), *India Migration Report 2012: Global Financial Crisis, Migration and Remittances*, Chapter 5, pp. 74–93, Routledge, New Delhi.`
Ramady, M. A. (2010) 'Population and demographics: Saudization and the labor market', *The Saudi Arabian Economy: Policies, Achievements, and Challenges*, 2nd ed., Springer, New York, pp. 351–93.
Ratha, D. and William Shah (2007). *South-South Migration and Remittances,* World Bank Working Paper No. 102, Washington.
Report of the High Level Committee on the Indian Diaspora (2001) Indian Council of World Affairs, New Delhi.
Report of the High Level Committee on Indian Diaspora (2002a) Chapter 13, The United States, http://moia.gov.in/services.aspx?ID1=63&id=m8&idp=59&mainid=23, accessed on 3 March 2013.
Report of the High Level Committee on Indian Diaspora (2002b) Chapter 21, Asia Pacific Region, http://moia.gov.in/services.aspx?ID1=63&id=m8&idp=59&mainid=23, accessed on 8 September 2013.
Roberts, G. W. and J. Byrne (1966) 'Summary statistics on indenture and associated migration affecting the West Indies, 1834–1918', *Population Studies*, Vol. 20, No. 1, pp. 125–34.
Rodriguez, N. (1996) 'The battle for the border: notes on autonomous migration, transnational communities and the state', *Social Justice*, Vol. 23, No. 3, pp. 21–37.
Rosenblum, M. (2011) 'USA Immigration Policy since 9/11: Understanding the stalemate over Comprehensive Immigration Reform', The Regional Migration Study Group, Migration Policy Institute.
Runnels and Nhu (n.d.) http://library.uwb.edu/guides/usimmigration/1970s_indochina.html, accessed on 14 January 2013.
Sahadevan, P. (1995) *India and Overseas Indians: The Case of Sri Lanka*, Kalinga Publications, New Delhi.
Sahay, A. (2009) *Indian Diaspora in the United States: Brain Drain or Gain?* Lexington Books, United Kingdom.
Sanjib K. B., 'Fresh foreign funds for Khalistan', *The Hindustan Times*, 7 April 2013.
Saudi Gazette. 'New Saudi labor law to end individual sponsorship', *Jeddah*, 1 April 2012.

Sen, A. K. (2012) 'Punjab-born Saund to laud Asian contribution in first India-American Congressman', *The Tribune*, 10 May 2012.

Seth, P. (2001) *Indians in America: One Strems, Two Waves, Three Generations*, Rawat Publication, Jaipur.

Shah, N. (2009) *The Management of Irregular Migration and Its Consequences for Development: Gulf Co-operation Council*, International Labour Organization Asian Regional Programme on Governance of Labour Migration Working Paper No.19, ILO, Geneva.

Shah, N. M. (2005) 'Restrictive labour immigration policies in the oil-rich Gulf: effectiveness and implications for sending Asian countries', United Nations Expert Group Meeting on Social and Economic Implications of Changing Population Age Structure.

Shah, N. M. (2012) 'Socio-demographic transitions among nationals of GCC countries: implications for migration and labour force trends', *Migration and Development*, Vol. 1, No. 1, pp. 138–48, Routledge.

Sheffer, G. (ed.) (1986) *Modern Diaspora in International Politics*, Crcom Helm, London.

Sherry, V. (2004) *Bad Dreams: Exploitation and Abuse of Migrant Workers in Saudi Arabia. Human Rights Watch*, July, Washington, DC.

Singh, I. P. (2013) 'North American Punjabi Association seeks special fast track court for NRI's disputes', *The Times of India*, 3 January 2013.

Singh, P. (2013) 'Baisakhi gains global significance', *The Tribune*, 13 April 2013.

Sinha, A. (2005) *The Regional Roots of Developmental Politics In India: A Divided Leviathan*, Indiana University Press, Bloomington.

Skeldon, R. (1997) *Migration and Development: A Global Interpretation*, Longman, London.

Statistics Canada (2011) *National Household Survey 2011.* Mobility and Migration, https://www12.statcan.gc.ca/nhs-enm/2011/ref/guides/99-013-x/99-013-x2011006-eng.cfm, accessed on 10 November 2013.

Tamas, K. (1996) *South to North Migration: Migration Potential and Economic Development*, cited in Hammar Thomas, Brochmann Grete, TamasKristof and Thomas Faist, 1997, *International Migration, Immobility and Development: Multidisciplinary Perspective*, Oxford University Press.

Terrazas, A. and Cristina Batog (2010) *Indian Immigrants in the United States*, Migration Policy Institute, Washington, DC.

Thomas, H., Brochmann Grete, Tamas Kristof and Thomas Faist (1997) *International Migration, Immobility and Development: Multidisciplinary Perspectives.* Berg Publisher, Oxford.

Tinker, H. (1977) *The Banyan Tree: Overseas Emigrants from India, Pakistan and Bangladesh*, Oxford University Press, New Delhi.

Tinker, H. (1993) *A New System of Slavery: The Export of Indian Labour Overseas 1830–1920*, Hansib, London.

United Nations (2009) *International Migration Report 2009: A Global Assessment*, Department of Economic and Social Affairs, United Nations, New York.
United Nations (2013) 'Total migrant stock at mid-year by origin and destination', United Nations Department of Economic and Social Affairs, Population Division.
The United Nations Organisations on Drugs and Crimes (UNODC) Report on Punjab and Haryana, 2010.
'US refused to declare 1984 riots as genocide', *The Hindustan Times*, 3 April 2013.
Vaidyanathan, R. (2008) 'Gujarat polls: the assertion of entrepreneurs', *Daily News and Analysis*, 2 January.
'Vancouver's Punjabi girl power', *The Tribune*, 3 February 2013.
Varadarajan, L. (2010) *The Domestic Abroad: Diasporas in International Relations*, Oxford University Press, New York.
Varghese, V.J. (2009) *Land, Labour and Migrations: Understanding Kerala's Economic Modernity*, Centre for Development Studies working paper No. 420, Trivandrum.
Venier, P. (2007) 'From Kerala to the UAE: emerging trends in a mature labour migration system', Maître de Conférences, Université de Poitiers, CNRS MIGRINTER.
Wadehra, R. 'Kabbadi world cup or a gimmick?' *The Sunday Tribune*, 9 April 2013.
Weiner, M. (1982) 'International migration and development: Indians in the Persian Gulf', *Population and Development Review (New York)*, March, Vol. 8, No. 1, p. 10.
Winckler, O. (2010) 'Labor migration to the GCC states: patterns, scale, and policies', *Migration and the Gulf*, Viewpoints special ed., Middle East Institute, Washington, DC.
Wood, J. R. (1983) 'East Indians and Canada's new immigration policy', George Kurian and Ram P. Srivastava (eds.), *Overseas Indians: A Study in Adaptation*, pp. 3–29, Advent Books Division, New Delhi.
World Bank (2011) *Migration and Remittances Factbook 2011*, World Bank, Washington, DC.
Yadav, S.N. (2005) *Journey of Overseas Indians: Labour to Investor*, Vol. 1, Global Vision Publishing House, New Delhi.
Zachariah, K.C., E. T. Mathew and S. I. Rajan (2003) *Dynamics of Migration n Kerala: Dimensions, Differentials and Consequences*, Orient Longman, New Delhi.
Zachariah, K. C. and S. I. Rajan (2008) *Migration and Development: The Kerala Experience*, Daanish Books, New Delhi.
Zachariah, K. C. and S. I. Rajan (2011) *Diasporas in Kerala Development*, Daanish Publishers, New Delhi.
Zachariah, K. C. and S. I. Rajan (2012) *A Decade of Kerala's Gulf Connection*, Orient Blackswan Pvt Ltd, Hyderabad.

Zachariah, K. C. and S. I. Rajan (2014) *Researching International Migration: Lessons from the Kerala Experience*, Routledge, New Delhi.

Zachariah, K. C., S. I. Rajan and Jolin Joseph (2014) 'Kerala emigration to Saudi Arabia: prospects under the Nitaqat Law', S. Irudaya Rajan (ed), *India Migration Report 2014: Diaspora and Development*, Routledge, New Delhi.

Zaidi, A. M. (1985) *Immutable Policy of Friendship and Cooperation: The Foreign Policy of Indian National Congress during the Last 100 Years*, Indian Institute of Applied Political Research, New Delhi.

About the authors

Dr. A. Didar Singh is Secretary General, Federation of Indian Chambers of Commerce and Industry (FICCI), New Delhi. He is a senior civil servant of the Indian Administrative Service (IAS) and retired as Secretary to Government of India in the HYPERLINK "http://moia.gov.in/" Ministry of Overseas Indian Affairs. Prior to this, he was Member (Finance), [Additional Secretary to Govt. of India], HYPERLINK "http://www.nhai.org/" National Highways Authority of India, Department of Road Transport and Highways at New Delhi. He was earlier Joint Secretary in the HYPERLINK "http://dhi.nic.in/" Ministry of Heavy Industries and before that in the HYPERLINK "http://commerce.nic.in/" Ministry of Commerce (Foreign Trade).

Alwyn Didar Singh did his schooling from St. Xaviers Delhi and Bachelors and Masters from HYPERLINK "http://www.ststephens.edu/" St. Stephens College, Delhi University. He also has a Masters in Development Administration from HYPERLINK "http://www.birmingham.ac.uk/index.aspx" Birmingham University, UK and has the distinction of having done the first PhD in India on the Policy and Administration of e-Commerce. Dr. Didar Singh is an international expert in e-Commerce and ICT development and has done several studies in the area of ICT strategy and e-Commerce for international agencies, including the International Trade Centre; World Health Organization; and South Centre, Geneva as well as the Commonwealth Secretariat, London. He authored (with Dr. Madanmohan Rao) a book on e-Trade for the WSIS summit at Tunisia. Singh is a regular contributor to the ITC Executive Forum series. Dr. Singh's book on 'e-Commerce for Managers' was published by Vikas in 2003 and his major treatise 'E-Commerce in India: Assessment and Strategies for the Developing World', was published in 2008 by LexisNexis Butterworths, New Delhi.

Dr S. Irudaya Rajan, is Chair Professor, Ministry of Overseas Indian Affairs (MOIA) Research Unit on International Migration at the Centre for Development Studies, Thiruvananthapuram, Kerala. He has thirty years of research experience in Kerala; has coordinated six major migration surveys (1998, 2003, 2007, 2008, 2011 and 2013) in Kerala (with Professor K C Zachariah), Goa migration survey 2008, and also instrumental in conducting the Punjab Migration Survey 2010, Gujarat Migration Survey 2012 and Tamil Nadu Migration Survey 2014 and has published extensively in national and international journals on social, economic and demographic implications on international migration. He had projects on international migration with European Commission, International Labour Organization, Asian Development Bank, World Bank, International Organization of Migration, United Nations Fund for Population Activities, Migrant Forum in Asia and Rockefeller Foundation; works closely with the Ministry of Overseas Indian Affairs (MOIA), Government of India, Department of Non-Resident Keralite Affairs, Government of Kerala and Department of Non-Resident Indian Affairs, Government of Goa. He is the coordinator of the Kerala State Development Report prepared for the Planning Commission, Government of India and also member of the National Migration Policy drafting group appointed by the MOIA. He is editor of the Annual Series India Migration Report brought out by Routledge. He is also editor-in-Chief of the Routledge Journal, Migration and Development.

Index

Abolition of Indentured Act (1916) 19
Academy of the Punjab in North America (APNA) 175
Africa 2, 5, 17, 19, 23, 27–9, 32, 79, 89–90, 97
Aid to Families with Dependent Children (AFDC) 10, 12
Alien land laws 159
Amerasian Homecoming Act 162
Anti-Terrorism Act 164
Appropriations for Vietnamese and Cambodian Refugees (1975) 162
Article 3 47
Article 10 48
Article 13 48
Article 14 48–9
Article 15 49
Article 128 49
Article 129 49–53
Asia barred zone 159
Asian Indians 34, 158–9
Asians 27, 33, 67, 158, 160–1
Atlantic Charter Act (1941) 67
Australia 29, 31, 41, 76–85, 89, 92, 114, 122, 150; Indian political connections 84–5; multiculturalism of 83–4; overseas Indians' emergence in 76–9; subcontinent ministerial consultative committee 85
Australian Citizenship Act (1948) 83
Australians 77, 79, 81, 83

Battle of Plassey 18
Belgium 65, 92, 126
Bihar Association of North America (BANA) 178
Bilateral investment treaty 109–10
Border Protection, Antiterrorism, and Illegal Immigration Control Act (2005) 165
brain drain 3, 8
Burma 17, 20, 29–30, 32
Burmese Indians 30

California's Proposition 187 163
Canada 89–98; India and, relations 91–4; political developments 94–8
Canadians 92, 94, 131
CDS *see* Centre for Development Studies
Centre for Development Studies (CDS) 42
Centre for Immigration Studies analysis of March 70
Ceylon (Sri Lanka) 29–30
Chandana Kannada Sangha (CKS) 175
Chaturvedi, Banarasi Das 31
Chinese Exclusion Acts 158
Chinese immigrants 74, 78, 158, 160
Citizenship Act 38, 77, 80–2
colonial emigration 18–21
communities 1–6, 81, 83–5, 88, 95, 97–8, 100, 102, 107–10, 121, 128, 141–2, 145–6, 167, 170–1

Comprehensive Immigration Reform Act (CIRA) 166
Constitution of India and Citizenship Act (1955) 38
country case studies 41–2; Australia 76–85; Canada 89–98; Europe 57–65; GCC region 42–57; Mauritius 107–10; Trinidad and Tobago 103–6; United States 66–76, 98–103
cultural organisation 169–70, 175–6
culture connectivity 128–9

demography 54–5, 71–2
Department of immigration (1945) 80
Detroit Malayalee Association (DMA) 170–1
developed countries 8–10, 12–13, 17, 35, 38–9, 113–14, 130
Diaspora *see* Indian Diaspora
Displaced Persons Act (1948) 160
domestic politics 8, 25, 112, 115, 137
Downer, Alexander 81
dual citizenship 38, 123

economic engagement 124
Eisenstadt, S. N. 2
emigrants 4, 20, 22, 97, 113, 134, 148
Empire Settlement Act (1922) 79
employment 5, 10, 12, 47–50, 77, 163
engagement 88, 117–19, 130, 135–6
Enhanced Border Security Act (2011) 167
Enhanced Border Security and Visa Entry Reform Act (2002) 165
ethnicity 92
ethnic politics 108
Europe 57–65
European immigrants 159
Exclusion of Asian Indians (1917) 158–9

Fiji Indians 29, 33
Filipino immigration 160

Fitzpatrick, George F. 106
food stamps 10–12
Foreign Exchange Regulation Act (FERA) 38
foreign immigrant worker 49
Foreign Policy Resolution 28
foreign workers 44, 46, 50, 53, 55–6, 76, 166
France 60–2, 78, 92, 107, 115, 119, 128

Gandhi, Indira 33–5
Gandhi, Mahatma 64
Gandhi, Rajiv 35
GCC countries 43–4, 50, 52, 133, 137, 146
Germany 62–3, 70, 78, 89–90, 123, 135
Ghan Express 76
Grassby, Al 82
Greater Carolina Kerala Association (GCKA) 168
Greater Richmond Malayalee Association Virginia 168
Gujarat 138–42; Diaspora 138–42; immigrants 141
Gulf 34, 41–2, 85, 113, 119–20, 123–4, 148, 150
Gulf Cooperation Council (GCC) 42–4

Hart-Celler Act 67
Hathaway, Robert 99
human and workers rights 127–8

Illegal Immigration Reform and Immigrant Responsibility Act (1996) 11, 164
illegal migration 58–9, 115–16, 120, 125–6, 134, 150
Illinois Malayalee Association (IMA) 169
Immigrant Act (1924) 160
Immigrant Act (1965) 161
Immigrant Reform and Control Act (1986) 163
immigrants 9–11, 13–14, 21, 44–6, 55, 58, 63, 67–70, 72–6, 78–9, 90–2, 96–7, 99,

104, 159–64; illegal 14, 73–4, 163, 166; integration 14; undocumented 11, 74–5, 163, 167; status of 55
immigration: illegal 163–4; laws 66, 76, 80, 97, 157, 165; policies 23, 41, 43, 46, 57, 61, 63, 66, 73–4, 76, 81–3, 97, 150, 163
Immigration Act (1990) 163
Immigration Act (1901) 78–9
Immigration Act (1917) 158–9
Immigration and Nationality Act (1952) 161
Immigration and Nationality Act (1965) 67 *see also* Hart-Celler Act
Immigration and Nationality Reform Act (1965) 33
Immigration and Naturalisation Act (1965) 67
Immigration Exclusion Act (1882) 158
Immigration Restriction Act 78–9
INC *see* Indian National Congress
indentured labour 17, 19, 23, 39, 61, 103, 106–7
India–EU migration 59
Indian-American community 98–100, 102
Indian-American Diaspora 102
Indian-American Leadership Initiative Public Action Committee (IALIPAC) 101
Indian-Americans 98, 100–3, 141
Indian citizenship 34, 38
Indian community 20, 24, 26, 30, 59, 62, 84, 98–9, 103, 147, 169
Indian community in France 61
Indian Cultural Centre 64
Indian Diaspora 3–4, 16–17, 22–5, 31–2, 34–7, 39–40, 54, 59–63, 65–6, 72, 76–7, 84, 88–92, 94–110, 112–13, 117–25, 128–33, 135–6, 138, 141–2, 145–9, 151–2, 156; administrative arrangements, post-independence 30–1; Africa and 27–8; associations 106; in Belgium 65; Burmese Indians 30; Ceylon (Sri Lanka) 29–30; communities 14, 27, 36, 100, 141, 146–7; demography and 54–5, 104–6; engagement 112–13, 121, 136, 142; Fiji and 29; in France 61–2; in Germany 62–3; groups 101, 122, 129–30; in Gujarat politics 140; historical background 23–5; Indira Gandhi's era 33–5; in Italy 64–5; migrant associations 53–4; migration of 17–23; Narasimha Rao's government 36–9; Nehruvian era and 25–7; organisations 112–13, 136; in Netherlands 63–4; policy 23–39; political mainstreaming of 88–110; policies 117, 130, 152; political policy perspectives, populations 110; post-independence 31–3; Saudi Arabia 53–4; in UAE 44–53
Indian immigrants 71–2, 95, 97–100, 105; population 72; *see also* immigrants
Indian immigration *see* immigration
Indian migrants 41, 43, 62, 66, 91, 97, 145–6; *see also* migrants
Indian Migrant Workers 44
Indian migration *see* migration
Indian National Congress (INC) 23–4, 137, 139–40, 148
Indian nationalism movement 62
Indian population 38, 67, 71
Indian Punjabi 96
Indians 16, 18, 20–37, 39, 42, 44–5, 53–4, 61–8, 71–2, 76–7, 84–5, 94–108, 113–14, 126–7, 147–8; in Australian politics 84; economy 37–8, 40, 89; emigrants 4, 20, 23, 25, 32, 42, 146; emigration 4, 18, 20, 22, 39, 43, 53, 85, 145; settlers 23–4, 26

India–the United States Civil Nuclear Cooperation Agreement 124
Indochina Migration and Refugee Assistance Act (1975) 162
Indophobia 27
international migration 2, 5–6, 8, 12, 33, 45, 132
international politics 147
Italy 64–5, 70, 90, 92, 114, 126

Jacob, M. M. 38
Jagatsingh, Kher 109
Jain, R. K. 17
Johnson, Lyndon 67
Johnson-Reed Act (1924) 160
Jugnauth, Aneerood 109

Kafala Sponsorship System 46
kafeel 46
Kanganis 19–20
KANE *see* Kerala Association of New England
KAPB *see* Kerala Association of Palm Beach
Kerala 45, 54, 63, 65, 112–13, 121, 132–8, 168–71; Diaspora in 134–8; economic engagement 137; engagement, forums for 135
Kerala Association of Greater Washington (KAGW) 169
Kerala Association of New England (KANE) 168
Kerala Association of Palm Beach (KAPB) 171
Kerala Congress and Indian Union Muslim League 136
Khalsa Diwan Society 95
Know India Programme (KIP) 116

labour: emigration 18, 20; immigrant 50; immigrants 58; laws 46–7, 49; market 1, 9, 48, 50–1, 55–6, 62; migration 12–13, 20, 148
languages, immigrant 93–4
leaders, political 58, 106, 108, 122, 139

legal immigrants 11, 65, 161
legal migration 59, 115–16, 126, 134, 151
liberalisation 35, 37, 39–40, 149

Magnuson Act (1943) 160
Maistry system 19–20
Malayalee Association of Greater Houston (MAGH) 169
Malayalees 136, 168–70
Mallige 175
Mauritius 107–10; Bilateral investment treaty 109–10; history and political mobilisation 107–9
Mehra, Ajay 141
Mexican Migration Project (MMP) 11
migrant Indian population 44
migrants 2, 9–10, 14–15; associations 53–4; communities 15, 41, 84, 146–7; in developed countries 9; illegal 13, 126, 134; integration of 14; international 2, 5, 42, 45; irregular 13; population growth and 12–13; protection of 151; undocumented 13–14, 76, 146; workers 2, 43, 45–6, 49, 51–2, 54, 121, 164
migration 1–4, 6–18, 20–3, 41–6, 52–3, 59, 73–4, 80–2, 84–5, 88, 112–42, 145–53, 157; colonial emigration 18–21; country case studies 41–53, 57–85; development and 3–4, 59; economic compulsions and 4–6, 8–9; history of 74, 157; in globalised world 145–53; issue of 66, 157; myths of 4–15; phases and patterns 17; policies 41, 46, 58, 73, 78, 151; political economy of 112–42; politics of 16–33, 35–40, 114, 129, 146, 150, 152; post-colonial emigration 21–3; return 8, 12–13; in South-North direction 6; undocumented 12

Migration and Development (1997) 3
Migration Act (1958) 81–2
Migration Policy Institute (MPI) 71
migration-related issues 115–16, 122, 125
migration resource centres (MRCs) 115, 128, 133–4
movement, myths of 1–15
MPI *see* Migration Policy Institute
multiculturalism 83–4
myths: of migration 4–15

NAPA *see* North American Punjabi Association
national amendments 158
Nationality Act (1920) 79–84
Nationality and Citizenship Act (1948) 80–1
Nationality and Citizenship Act (1955) 81
Naturalisation Act (1903) 79
Naturalization Act (1790) 157–8
Nehru, Jawaharlal 25–7, 28–30, 32–3, 37, 148–9
Nehruvian policy 31–2, 36–7, 149
Netherlands 59–61, 63–4, 90, 92
Non-discriminatory Australia (1949) 81
non-profit organisation 172–4
North American Punjabi Association (NAPA) 120–1

Oklahoma Malayalee Association (OMA) 169
Omvedt, Gail 18
Opperman, Hubert 81
Overseas Indian Facilitation Centre (OIFC) 116
overseas Indians 22–8, 30–5, 39–40, 59, 62, 66, 76–7, 85, 102, 110, 149
Ozawa v. United States (1922) 159

Pacific Islander Labourers Act 79
Panday, Basdeo 106
patterns of emigration 21

Persons of Indian Origin (PIOs) 16, 35, 38, 59–64, 91, 104–5, 107, 110, 113, 123, 151
philanthropic engagement 125
policies: localisation 55–6; multicultural 83
Political mainstreaming of Indian Diaspora 89–92, 94–7, 99–110
Post and Telegraph Act 79
Pravasi Bharatiya Divas (PBD) 64
Punjab: Diaspora from 113–15, 119–29, 131–2; supplementary policies of 116–19
Punjabis 92–5, 113–14, 116, 123–4, 127–8, 132, 175

racial discrimination, elimination 82–3
reforms 37–8, 74, 163–7
Refugee Act 162
Rao, Narasimha 36–9
returnees 126

Saudi Arabia 53–4; Indian Diaspora in 53–4; labour localisation policies 55; Nitaqat law and 55
Saudisation 56
Saund, Dilip Singh 115
Sikh Diaspora 122, 129
Singh, Rabin Baldew 64
social capital 129
social issues 126–7
South Asian immigrations 159

Tamil Association of Colorado (TAC) 177
Thakur, R. 37
Tobago 103–6
Trinidad 103–6
Tri-State Kannada Cultural Association 176
Tydings-McDuffie Act (1934) 160

UAE 22, 42–6, 48–52, 126, 137; Indian presence in 44–53
United Nations 45
United States 66–76, 98–103; demographic and socio-economic

overview 72; immigration policies 73; Indian-American community 98–9; Indian government's attitude 100–3; Indian population in 71–2; legal Indian immigrant population 72–3; migration, estimates of 68–71; overseas Indians' emergence in 66; political mobilisation, causes for 99; from 1790 to 1929, migration 73–6; unauthorised Indian immigrant population 72–3

Vishal Bharat 31

Welfare Reform Act 11
White Australia Policy 78
Whitlam, Gough 82
World Bank 3